Debbie,

Anything you believe,
you really can achieve!

Believe Debbie

DeJuann

DA JUANA BYRD
GHOSTS TALK

BYRD PUBLISHING

FIRST EDITION

Library of Congress Cataloging-in Publication Data
Byrd, Da Juana
Ghosts Talk/ by Da Juana Byrd

p. cm.
ISBN 0-9702663-2-4
Library of Congress Control Number: 200119209

The names of some people involved in incidents in this book have
been changed to protect their privacy.

Dedicated To:

My friend, Carroll,
taken for granted but always loved, and who sent
me kicking and screaming from the psychic closet.
My friend, Muffin,
who saw me through the rigors of writing
many nights.
To her re-incarnation,
Mysti,
who waits patiently under the desk
as I write, and her sister,
Madeline,
who is never patient.
My daughter, Mickey,
who without knowing it made
me face the reality of who I was.
To my very special editor, friend, lover and husband,
Claude,
who has almost always believed in
me and my abilities,
and to the one who is never least in my life,
the man who helped me always
and is my ghost friend
John.

TABLE OF CONTENTS

Section One
DA JUANA

Section Two
GHOSTS

TABLE OF CONTENTS

TABLE OF CONTENTS

ACKNOWLEDGEMENT

Many people, especially my family, deserve my genuine thanks for assisting me in the publication of this book. All my life, my father and my two brothers gave me inspiration by loving me and standing behind me even when they didn't understand what I was doing.

My husband, Claude, has worked long hours editing and enticing me to use the correct words in expressing my desire to educate people about the metaphysical.

Our daughter, Mickey, has proofed and asked intelligent questions on the content so that I might give greater sources of information while writing this book.

Al Brumley used his considerable knowledge and time in editing my book so that I might write with fewer words and more understanding.

To all of you and to everyone who buy this book, my greatest thanks.

PROPHESY

The Bible

1 Corinthians 14:1-5

Follow the way of love and eagerly desire spiritual gifts, especially the gift of prophecy.

For anyone who speaks in a tongue does not speak to men but to God. Indeed, no one understands him: he utters mysteries with his spirit.

But everyone who prophesies speaks to men for their strengthening, encouragement and comfort.

He who speaks in a tongue edifies himself, but he who prophesies edifies the church.

I would like every one of you to speak in tongues but I would rather have you prophesy.

About the Author

Da Juana Byrd has communicated with ghosts or spirits from the "Other Side" all her life. Immediately after deciding to declare to the world she was psychic in 1987, she has had unbelievable success and notoriety as a professional psychic. Within six months from coming out as a professional psychic, she was doing a regular radio show and interviewed on several television shows and written about in newspapers. Da Juana does a daily psychic advice column that is found on her website, along with world predictions that she makes in December for each coming year. Her accuracy with predictions has made believers of many. She not only reads with amazing accuracy for people, but communicates with pets as well. She has devoted many hours, at her own expense assisting various law enforcement agencies in solving crimes and locating missing persons. Da Juana is an author, lecturer, columnist, radio and TV personality and professional businesswoman. Her goal is to help people help themselves and prove that the gift of prophecy is real and that it should be used to help mankind.

SPIRITUAL GIFTS

The Bible

1 Corinthians 12:4-11

There are different kinds of gifts, but the same Spirit. There are different kinds of service, but the same Lord. There are different kinds of working, but the same God works all of them in all men.

Now to each one the manifestation of the Spirit is given for the common good. To one there is given through the Spirit the message of wisdom, to another the message of knowledge by means of the same Spirit, to another faith by the same Spirit, to another gifts of healing by that one Spirit, to another miraculous powers, to another prophecy, to another the ability to distinguish between spirits, to another the ability to speak in different kinds of tongues, and to still another the interpretation of tongues. All these are the work of one and the same Spirit, and he gives them to each one, just as he determines.

Foreword

Generally people believe in things they can see, hear, smell, taste or feel. The sixth sense is not tangible but some things are true whether you believe them or not.

When a person who has been blind since birth looks at the world, they see only the darkness that has engulfed their sight. Needing others to explain the world's sights, they create in their mind a picture by listening to the descriptions of sighted people.

Having never experienced the ability to see, the blind are left to imagine the sights explained to them. The blind sighting experience is only as magnificent as the sighted persons detailed explanation.

Their dependence on others to perform the act of sight makes the blind learn the process of complete trust. Thus they access an intangible sense called "faith" in those who see for them.

Most of us believe in the existence of God or a higher power. Have we ever seen Him? The majority would say they have not but they still know without a doubt that there is a Supreme Consciousness. What they do not agree upon is whether God is one to fear or one to love. Love and respect are what we want from our children, not fear. If the perception of God is that He is our father, as many believe, then why should he be so different from us? We, then, are part of his spirit as our children are part of ours.

Spirit is one of those true things whether you believe it or not. It is the thread woven through the fabric of the universe that makes all it touches part of the tapestry of life.

Without the insight of a person believing that the body is a mass of cells, we would still believe that we are one complete body, instead of the multitudes of cells that go about their individual business of making the whole body exist. Medical science came up with the microscope that could see those little cells. Then humans discovered there was more to the body than originally thought. Had man not invented that powerful tool, humanity would still be under the illusion that the body was not a wonderful working colony but instead a single mass as it appears.

The sun with its beauty and light is, like God, one huge energy entity that gives off light brightening a vast darkness. Each ray of the sun breaks away from the parent in order to find darkness and erase it giving instant light.

Foreword

The individual rays of the sun are still a part of the vastness of that celestial being. They continue to emit light and heat wherever that golden ray may travel. Its energy is effervescent, dancing in the darkness with the happiness of a small child learning a new subject. Where there is light, one can see and Believe Without Fear.

Loved ones who have gone before us in death are within our reach to communicate with, though they died long ago. Angels are not beyond belief. Using your psychic ability in everyday life is part of the gift given to you when you return to life on earth. Believing without fear is an ability you have to learn.

Logic has always dictated that I was and am skeptical of everything. Skepticism has bred a great respect for my learning. Being a person who has to taste, hear, see, feel and know it is right, I learn and teach in the same manner.

In my quest for knowledge, I found there is no one, right way to do anything. Teaching allows me to bring out the psychic knowledge individuals have possessed all along without their awareness of it. Taking one's psychic ability and dissecting it into the smallest degree helps those seeking education to be able to see psychic abilities in themselves.

Knowledge makes one stronger. Listening to the inner spirit is the key to psychic ability. The inner guide will never fail a person.

Psychic ability is not hard to possess. Everyone has it, although some use it more than others. Most people think psychic knowledge should come with such force it could knock them over, when in fact; it is usually gentle as a whisper. Focus and concentration will allow one to listen to the whisper.

In this book, I strive to reach out to as many people as possible. To answer questions I have asked and been asked, down through the years, is my reasoning for writing this book. Having been where you are, I understand the feeling of being alone. You are not alone.

My prayer is that this book helps others to understand themselves better. Together we can make a difference. We can make a better world.

DA JUANA

Chapter One

A TESTAMENT

As a child, I saw and talked with Jesus Christ. This was such a personal experience, I did not even tell my father until much later on.

According to our church, it was okay for me to see and talk with Jesus or the Holy Ghost. If I admitted speaking with other ghosts, I was told I was being influenced by the devil. My problem was that I had to wonder how the church knew which ghost was holy.

When I was about six years old, I had what we, in my church, termed a vision, not that I hadn't had them before, but this was a special revelation. A vision is an image that is happening in another dimension while a person is doing something ordinary too. In other words, I was in two places at the same time.

Actually what had happened was, that at this young age, I no longer wanted to live and sent that message out, so Jesus came to see me.

Lying in bed one night, I was looking into the darkness. The dark has always frightened me because I needed to be able to see who was in my room with me. Having had numerous ghostly visits at night, I preferred to have a light on when sleeping. (It's a good thing that my husband does not mind sleeping with a light on because I still do.) Since my father kept the rooms dark at night, I usually would pull the cover over my head even in the heat of summer, just to be safe. This was before air conditioners were commonplace.

The vision occurred in our front yard. It had every kind of flower known to man. The scents were wonderful. Our front yard had turned into a garden paradise. During that time period hardly anyone's yard had flowers, especially in such abundance.

The landscaping was gorgeous. Jesus sat beside me on a concrete bench, which was centered in the garden. Behind Him, to His right, was a golden stairway that led to the sky, with beautiful angels standing at intervals on the steps.

Jesus asked me why I wanted to see him. Replying to him without fear, I told him I didn't want to do what I had said I would come here to do. Rather than go through with it, I wanted to die. The "It" I was referring to was being ridiculed, persecuted and maybe even dying for my beliefs again. As a child, I had memories of dying for my beliefs.

He told me that he would take me if I really wanted to go. Ready to leave this earth plane, his words made me very happy. After His having told me he would take me soon, the vision ended.

Without fear and with the self-importance of a six-year-old who had a secret, I walked through life waiting for Jesus to come to take me back home.

Three days later, Jesus came back to visit me. He told me that my father was really upset over the fact that I was ready to leave. My words to him were that daddy didn't even know.

His next question made perfect sense to me. He asked if I had not noticed that daddy had gone into his bedroom and stayed for the last three days, only appearing outside to go to the bathroom or to work.

In our religion, you went into a closet to pray, and you also fasted when you were worried about something in order to get closer to God. God is supposed to listen to you better since you are giving up something for Him. This is usually done when you are upset or really want His attention.

When Jesus asked about the bedroom, I thought about daddy

A Testament

not eating for the past few days. He had my attention. At that point, he told me that if I died then, I would change my father's life. Reiterating what we had talked of on the previous occasion, Jesus repeated that he would take me with him if I really didn't want to go through with my life this time.

In my little mind, I was trying to understand how it would make a difference to my father. In essence, I would be going back home with Jesus. His religion taught that the definitive good was to go to heaven to be with God. My father should have been happy for me because I was achieving his religion's ultimate goal.

Even as a child, I knew that it was not my right to change the direction of another person's life. Torn between the fact that I wanted to go with Jesus, but I didn't want to change the path my father had chosen, I was in a dilemma.

Though I did not want to be ridiculed for my beliefs, I told Jesus I would stay. Even at six years old, I felt sure that I had been ridiculed and died in prior lives for my beliefs. In this life my thought was that I did not want to go through those times again.

Looking back I realize that Jesus spoke with me as adult-to-adult rather than adult to a six-year-old.

Jesus then told me that if I stayed, I would be very ill. He told me to remember that I would not be permanently damaged and would come out of this illness as if nothing had happened. Three days later, I was rushed to the hospital and was found to have one of the first cases of polio.

I had taken the vaccination the day after Jesus had talked with me about the illness. My father did not want me to have that vaccination but my mother did. To this day my father still gets very upset for allowing my mother to talk him into my having that vaccination.

According to my father, he thought that in giving me the vaccine, I would contract the disease. He had a psychic revelation to this effect and was frightened. For him, it was a test of faith. Daddy thought that God did not want me to have the vaccine. In going through with the shot, he felt, he had forced God's hand and it was his fault for my having polio.

In actuality, no one was to blame. This was a lesson for us. By allowing the disease and getting over it, my vision was coming to pass.

GHOSTS TALK

My father needed to learn to turn loose of the guilt he felt for letting me have the vaccination. The disease was not his responsibility but was an experience from which to learn.

When I went into the hospital I told everyone that I was going to be okay. Even the nurses' thought I was a little odd with my beliefs but I think some found it strangely comforting too. The needles hurt and the stay in the hospital left a little to be desired but I was able to stand it.

With the knowledge from Jesus that I would be fine, I believed him. I got those looks from the nurses that said, *Oh, I feel so sorry for the poor baby. She thinks she talked to Jesus and that has given her such faith that she's going to be all right, but we know that there has been more disasters than good results related to this disease.* I knew from those looks, even as a child, that they thought I was unaware of the way life really was. Yes, they believed in Jesus, but they didn't believe he would talk with a child.

With child like faith, I continued to tell them that I would be fine because Jesus had told me I would be, and I knew it was so.

Within three months, I walked out of that clinic with no signs I had ever had polio. Most would call it a miracle but it was not a miracle to me, simply a fact. Jesus told me I would be well, so I believed him.

Jesus has always shown himself to me surrounded in a blue-white light wearing blue-and-white robes.

The feeling he shares with me is one of total peace. He sometimes uses spoken language as we did when I was young. At other times, he speaks to me telepathically.

Why did Jesus come to visit me in my time of need? Maybe it was my church upbringing that made him become my angel or guide or maybe it is because we know one another.

If I were Buddhist, Muslim or any other religion, another deity from that religion might be the savior I would expect to see.

People believing in Mohammed, Buddha or other religious figures would ask those people for help in the same light as Jesus did for me.

Great guides come in human form so that people can learn from them while they are on the earth. It is and has been our privilege to walk, talk and be educated by them. They all have similar philosophies.

Jesus taught the most important lesson of all time when he was on this earth. The lesson is to love everyone as you love your self. If we do this, then there is no need for any other law in society.

Many earthly spiritual teachers have taught us how to live with others in the best of harmony. Jesus happens to be one that I recognize most because I was taught his teachings by my father and by my dear dead friend, John.

Growing and learning on this earth plane, there are guardian angels here to help us at every step. Jesus is one of mine on occasion. He can be there for anyone else who needs Him and request his services. As a part of God, just as we all are, He tries to help others because it helps Him too.

Part of our lot in life is to help others in order to help ourselves. It is the same with guides or guardian angels. When they help others, they assist themselves.

As God said in the Bible, "He knows every falling sparrow." I believe He pays attention to something so small and so taken for granted as the sparrow because it is a part of Him.

We, on earth, reap the benefits of all those angelic forces being there to help us as God said.

Celestial visits are good. They remind us of our heritage as spiritual individuals and bring us hope when there seems to be none left.

Jesus and I have something in common too. We were both called insane by people who knew us.

"Then Jesus entered a house and again a crowd gathered, so that he and his disciples were not even able to eat. When his family heard about this, they went to take charge of him, for they said, 'He is out of his mind.'"

"And the teachers of the law who came down from Jerusalem said, 'He is possessed by Beelzebub! By the prince of demons he is driving out demons.'" Mark 3:20-22

Even my family, with whom I am very close, and who knew that psychic events are real, tended to make fun of my abilities when they finally found out I was using them openly. For years, I did a wonderful job of covering them. Only my father suspected. A family looks at you as one of them and can usually never see any hidden talent. We are all taken for granted by family.

As you can see by the New Testament text above, Jesus had his hard times too. Not only did his family think he was insane, but his detractors thought he was a demon. The Bible states that He died for his beliefs.

According to the New Testament, Jesus gave us a road map to live by. His life was supposed to be it. Although people seem to be afraid to look at Jesus as a mortal, he was. Everyone has the mortal and spiritual part of their being in common with him.

Like Jesus, I have had my share of detractors. One woman at a hotel where I was working passed my table, and in a loud voice to be heard by all, said, "Someone ought to call the sheriff."

My husband was seething. His need to protect me was overwhelming.

I smiled at her and said, "God bless you."

There were two reasons for my saying that. One is, she really did need God's blessing. We all do.

The other was that I wanted her to take a look at her Christian belief system. Her thoughts of me were her business. If she wanted to believe I was the worst person alive, it was her right as long as she kept it to herself. The moment she spoke aloud, as she walked past without looking me in the eye, she made it my business.

Condemning me on assumption, she did not even know my beliefs. Had she stopped to talk and learned how I believed, she could have made an intelligent decision instead of an unwise remark.

For me, her attitude was not the mark of intelligence. If I know nothing about a subject, then I am apt to ask questions. I question everything, even my abilities.

Hopefully, I gave her reason to think about what she did and said without hurting her with words of my own.

After coming out of the psychic closet, I lost what I considered several good friends. Before they knew I was a psychic, they valued my advice. When I accepted the psychic label, then, it seemed, I became evil in their eyes.

This explains the fear I felt as a child. I knew that one day I would have to tell the world who I was. When I did other people whom I valued would look at me differently.

Jesus had to prove himself when he was on the earth too. If he came back to today's environment, he would have a harder time than

A Testament

he did before. People are so well educated today that it is hard for them to believe in miracles because they are suspicious of anything different. His gospel of loving everyone is enough to make them suspect of his motives.

Is Jesus a ghost? Is He the Son of God? Who is He?

Jesus is the Son of God, in my belief, just as I am a daughter of God. We are all God's children, which is confirmed by the Bible. In following those beliefs, then Jesus is my brother.

Is He holy? Yes He is, as we all are in God's image.

Many believe that we may be made in God's image but as man we are full of sin. I believe "sin" is a fallacy promoted by people who want to remain in control of the lives of others.

Sin is a word invented to promote guilt. Everyone with a conscience at one time or another feels guilt. What better way is there to control man than by guilt?

For instance if a man takes another man's wife, then according to most religions, he should feel guilty because it is a sin.

He forgets that there were three people involved in that little experience and takes all the guilt upon himself. What did the wife feel was lacking in her husband or herself and thus made her stray? As for the other adulterer, how could he take someone who had a mind of her own? Did he kidnap her? Could the husband have done anything differently to make his and his wife's life better?

These people could have lived those lives experiences a little differently but they didn't. If they had, then they would not have had to deal with guilty consciences. Each was in complete control of his or her life and thus retained some responsibility for what happened. Sin was not there, but there was an opportunity for learning. Because of their actions they had new experiences in their lives, educating themselves through tears, anger, remorse and happiness.

Jesus is now and always has been a spirit, which is part of All That Is. Being a helper and guide to others is still His place in the scheme of things. He has helped me when no other could.

Chapter Two

OPENING THE PSYCHIC CLOSET DOORS

Coming out of the psychic closet and letting people know that I was a psychic so unnerved me that I did not do it until I was thirty-six years old. This was simply because I was afraid of being ridiculed.

As most are well aware, *the church tells us psychics are supposed to be of the devil.*

When I was a little girl, people looked at me as if I was different. At times I thought it was because my parents were divorced but I can't remember the number of times an adult told me I was mature beyond my years.

As a very serious young lady looking at the children my age, I knew I was different. Even my classmates treated me more like an adult. Needing to know the answers to any question that crossed my mind, I pestered my teachers constantly. One or two even gave me a philosophers nickname, Aristotle.

Although I knew I was different I didn't want anyone to look at me that way. Because I saw things others could not, I stood a little aloof and watched my fellow classmates as if I were watching a movie. I was part of that real life movie but was able to watch the action from a different prospective.

Because I could see things that others had given up the ability to see was no reason, in my estimate, for others to look at me as if I were a bad person. Still that little nagging feeling was there that when I started to really open up and talk about what I believed, the people in my world would look at me totally differently.

At an early age I had realized that if someone wants to talk badly about you, they will.

My mother and father were divorced in the 1950's, a time in which divorce was not supposed to happen. Consequently, my brothers, my father and myself were isolated and looked at scornfully by most in my world.

My world was the church. Because of the divorce, the church could no longer recognize my father's ordination. He could, however, continue to preach as an evangelist. Living for those days, he kept his ministering powers in tact by preaching to his children.

As a member of the Assemblies of God, I was used to being called names such as Holy Roller and a few other not-so-nice names. We were taught to be peculiar in our church, not to be like the world. As a result we wore those names as a badge of our Christianity.

At that time the church did not want women to cut their hair, wear makeup, or show their limbs (arms and legs). Women could not cover those appendages with pants because that would put them in a man's clothing. Being unable to tell the sexes apart was a sin.

My contention was that in Biblical times everyone wore robes and had long hair. That little shared tidbit of mine brought dire consequences for me.

According to our church, no one should question those beliefs but instead they were to practice blind faith. My problem with this doctrine was if God gave me one thing for sure; it was intelligence, the intelligence to ask questions. If He had not wanted me to look for answers, why would He have given me this questioning mind?

We were also taught that works took you to heaven. The only way you could see the streets of gold was to be sinless at the time of death. That brought up another subject for me. Just how many people do you know who are perfect on a daily basis, let alone at the time of their death? I wondered just how lonely their heaven was going to be.

At an early age, I knew that I wanted to learn about all religions, but in the United States at that time, there were only a few considered as "real" religions. This was only because they were the largest established religions of the time.

Those religions were the Catholics, Methodists, Baptists, the Church of God, the Church of Christ, Pentecostals, and the Assemblies of God. I hope I am not leaving anyone out but these were the ones who stood out in Louisiana and only one was really recognized by our family.

The reason I didn't mention the Jewish religion is because we were taught they had no religion. They were just a group of people who were held in awe by our church because they were the group Jesus was born into. My church considered them heathen because they didn't believe that Jesus was the Son of God as we did.

That philosophy posed definite problems to my way of thinking.

In studying each church, I found that each has a tendency to think they are the only ones who are right. Without putting it into words, they seem to suggest that their church members are the only ones going to heaven.

As I told my minister father, people in all religions and even those who are not religious are going to go to what he considered heaven.

Daddy looked at me many times in disgust for his failing to teach me appropriately, and then he tried to use his knowledge of the Bible to correct my mistaken ways. (He would also ask me if I had been hanging out with those Catholics again.)

As I look back, I know my father had a hard time living with me. Anyone who has ever lived with me had a hard time for obvious reasons. My mind gives me the ability to ask questions and expect to get answers that would alleviate the questions.

I was constantly bringing up other religions and telling him about things that were going to happen in the church. It was all right for me to see future events in the church. They called it prophecy, but according to them prophesy only happened within the confines of the church.

I would also hypothesize about such things as UFO's and their involvement in religion.

GHOSTS TALK

Saying to my father just for the sake of argument, "What if people in UFOs came down to earth? Would we not consider them gods since they obviously were of higher intellect than we were? After all, they were in flying machines much greater than ours. Even the Old Testament spoke of these flying machines and people who were in them in II Kings and Ezekiel. What would they have looked like to people from the Old Testament times who had never seen an airplane?"

Daddy always had to be on his toes for me. A lot of prayers were said for my salvation. Because my father was under the opinion that if you "Spare the rod you spoil the child," he really wanted to make sure I was not spoiled.

When I was very young, I told him about reincarnation. This was not the best thing to say to my father. I learned to keep my mouth shut until I was old enough to speak my mind without fear of reprisal. At thirty-nine, I brought the subject up to him again.

The Assemblies of God did not teach reincarnation. It makes you wonder where one so young could have gotten a belief such as past lives.

Metaphysical events were a constant in our house. Strange lights would come through the house, usually in threes. The Father, Son and Holy Ghost was the way my father described it.

My father saw them and so did my mother. One of my father's favorite stories was about the trinity of lights coming into his room and going through his body while he lay in bed beside my mother. Of course, she had a small problem with this type incident. This may have been one of the reasons for their divorce.

The divorce of my parents might have had an impact on my decision to stay quiet about my abilities all those years. Being psychic is not the easiest path to take in life.

Chapter Three

HIS NAME IS JOHN

Ghosts have always been a part of my life. They may be telling me about Aunt Lou's gout or that Uncle Billy should be careful driving his pickup today, but they were always talking with me. My thought was that they were going about the every-day business of living just as I was.

When I was a child, I had one ghost friend whom I referred to as God. Like a good parent, though he wasn't my parent but a dear friend, he was always there to talk with me, teaching me right from wrong and helping me to see the other person's point of view.

For example, if I were to let jealousy into my thoughts, he would instantly give me a very logical talking to, but he did it in such a way as to get my attention rather than to make me want to shut him out. He made me see that there are always two sides to every story and that my feelings were not the only feelings involved.

He was my rock. When I needed a friend, he was there. Ever vigilant in my spiritual growth, he helped me through my childhood years.

GHOSTS TALK

This glorious man taught me to always stand for my word, to be kind to others as I would want them to be kind to me, to love everyone and to stand up for my beliefs though I may die for them. He held Jesus in high esteem and had great love for the man and His beliefs.

When, unable to speak with my father for fear of being misunderstood, he was there. Guiding me gently but firmly, he helped me grow into the person I am today.

Even though a golden white light surrounded him, I never thought of him as anything but my friend. Instinctively I knew he was a little different. Taking his name for granted, I called him God. It never occurred to me that people didn't speak to and hear God's voice speak back on a daily basis.

Daddy had taught me it was all right to see ghosts but he also tried to teach me to fear them too. He seemed to fear the unknown. Although he never said fear them, he said that the devil came in ghostly form even as "The prince of light." I did not know the devil but wanting to take my father's word for it, I was careful. This man, who seemed to be only visible to me and with whom I spoke on a daily basis, was my friend. He helped me. It was unfeasible that he had anything to do with the devil.

When I called God, my friend was always there. As I grew into an adult, his appearance never changed. He was always with me.

Patiently waiting for years to tell me his name, he told me when I was thirty-six. Not only was it a shock to my system, but it also left me feeling as if someone suddenly took my childhood teddy bear away.

The day I finally decided to come out of the psychic closet, he told me who he was. This man had always been closer to me than anyone other than my present husband, Claude.

My life with this man had prepared me to open those closet doors but the way it happened made me realize I had been walking towards this event all my life.

Telling my husband of about six years that I could see the future was not easy. A series of events served to send me bolting out of the psychic closet. To a certain extent, I felt as if it were out of my control. Now I know better. Looking back over my years in this life, I have learned that I was in complete control of my situation.

One morning I woke to say to my husband, "I have to have you

His Name is John

believe me now." At that instant, my life took the turn that put me on the path to do what I came here for.

Then I proceeded to tell him about the dream I had the night before.

Tentatively, I told him that a plane crash would occur in the next few days, involving two planes. I explained to him exactly how the smaller airplane would hit the larger one right behind the wings, close to the tail.

Holding my hands up to show him how they would collide, I informed my husband how the midair crash would occur. I told him how the smaller airplane would look after it had fallen to the earth. Continuing I told him, that from above, it looked as though it was flattened out in what I perceived to be a pasture. The reason I thought it was a pasture was because I could only see grass around it.

I explained that the larger plane would hit a subdivision because I could see a man who was very upset talking about the disaster. Fire raged in the houses behind him.

Explaining that there was a second smaller plane that would not be hurt but would be a part of the whole scenario made him look at me as if I were crazy.

He lay there silently and with the way he was looking at me in total amazement, it took no psychic to know that he was thinking to himself, "Oh my God, I am married to a loony tune."

In most second marriages, spouses do not usually want to fail again so they work harder to stay together. Thankfully, Claude felt that way.

At least this was not going to be an easy decision. Do I leave her or do I stay? His fear of having to start over again didn't change the look on his face though, or the impression it made in my heart. Though I tried to understand it, it did still hurt. After all, I had learned to deal with this type thing in my life but not from someone I thought loved me as much as Claude did. He knew I was not a liar, nor could I stand anyone lying to me. That helped.

Looking back he remembered the times when other people had lost some item and couldn't find it. He was always telling them to get me to find it because I was good at that sort of thing. Most people would have taken that as an indication that I might be just a tad different.

My aircraft disaster prediction came true three days later and was on a special news report with the man in my dreams speaking as the

GHOSTS TALK

flames in the subdivision raged behind him. Exactly what I had seen and explained to my husband was now on the television. He turned to me with one statement, "They said nothing about the third plane."

All the evidence was there except for that one plane. I would have thought the information I had given him would be enough to get his attention at least. Here he is asking about the only plane that did not mean that much in the scheme of things. After all the people in it were still alive.

With exasperation, I said, "Give them a couple of days and they will."

The disaster happened in California with the larger plane crashing into a subdivision.

The small plane in the pasture was actually in a schoolyard. There was nothing around but grass. Had someone been flying over and looking down at it, as the reporters and I had, it did look as though it were a pasture instead of a schoolyard.

My husband, still in a state of disbelief but open to the possibility now, came up with something new. He told me to make this ability grow.

The next day news reporters talked of how the air traffic controller had taken his eyes off the two planes involved in the crash to look at a third, small plane in the same air space. When the controller looked back, the two planes were gone.

My husband was quite uneasy with what he thought were the newfound abilities of his psychic wife but he was also realistic in terms of what that meant in our life. He started hesitantly to encourage me to expand those abilities and to look for others like me.

Just as God always does when asked, He sends the person you need to guide you when you require it.

A neighbor of mine, who was taking lessons from a numerologist at the time, told me I was a psychic. Barely knowing my neighbor, I did not understand how she knew I was psychic.

To put it bluntly, she told me that if she had my gifts, she would be using them. Giving it a name, she called people who had these gifts, "Psychic."

Now I knew what I was. This word felt good. Thank God there was a word I could live with. I was a psychic, not a witch, not a Satanist,

His Name is John

just a psychic.

In my church, the gift was called prophecy. It was all right to use it within the confines of the church. According to Romans 12:6, "We have different gifts, according to the grace given us. If a man's gift is prophesying, let him use it in proportion to his faith."

People within the church called this gift used outside the church "of the devil," as if God only did blessed things inside the church. Not only that but God also only gave those gifts to people who worshipped in the church. For me, a building is only a structure. There is nothing that is not God's church in my way of thinking, so the world was open to me.

In Spanish, French, Italian and Latin, my name means "Of John," not "of the devil." Having no league with Satanism or Witchcraft, the name "Psychic" felt good.

My neighbor's psychic friend gave me a mini reading. She told me that I was psychic, but not someone who would really use the ability in their every day life. This left something to be desired. I knew better because it had been with me all my life.

Psychics are not always one hundred percent correct. I wish we were but we are not. Thank goodness for her, though. She suggested I go to a psychic fair.

There is always a lesson to be learned, no matter how small. She pointed me in the right direction.

My husband and I went to the psychic fair. Neither of us had ever been to one. Unsure of what I might find, I was excited but also a little apprehensive.

Amazingly enough most of those people looked just like us. There were a few who I would consider bizarre. One man wore a turban and made me think of running as quickly as I could out of the building. My husband, upon seeing this man, made the statement, "These people ought to be locked up. They are dangerous." Curiosity kept me there.

I went straight to a blonde lady who looked sane enough. She was someone's mother and it showed. With a smile, she held out her hand to us.

We were going to get what they called "A reading." Because I had a reading from my neighbor's friend, I had learned what a session with a psychic was called. This psychic would be talking with us directly. I liked this but was also a little anxious.

The energy in the room was phenomenal and thus energized me. It made me feel rested and ready to pursue any task eagerly. It was exhilarating.

Trying to be a nice person, I let my husband get the first reading. Quietly I stood behind him while she gave his reading. She kept saying things about me instead of him. Frustrated and thinking we shouldn't be there, he told her everything she was saying applied to me, not him.

Very strongly, she told me to get away from her table. Then she thought of how powerfully she had said, "Get away from my table" and tried to explain. She said that my presence was so strong that I was interfering with his reading. I understood exactly what she meant. Not having to ask questions as to how I was interfering, I left without having my feelings hurt.

For someone who started so terribly wrong, when I left the table, she became amazingly accurate. When she finished with Claude, he couldn't believe it. He told me there was no way she could know the things she did. Of course I wanted to know everything she had said.

He was shocked at her accuracy but still skeptical. Still he was not convinced that his wife was really "Psychic." Though her air disaster dream had come true and she could find lost objects for others, he needed more proof because the memory of them had faded. It was okay for a stranger to be that way but not his wife. It's nice for a man to be able to see another man's wife wear the bikini, if you know what I mean.

We got readings from about four other people that day. Too logical to believe without the aid of more than one test, I was most impressed with the blonde lady. Needing confirmation of my own abilities, I wanted to see if she saw the same ghosts in our house that I did.

I asked her to visit our house. She did for a fee.

The Tuesday the blonde psychic lady came was on Super Tuesday and I had gone to vote. My husband was home alone. By the time I got back home, she had been through the house showing Claude where ghosts had appeared.

After finally coming out of the psychic closet, I had been telling Claude about several ghosts in our home. Her confirming exactly the same thing I had said about the ghosts made him a little more ready to

His Name is John

listen, when I finally made it home.

Upstairs, in one small area, we could smell the distinct odor of sawdust. There were no visible renovations going on at our house.

Having asked what this was, a ghostly voice told me they were building on my abilities. Looking back, I remembered that at about five o'clock every morning, I was awakened to sawing and hammering.

One morning, they even woke my husband up. He is a bear when awakened that way. Throwing on his clothes, he went outside to see who was making that kind of noise so early in the morning. No one alive was and for that I was grateful.

I liked our neighbors and I didn't want my husband to harangue any of them after having been awakened so rudely. Now I know, the ghosts were affecting my husband's abilities too because he could hear and smell their renovations.

In order to make us more focused and to let us know what we had smelled and heard was authentic, they allowed the odor to be smelled by the visiting psychic only in a localized area. This space was about two-foot by two-foot and at head level.

We went downstairs and sat at our breakfast room table. Once seated, she asked that I get a piece of paper and write the first thing that came to mind.

Well, I had been doing this all my life although at the time, I did not know it had a name. It is called automatic writing.

I wrote the name, "John."

For me, John was not a spectacular name. Being a common name it was no big deal except it was the name I heard. (No offense to any Johns out there. All you Johns or lovers of John, please read on before you get angry with me.)

When she saw the name, she asked if this was a guide. The answer came back, "Yes," from him.

While she was talking to me aloud, I was talking to him with telepathy. As a matter of fact, we were in an argument. I told him not to come here changing his story after all those years. His name was really God and I didn't want to hear him surface now with this John name.

With all those years of experience in dealing with me, John knew I was not a stubborn woman if given information and having the time to contemplate it. With the patience of Job he answered, telling me to get my Bible. He would explain.

I started to get up. My husband, who was now getting into this, asked what I wanted. He decided he would get the Bible for me. Later he told me he was so fascinated by what I was doing that he didn't want my concentration broken. There was no concentration but an all-out argument going on between John and me.

Questioning me, Claude asked, "Which Bible do you want, yours or mine?"

"Mine," I answered. So he got my Bible.

Putting the Bible between my two outstretched hands and with my eyes closed; I let my Bible fall open. I placed my finger on a passage. Upon opening my eyes, I read the verse aloud. It said: "**He motioned for a piece of paper and to everyone's surprise wrote, 'His name is John!'**" Luke 1:63

My husband almost fell over. He freaked. The blonde psychic woman looked kind of shocked. Neither my husband nor I realized that passage was in the Bible. (For that matter, neither did our Baptist minister.) To say it was unexpected was an understatement.

Her next question was "Are you the only one there?"

He was answering before she was able to finish speaking the question. I was dumbfounded but relieved. Now I was getting the answers. If I had known how and what to ask before, I realized, I would have gotten them all along.

"No," came the answer. "There are all these others to help you now. You are no longer a child. You don't need me any more. I've got other things to do."

John had never tried to push psychic ability on me. He had allowed me to grow on my own and at my own pace.

When we spoke it was always about mundane things, not what I would call spiritual or psychic. Now I realize the mundane is both spiritual and psychic.

Learning who I was made me elated but heartbroken too because I was losing my life long friend and companion.

Ever my teacher, he reminded me telepathically of the times I had heard the others speak to me also. They would be talking all at once but each was saying something different. It was very difficult listening to and answering them, I remembered. Besides they were ghosts. John was not a ghost to me. He was my friend.

Trying to be a good Southern woman listener, I would seek to answer all of their ghostly questions even while talking with a live person such as my husband or a neighbor.

More than once before I even knew I was a psychic, people would tell me that I was off in another dimension instead of being with them. Nothing changed. They still say it. It didn't matter that I had answered their questions as if they had my full attention. They knew I wasn't with them totally. My husband has a tendency to say I am out in space again.

John told me that these people would help me. As the need arose, others would take their place.

All my life, I had known that there was a difference between John's world and mine but I seem to be able to bridge both. Though I am in a room with multitudes of people, I can use a part of myself to step though to the other side where John lives. While I am speaking with the people on the physical side, I am able to communicate with people on the other side.

Communicating with the other side has always been quite easy for me. To make this easier for others to understand, I equate it to a room.

Imagine that you are in the center of a room with a line running through the middle on either side of you. People from the physical side of life are behind you and people from the Other Side are in front of you. Neither side can cross through the center or hear people on each side of the room. Only you can cross the center boundary or hear either side.

Now suppose you hear someone directly in front of you from the Other Side wanting to speak with a physical person in the room.

They ask for your attention. Naturally, you take a step forward to hear them better. The divider is crossed yet still in place. Being able to step into either part of the room is easy from where you are located.

Now you are able to listen to either side and interpret what is being said to the person who needs the explanation.

That has always been my position in life.

John was what some would label a guide to me. A guide is someone who agrees to help you by guiding you through the every-day world while you seek to become more Godlike. They may be called guardian angels or other names but they are helpers. Now there are others I allow to help me, as John said, who come in and out of my life at will when I need questions answered.

They have always been there, but I was not ready to receive them as people that could help me. In looking back, I remember a woman who did not call herself psychic that I went to see while living in Louisiana. She told me of my future and what she said came true. In my way of thinking, she did not regard her ability as a good thing, and I don't know if she even knew what she was. Certainly, she did not call what she did a reading. For her, this was a burden she carried rather than a wonderful gift.

I realize now that she could have been a guide to me then, had I questioned her, but undoubtedly I was not ready to open those psychic doors at that time.

My guide, John, was my friend and still is although I no longer see him. He is just off to other pastures now helping someone else become enlightened. I can't express the love and admiration I have for this man. He was and still is one of the most admired teachers I have ever had.

It is possible that some will have the same guide all their lives. If I had not come out of the psychic closet, then John might still be with me, trying to enlighten me with his wisdom.

People are quick to tell me they have a guide. These people are proud because they know their guide's name. People naturally have a tendency to want to know with whom they are speaking. If that is what they want and their guide is willing to give them a name, I am happy for them.

When working with guides now, as with John, I rarely ask their names unless it is for the person I am working with. There is usually no need to know the name unless that person or the spirit wants me to know, but I don't take for granted that they are God any longer. That is a lesson I had to learn even though as spiritual entities we are all part of God.

Guides come to us in a manner we can understand so they won't frighten us. This is for our comfort.

If you ask their names, they, like John, will tell you who they are. They don't necessarily volunteer the information. This doesn't mean they are bad, it just means they are trying to make you feel more at ease.

After all didn't God tell us he would send an emissary to help us?

His Name is John

John was part of that Holy Spirit, just as we all are.

People on the Other Side are more matter-of-fact than we are on this side. Not to say that they don't have a sense of humor. They do. Knowing the outcome, they see more details than we do. They will usually inform us if we act interested and listen.

It was really my fault that John had never told me his name. I had never asked. I took it for granted his name was God. When I asked for God to help me, he would answer.

His answering as God had its implications, because I told my husband that God spoke with me. Thinking that everyone did the same thing in talking with God and receiving an answer, I inquired of my husband if God didn't answer him too.

My husband informed me that not only did he not get an audible answer from God, but no one he knew did either. This was entirely wrong to my way of thinking, but he told me to ask the neighbors if they received spoken messages from God too. I asked two neighbors, found out they didn't, and stopped before the rest of my neighborhood thought Claude should have me committed. John taught me to protect myself.

Had John, a very serious man of authority with a great voice, not come to me in a masculine tone, I would have discounted him because when I was growing up, I knew God had to be masculine. That's what I was taught.

Otherwise, if the person speaking had spoken with a female voice, I would have thought it was just me, even though the voice was different.

It did not occur to me until later that John was that great man who also taught me between lives, while on the Other Side, before I was born to this life.

Now I have both male and female guides talking with me. (I always did but now I don't discount the female voice.) I have told them to speak one at a time or in unison. With them speaking as individuals, it is not so hard for me to understand and keep up with them now. Sometimes there are relapses though. They try to grant my wish but like all of us when we have something to say, we want to be heard.

Sometimes it's like a grammar school classroom where everyone knows the answer to the question the teacher has asked and all the guides try to answer at once. Thus they fail to sound as if unison. That is what I had heard all my life. My only problem, now that I look back on it, is that I thought this type communication was natural.

I miss John. He is no longer with me but I heard from him through someone who didn't even know they were giving me a message from him.

A tendency of mine is to ask my ghostly friends to watch out for my earthly friends. One of our psychic friends left our house so late one night that I asked someone from the Other Side to go home with her. I didn't specify anyone but just asked that they take care of her on the drive home and to make sure she was all right.

The next morning she called, and asked, "Who is this John person? He has been preaching to me all night." She must have needed the preaching. John did enough of that with me.

I cried.

Thank God I had him for the time I did. He helped me become who I am today.

Chapter Four

PSYCHIC LIFE CAN BE REWARDING AND FEARFUL TOO!

E
ven though most people say that they want to become psychic, to see and speak with spirits, it takes a very special person to give into that life. Once you make the decision to become a psychic minister to others, you open yourself up to a whole spectrum of life you never realized existed before. Never again will your life be just yours for the asking.

From the time you express your desire to use your psychic abilities in a constructive way for others, your life is no longer yours. Maybe that is one of the reasons I was afraid to open those psychic closet doors. Knowledge is always there for the true psychic whether they want to admit it or not. They can see into their own future but are sometimes afraid of what they are seeing. As with any human, they pretend that it doesn't exist by exclaiming that they cannot read their own lives.

Putting limitations on their gifts, they tell others that they did not know this would happen to them, but they really saw it before it ever took effect. Or at least I did. Somewhere in the back of my mind I knew that once I opened those doors, my life would never be the same. Because people look at something they don't understand with prejudice, I knew that people I loved would look at me totally differently. This was quite unsettling and something I did not relish happening for a time.

We, as humans, though, put into action the events we need so that we can grow and mature into the person we intended to become in our lives. Most of us do not want to take this responsibility. Rather we would pretend that we are driven by circumstance more than the divine plan for our lives. Incidentally, we were the ones who made that divine plan for this life while living on the Other Side.

Living the life of the psychic can be rewarding as well as unsettling until you reach your comfort level. Even then there is very little comfort for the good psychic. Always being tested not only by those you don't know but also by those you love is part of a good psychics life. A psychic is always on guard and rarely finds a place to let their hair down and become the chosen human they became at birth.

People you love and who love you become scared of you because of your gifts. It is not that they don't love you but rather listen to your every word to see when it might be one of prophesy. Humans have a tendency to believe the worst is in store for them most of the time. So your friends do not take your words lightly as they would their other friends. A joke coming from the psychic friend is not necessarily as funny as one coming from someone else.

In living with this gift, you have to be aware that words carry extreme importance to those who know you are gifted. As such, you will be constantly on guard to watch your words and can never be completely comfortable, not even with someone who has been with you for years. This is only part of the psychic's world.

Psychics have a tendency to go through three phases in their lives. This can be a day-to-day or month-to-month process and does not have to be in a consistent order. They are the "Happy Psychic," the "Militant Psychic" and the "Suppressed Psychic."

When I first came out of the psychic closet, I was the happy psychic and still am at times, quick to tell the world that I am a psychic. The joy of being a psychic far outweighs the hardships accompanying

Psychic Life Can Be Rewarding and Fearful Too!

the ability. A happy psychic wants everyone else to know how great this gift is. We go about gaily offering advice to anyone listening and trying to teach those same people that they can use their gifts too.

Great joy is felt when psychics give freely of themselves. Walking on cloud nine, they go through life dispensing metaphysical information to all who want it. In a euphoric state, they stay on a psychic high while giving out their advice. They are proud to be alive because of their endowment and want everyone to know it.

The "Militant Psychic" is the one who wants everyone to know about their psychic ability because they don't care what the other person may think of them. They are tired of trying to save everyone else's feelings to their own detriment. Sorry to say, I have been this one too.

After hearing that psychics are "bad" enough times, this psychic has a tendency to be quick in offering advice some may find a little hard to take. Not only do they tell the person they are speaking with that they are psychic but they usually add little tidbits that the recipient may have felt they were better off without.

On one occasion I listened to two young women at a restaurant I frequented talking about me. One of the ladies was quite sweet and innocent. The other had known much of the world or so she thought. Her estimation of a psychic was not very good and she was proceeding to tell the other sweet lady this as I walked up to them.

Hearing the sweet lady talk about me made my heart warm but the other lady left a little to be desired. She didn't believe in psychics and didn't care that I knew. Not believing in psychics is not a bad thing but having a closed mind is.

Teaching her a lesson came from the "Militant Psychic," I am sorry to say. Even though I knew her heart and knew that she was not a bad person, my mouth opened to start the words. "Buckle up when you are riding with her," I told my sweet little friend, "Because the two of you are going to be in an accident within a few blocks of your home. Neither of you will be hurt but it is because you will be wearing your seatbelts, which you," I said while pointing to the nonbeliever, "do not like to wear but you will be this time. Stay buckled up."

Proceeding, I told them that this would happen on a misty day and what color car would hit them.

Smugly, the "Militant Psychic" left the restaurant. She didn't try to soften the blow of the ensuing car crash as she generally would but instead left with a smile on her face because she had removed the smile from the nonbelievers face.

The "Militant Psychic" forgets that she can get more flies with honey than being bitter because someone has a problem with her. After all, that is part of the psychic life. Not everyone believes in you. A good psychic knows that this is better than having everyone believe so much that they try to make the events their psychic describes happen.

A skeptical mind is a good thing to have, especially with so many charlatans in the world. Even I am skeptical. Until I have done it, I have a hard time believing it. Yet, there are times it is more than I can bear to hear bad words about myself or another psychic that I know is good at what they do.

Needless to say, when I visited that restaurant again, the nonbeliever came over to me with her friend and told me how what I had said had come true. She also told me that as they got into the car, her friend told her to remember what I had said about the misty day and to buckle up. The accident occurred within two blocks of their home.

Smugness left the "Militant Psychic" as she said she was sorry that her prediction had come true. Although both of them were safe, it is not always easy to hear that a dire prediction you have made has happened, especially when you made the prediction without much tenderness.

Psychics always need to remember that they could possibly be on the other side of the coin with their future being read to them. Some things are more easily swallowed with a little sugar. The lesson here is to always watch your words. They are creations as surely as the physical planting of a tree. By telling them about the accident, I insured that they would buckle up and that probably kept them safer than if they had not been wearing seat belts but the way I said it could have been gentler.

Sometimes though the message is more important than the way you deliver it.

The "Suppressed Psychic" goes through her days being very silent about who she is when meeting new people. Because she is tired of fighting the fight for a while, she becomes introverted when people ask about her life and her calling. Even if they know who she is, she tends to step back into an emotional corner and try to hide who she is.

This person is well aware how people will hang on her every word

Psychic Life Can Be Rewarding and Fearful Too!

and will either fear her or hate her without getting to know the person behind the psychic talent.

The "Suppressed Psychic" may feel uncomfortable herself because she knows the feelings of others. As an Empath, she takes on their hurts and joys as well.

Tired and wanting a vacation of sorts, not from the gift, but rather from the people it involves, she refuses to tell those around her who she is because she knows they want more information about themselves. This is not a bad or selfish thing for them to want, she knows, but only curiosity about their own lives and whether she does really have metaphysical abilities. There again, she has to prove herself.

The fact is most good psychics can't help themselves when asked for advice. They tend to give it even when it may be detrimental to them at the time. Sometimes working while ill is part of this. Those people want to know so much that they don't consider the psychic human may be unwell. Needing to know about themselves, they do not think that they are being inconsiderate even though if they were ailing, they would want to curl up on a couch and hibernate. These people see only the gift and not the person. The ability should never stop and they know it even though the container might need a break.

Psychics go through these three times in their lives over and over again but most acknowledge that the gift of prophesy is one of the best in the world and well worth having.

Another part of psychic ability may appear cavalier but is not meant to be. I am frequently caught this way. It is not because I don't value another person but because I am simply doing my job. As with anything else, we sometimes take this ability for granted and speak out at times it would be better to remain silent.

Ask any good psychic and they will tell you that there have been times that they heard precognitive words being spoken and realized that it was coming from their mouths and was something that could change a life. This happens to me all the time.

People think you know what you are saying and have a hard time realizing that you don't necessarily know when you are the one speaking about something or someone close to them.

While speaking with an insurance agent friend of mine about one of my husband's policies, he brought up a person without using their

47

name. Without thinking my mouth started and I heard, "He really does need an insurance policy. He has a very bad disease."

The next thoughts were, *Oh my God. Is this a friend of his? What did I just say?* You can see how being a psychic sometimes has its effect even on the psychic. Unable to crawl under a table out of sight, then you have to deal with what you said.

Because I was on target with things relative to the insurance agents friend, he knew that I was able to advise him on his friend. This may be why people sometimes feel uncomfortable around psychics. If we can see someone they are only speaking of, then it is totally possible that we see so much more about them because they are in the room with us. This can be scary for people in close proximity to a psychic because they are never sure what we will say nor how we will say it. Perhaps we might say something about them in much the same way.

Another feeling that a psychic may have is that people don't want to get to know them as a person but would rather get to know their gift instead. They only tolerate the metaphysical container in human form in order to receive the gift. Failing to notice that a human being is the possessor of the gift, they hang on the psychic's every word to see if something is going to be said about them.

Again, let me reiterate that this does not make people doing this bad. Instead it only makes them human. After all, most of us like hearing about ourselves especially if it is something wonderful in our futures. Other psychics want to know what is happening in their lives as well and tend to question the psychic of their choice about those matters.

The problem with this behavior is that it can wear a psychic out by having to constantly be at another person's disposal, especially if being a psychic is the chosen field of employment. Who wants to work all of the time? Everyone needs a little time off to recuperate.

If the psychic is an Empath, it is hard enough being able to feel the feelings of that person without having to explain what you are feeling to them while you are together. Knowing what they expect from you can be a drain in itself. It can wear a psychic out just as physical exertion can. For a psychic Empath, touch of any kind is felt as if it were physical.

Some years ago I had to go to Hawaii to work a convention for a major radio station. Just so you know, I am not complaining. If I had

Psychic Life Can Be Rewarding and Fearful Too!

to work anywhere, Hawaii was the place to be.

The people were wonderful. They have great respect for psychic work and made it quite evident but that was the first time I have ever been physically touched so much. Of course, they asked if they could touch my face, hands or arms but it is still giving a piece of yourself each time you allow this to happen. With each touch, I was able to read that person, his lives and his wishes as readily as if someone was shaking me. Psychic ability allows you to become that person for a moment, and therefore you feel all that he feels. That can become overwhelming for some psychic people.

Gambling casinos are especially hard for me but I know other psychics who have no problems at all in that environment. The flood of emotions from the people who are gambling is so overwhelming that it is hard to contain myself. Some psychics are better able to insulate themselves than others. My abilities are left open all the time because it is like one of my other senses making me very sensitive to the feelings of others. Coming to rely on this ability just as with my other five senses at an early age makes it very hard to turn off now. Without it I would feel lost. For me, it is just as important to my life as breathing. Just because I did not come out of the psychic closet until later in my life does not mean that I was not using it all the time anyway.

Another point to consider from the psychic viewpoint is people who hang around psychics only to hear what the next prediction for them might be. They are so excited to be close to the gift that they can't get enough of it and thus prod the psychic for more and more. Getting proof that there are most certainly metaphysical events can be a heady experience especially when it can be proven in your own life. Even I, as the teacher, test the psychic.

After teaching a class some years ago, I had a very nice, well known man in computer technology continue to ask me to do readings from little notes certain people gave him. This was fine for a while but after the third or fourth note, I had to tell him that I could no longer do this for him because it was as if he wanted to read their diaries. "Oh no," he exclaimed, "I don't read what you are writing. I'm giving them the notes that you write back because I want them to know how good you are and that this is real."

The reason for his believing I was good is because I taught him to see auras, something someone into computer technology could not believe. He came to my class with his arms crossed daring me to teach him and left with the knowledge that there was something to this psychic thing after all.

Giving me the notes to work up and send back with a reading was his way of teaching his colleagues that there was indeed something to metaphysics.

When people are with me, I do not always tell them what I am seeing in reference to them. Oh, sometimes something may slip out about their lives or someone they care about, but I usually try not to let that happen unintentionally.

One such incident happened when my husband and I were out to dinner. Someone told one of the waiters at the restaurant that I was a psychic. He wanted proof. I mentioned something to him about the new television he had just bought a couple of nights before. If someone he had known had mentioned the television he would have been all right with it but he didn't know me. He looked at me as if I were a stalker instead of a psychic.

Over the years I have learned that my interjecting intuitive comments into the conversation has a tendency to alarm some people. Generally when people become alarmed, they begin to fear the source. Also they have a tendency to believe that I may be able to read their minds, which is not always good, because I sometimes tell them what they were talking about prior to coming to my home. On occasion, I do read minds. This does not make it easy to be my friend.

Being friends with me is not easy. If I am not making a friend uncomfortable with the thought that I am reading her mind, then I am talking to the Other Side. People have a tendency not to feel comfortable when one is speaking to dead people.

My best friend tells me that when another dimension tries to get my attention, she knows that it is better to stop whatever we are doing and let me see to whatever or whoever was paging me. She realizes that until I am able to deal with the supernatural, I am only giving her part of myself.

This usually happens when we are on the phone since she lives a few states from me. While we are talking, one of my ghostly friends or even one I don't know may come to visit. Usually they are very considerate but if they have a need to let me know something pertinent to her, they are not adverse to just showing up in some spectacular way to get my attention. Even though I try to hide this from her, she is wise enough to know the signs and will tell me to take care of the intruder to our conversation before I get back to her because she wants all my attention.

On the other hand, she also says that knowing I can read her mind makes her uncomfortable at times but that my friendship is worth it. By the way, she rarely asks me to read for her unless it is an emergency. The lady is a true southern woman. She does not want to make anyone uncomfortable.

Friends of mine have to bear being ready to hear things that they may not want too. There are times that I inadvertently say words that were not what I thought I said. After the words come out and I am two or three sentences ahead, I realize that the words were not what I had considered them to be. When the realization of the words hit me, I am generally looking at someone with a very unusual expression on their faces.

This happens to Claude constantly and it is not just the everyday husband and wife stuff. This may be about one of our children or it could be about a business transaction. Any number of situations may evolve with my unconscious prognostications. Living with me is not easy but it can have its rewards.

My first husband did not find it rewarding. While we were married, I generally told him about the lady he was out with the night before. He didn't like that.

Knowing the future is not always the enlightenment that some want. It can be a burden as well.

Claude, my husband, can become quite frustrated with me about my ability. Not being one to take metaphysics lightly because it has to be proven to him and after having seen my abilities over the years, he has a tendency to keep me under the microscope as well. Listening to the hidden meanings in all my words is not easy for the two of us.

If I mention one of our children, he is immediately interested as any father would be, but this is more. My ability to be concerned over my children without the third degree is gone. Upon voicing any apprehension, he instantly asks, "Why, what do you see?" Generally when he asks that question, I get the answer but sometimes am not willing to share because in my estimation I am in trouble if I do answer and in trouble if I don't share. There are some things naturally that a parent does not want to know.

Within a few moments of the question, my normally sweet husband and I are in an-all-out argument. A pouting "Cancer" is not easy to take especially when you love him. Not wanting to hurt his feelings, I try to phrase my words so that they are not as disturbing. He feels that since he is married to me I should not keep secrets of any kind from him. These are not secrets. It is sometimes easier for some to go through life not knowing until the problem arises. Once he learns the problem, then he gets frustrated and takes it out on me because I am the one with which he has to talk. He and I are best friends and we talk about everything. Knowing about your loved one's problems is not always easy and he doesn't leave me the room to ignore the predicament until it occurs.

My husband tells me too that I am no fun when it comes to him buying me gifts because I generally know what he has bought me. I try not to think about the gift but if he makes comments about it or ask a question about it, I frequently realize what it is.

Both of us love playing games. Though I am psychic, normally I try not to use it with the games we play because I don't feel it is right to do so, but I have had the occasion to ask for a little assistance if he or his mother is getting a little arrogant about how well they can play.

On one occasion while playing eighty-four (dominoes) with his family I must say that I did use my abilities because I didn't know how to play the game well and my mother-in-law bid two marks. She knew she had everyone at the table that knew anything about the game beat except for me, who knew nothing except to follow leads.

Well after asking my guides, they told me to hold the double two which would normally have been played earlier in the game by anyone who knew how to play the game.

My mother-in-law doesn't curse but she wanted too. At that point, she had a very hard time with my being psychic and told me constantly that she didn't believe in it or that I was. She lost two marks. Maybe that is one of the events that made her believe.

When someone you know is about to die, do you really want to know? I try not to tell anyone that someone they love will die but have been known to make the statement that they should spend more time with that person in a certain time period. Giving them this information does not tell them that the person will die but gives them the chance to be with them before they go to the other side.

Some of my clients have told me that I did this for them and that they were eternally grateful because they were able to be with their loved ones when they were needed.

As a psychic though, I do know about the ones I love dying. When put on the spot, my guides always tell me. It is not necessarily me that does the asking either.

A good friend of mine who was in radio for years asked me at a party one night how long he had to live. I had not looked at that subject until he asked because I had not wanted to. Instantly, I heard the answer of how long and how. My reply to him was that he had as much time as he needed and that he needed to live and quit thinking about death. At the moment of his death, he came to my home to see me. That is how I knew he was dead. Incidentally my guides had told me correctly.

My schnauzer dog, Muffin, who I dearly loved, was one that was particularly hard. Upon cutting her hair for the last time, I heard that this would be the last time that I would cut her hair. She wasn't showing any sign of it being that way. This countdown continued until I gave her a bath at which time they told me it would be her last bath. She was bathed frequently. They were right. Not many people can live with this knowledge but I would not know how to live without it.

My husband had to know four months before his father died on which day it would be, so he asked me. Again I knew but would not tell him until he kept on and on. Then I told him that it would be on the eighth, and I even knew the time of day, but he did not ask that. He says I helped him by telling him, but he had to live with that knowledge for four more months. Human beings typically do not want to have this type information.

Living with me has brought more than a regular husband and wife team normally has to deal with. The psychic seems to be there for him too, so that he is unable to walk unexpectedly into situations as well. Grabbing future knowledge is so overwhelming that one literally cannot help but want to reach for it.

The negatives I am sharing in being psychic is so that you can be well-informed before you ask that the gift become more evident. Once you ask for this gift, the doors will open and you will receive it.

My love of the metaphysical is so overwhelming that I would take all this and more to continue my work but it does cause me to challenge every thought and inspect thoroughly every meaning.

Once when I was feeling especially sorry for myself because I thought people saw only the ability and not me, a friend asked if I would be willing to use this gift if people did not know who I was. He said to pretend that there was a stage with a curtain in front and that I had to stand behind the curtain and prognosticate for the audience. In this way they would not know who I was and I could go on living in anonymity.

"Would you be happy then," he questioned?

After thinking for a moment, I told him that I would want to be able to see their faces as they learned what I had to tell them. They would not have to see me but I needed to see them. That was my selfish reward.

He then admonished me to quit feeling sorry for myself because people didn't notice me but only my gift. The endowment of metaphysical ability is what I was here to teach. Whether they noticed me or not was just a human emotion and had no business interfering with the job of teaching. Humility is something John always told me that we as humans should learn and obviously I have had my chances to do so.

Another emotion concerned with metaphysical activity is one most relate to it, that of fear. In dealing with that emotion, we need to look it over in context and deal with it on a primary basis. Fear will cause one to limit their abilities and themselves but seems to be something at times a person cannot control. In reality, we are in supreme control over our mental faculties and emotions.

For so long, I was frightened that I would be looked at differently in the human sense that I concealed the metaphysical senses. Constantly trying to relegate those senses to the posterior regions of my life, I felt that a most important part of my life was missing.

On the outside people saw a happy-go-lucky façade for a person who was very serious minded really. Trying to be the life of the party for everyone else kept me busy enough that I could mask my metaphysical talents about fifty percent of the time. Even when they appeared, I lacked the courage to tell anyone about them unless I was imbibing a little from the grape.

At those times, I did notice my audience would grow and be in rapt attention as I spoke of different other worldly events in my life. As I watched the audience grow, I remembered, even in the alcohol haze, to watch how much I said. Unlike when I was a girl and without thinking I told my classmate that I knew at what time her father had died the night before because he came to tell me so. That type of admission can lose you friends.

What my classmate didn't know is that I was concerned too, because he came to see me. Her father was a wonderful man who had three sons and two daughters. I greatly respected him, and it was out of this respect that I told her about his visit (and because I was testing my own ability.) He had shown me the time of his death and I needed to confirm that it was real but that didn't help her. I was not trying to upset her but could probably have chosen my words better.

The look on her face made me know that not everyone is as accepting of this ability as I am. Not only had she lost her father but here her best friend was telling her that he had visited her at the time of his death. She was very upset with me. In her defense, it was understandable that she should be. Not only had she gone through his death but was still in the grieving process when I made her remember her loss.

Looking back on the situation, I can now understand that I lacked certain metaphysical manners at the time but was proving to myself how correct my abilities were. As a skeptic, I am always testing those talents to make sure that they are genuine.

Being a metaphysician has it's own set of fears. According to your talents, your fears may grow in size.

Psychics who do not see the Other Side may only be concerned with their readings for others. The responsibility lies in telling others what you see in their futures in a conscientious way. These psychics may feel anxiety about accountability of themselves and to the universe.

Fear doesn't have to be physical to be felt but can cause physical reactions in people. For example, think of a time when you were most frightened in your life. Think of the physical response to the event. Probably, you breathed harder, your heart pounded and you were looking for escape. All of the circumstances concerning your dreadful event led the body to emit physical responses.

Being scared has its uses. In a dangerous situation, fear can propel you into action so that you can escape harm. Less hazardous conditions will allow the dread to start building so that you prepare yourself for flight. All fear does is to give you the impetus to move quickly. When there is someone physically close enough to hurt you, this can be a good tool to have. Putting you on notice quickly gives you needed time to help yourself.

In the metaphysical world, fear has less good effect. Though it can be part of the equation, it does no good other than to alarm you.

As a child, there were some fears in my life in connection to the Other Side. My friend, John, whom I was never afraid of, didn't explain to me that the other ghosts around me shouldn't alarm me. I never brought them up because I tried to ignore them. Because of that, he never had the opportunity to educate me about them. We were usually too busy talking about other subjects. They generally always remained in the background while he was around and I felt safe then.

It looked something like this. Imagine a small child hiding behind her mother's skirts, looking out from behind them timidly while studying the people trying to speak to her. She wants to talk but needs to learn whether they are friendly souls. Until urged by her mother to proceed, she stands firmly behind her. This was my way with John. Continuously patient, he waited for me to get over my concern. Had I ever brought up the question as to whether I should have been alarmed by them, he would have told me. They were always there but took their cues from my friend John.

With him, I felt safe. The others, though, made me just the least bit apprehensive. As a child, when I was going to another room in the house, I always looked straight ahead to avoid the eyes and cries of those who were dead.

Going to the bathroom at night was especially difficult for me. I had to build up the bravery before running as quickly as I could to the bathroom and turning on the light so that they would not be as evident. The only problem with that is although they allowed me that little bit of privacy they were still there. They were always there and I knew it. For me turning on the light gave me a little time to catch my breath.

Sleeping at night could be a time of sweating too, not only

Psychic Life Can Be Rewarding and Fearful Too!

because of the others but also because of the heat of summer nights without air conditioning. In my childhood, hardly anyone had air conditioning. So on summer nights, we opened the windows. The only problem with that was that I kept the covers pulled up around my face thinking that it would give me peace.

Had I ever asked John for help with this, I am sure he would have explained the situation to me. Maybe he didn't offer because I had to learn on my own to overcome the fear of strangers in my house.

There was never a time I didn't remember John being with me. The others came into my life and went out just as quickly. People whom I knew alive often startled me when they visited me after they had died, sometimes to the point of my heart racing. I was able to get over it. The fear of it only made me more aware of the event.

Sometimes I think that is why fear is part of the metaphysical world. It brings emphasis to a situation that you may have let go by just giving some weak explanation without challenging it meanings. Fear makes it physical. After having a bodily reaction you are much more likely to remember the event. Your body saves the happening using the fear to enhance the process.

Fear of psychics is something else entirely. People fear what they don't know. As with any prejudice people have a tendency to want to eradicate what they don't understand instead of seeking to learn from those individuals.

Superstition is based on fear and is attributed to the metaphysical. Looking for curses and other weird myths, people then think they have a reason to act upon those fears by transferring their anger to the object of that fear. Getting rid of the object will stop the fear, they think.

Fear causes abnormal thinking. A lady wrote me not long ago with what I guess to be a superstitious anomaly concerning a crow. The reason she wrote was because this bird had been hanging around her back yard, even trying to get into her screen door. She wanted to know if I could make the crow go away or send her in the right direction to get the crow removed.

Well if I wanted a crow removed, I guess I would call someone who knew birds to do it. However, I am not into removing birds because I love them. Crows are not a favorite bird for me like the songbirds but like the songbirds they are interesting in their behavior.

GHOSTS TALK

This lady would not be satisfied with my explanation that the crow probably was raised by someone who looked like her or that the crow had been fed by humans and was thus unafraid. For her that crow meant that there was some sort of dire circumstance associated with it. She could not enjoy the bird for what it was, just a bird. No, she had to ascribe some macabre reason for its visits. She thought the worst of the poor creature and thus, was ignorant to the plight of the crow.

Ignorance is dislocated fear. Once a person is educated, then there is no reason for fear. Illumination cancels darkness.

Lack of knowledge and the unawareness of that fact is a serious enemy to the advancement of intelligence. People who are stuck in their beliefs without question are generally unaware that they may have a considerable lack of knowledge. That's why I try to teach and to keep an open mind to all possibilities even though a healthy amount of skepticism is good.

Hitler used religious prejudice to unite a nation one person at a time. Perhaps very few people know that this man wanted to become a priest. He took his religious feelings to a new high in vengeance. This man sought power in order to avenge the death of Jesus Christ, or so he thought. In seeking this, he united a kingdom to do his bidding because the people of Germany came to believe in a man who taught them that the Jewish race was bad and had no business on this earth. This man was so charismatic that he talked a democracy into giving up that democracy and allowing him to become their sole leader.

Not only did Hitler have religious convictions, but thought of himself as a prophet also. In his speech of January 30, 1939, he said, "In the course of my life I have very often been a prophet, and have usually been ridiculed for it. During the time of my struggle for power it was in the first instance only the Jewish race that received my prophecies with laughter when I said that I would one day take over the leadership of the state, and with it that of a whole nation, and that I would then among other things settle the Jewish problem. Their laughter was uproarious, but I think that for some time now they have been laughing on the other side of their face. Today I will once more be a prophet: if the international Jewish financiers in and outside Europe should succeed in plunging the nations once more into a world war, then the result will not be the Bolshevizing of the earth, and thus the victory of

Psychic Life Can Be Rewarding and Fearful Too!

Jewry, but the annihilation of the Jewish race in Europe!"

To hear that this man thought he was a prophet was bad enough, but to realize that he almost fulfilled that prophecy is thoroughly terrifying. The reason I used his speech here was to bring home to everyone reading this text how easily a mass of people can be swayed by someone who professed to be a prophet. It took individuals to allow their freedom to be lost in mass. That is why I think that we all should be open minded but also we must use a fair bit of skepticism so that we are cognizant of all the issues before we make up our minds on an issue. Never follow anyone blindly. Use your own innate psychic abilities and ask questions. When you feel that those queries have been answered sufficiently and you feel that your suspicions have been allayed, then and only then make up your mind.

Fear and reward are tied to the psychic when I am working murder cases. In taking the victims point of view, which I generally do, then I can feel all the circumstances leading up to the death including the fear felt by the sufferer. The reward comes in helping law enforcement find the person who committed the crime.

Being psychic has it's own fears and rewards, but I am so glad that I am able to use my abilities in this life. For me they are like breathing; without them I don't think I could live. These experiences give so much more than they take, although the responsibility for them is high. They are the wonder of wonders to me.

Chapter Five

MY NEAR-DEATH
EXPERIENCE

To understand a near-death experi-
ence, one has to understand what the scientific description of death is.
The dictionary describes death as the cessation of all vital functions. It
is described as the cause or occasion of loss of life. Near-death then
would be close to the cessation of all vital functions or the cause of loss
of life.

When a person is close to death, they are more strongly aware of
the other side. Being able to see people on the other side and speak
with them is part of the process.

Sometimes those otherworldly people invite the passing loved
ones to come with them making it easier for them to leave the worldly body and become reborn in the spirit. The dying person goes on to
their heavenly bodies and do not return to the physical body in the
same way they were before.

There are some death experiences that do not necessarily end in
the complete departure of the physical body. The spirit of that body

may visit the other side and return to the body without completing a physical death and thus becomes a near-death experience.

Accidents, surgery and other experiences may be the cause of near-death experiences. Though the body goes through physical changes, which causes the near-death experience, the spirit is still able to continue residing in the bodily encasement.

The spirit has seen both the mundane world and the supernatural side while in an earthly life cycle. Being able to derive information from both sides helps the entity to lead a better life upon its return to what most consider the real side of life.

There are reasons for the near-death experiences other than just to see what the other side looks like. Those experiences teach us lessons we would not be able to get under normal circumstances.

Near-death experiences allow one to see a different side of life. In most instances when we see dead people, we focus totally on their being dead. We don't take the time to notice where they are and how the place they are in affects them. All we know is that we are seeing a ghost.

When having a near-death experience, we focus totally on ourselves as part of the whole.

We are able to see everything that pertains to life and living. All knowledge is gleaned as soon as one permits themselves to go to the other side. Life truly does flash before their eyes.

Aware of all circumstances in their life, people see what effect they have had on themselves as well as others. Seeing how one action reflects another, they understand that they are capable of commanding great power in their relationships. They also comprehend that the whole universe is one big relationship. **We are not alone. We are one but separate.**

A near-death experience put me on both sides of this equation, because I died for fifteen minutes on an operating table while having surgery in September 1980.

Before going into surgery, I decided I no longer wanted to live in this world because I was frustrated with the human race as a whole as well as myself. This was the second time I had this revelation in this life.

Looking at the way people got along with each other, I felt there was too much prejudice. Everyone judged others by either the color of their skin, sex, sexual preferences and cultural or religious differences.

My Near-Death Experience

It made no sense to me, but I had lived with this sort of philosophy espoused by others most of my life.

Human beings hurting one another in order to feel more powerful was one of the human traits I saw in others at a very young age.

My favorite cousin once exhibited this type behavior when we went fishing with my father. We went to the dam to fish but instead were in the middle of an emergency. Fire engines were everywhere and they were dragging the raging side of the dam for bodies.

Someone who had been watching the whole tragic scene told us that they were still looking for an uncle of a little four-year-old boy whose body they had found. The person relayed the story of how the little boy had fallen into the churning waters and the uncle who could not swim had dived in to save him. Instead they both died that day.

The fireman brought up a young man who was in his early twenties. Life, which should have really just started for him, had ended in such a tragic manner. He was about six-foot tall, weighing about two hundred and forty pounds, with short-cropped hair and beautiful black skin. The fireman laid his body out on the ground and covered it with a tarp.

Thinking of this man's selflessness and the useless way two souls had died made me start to cry.

My cousin did the unspeakable. She looked at me with no concern whatsoever and questioned me, "What are you crying for? They are only N-----s!"

Not believing my ears, I stared at her in confusion as the tears came more readily. "I am crying for two human beings that died so uselessly today."

My father had never taught me to believe in the manner in which this person had just confronted me. She was my father's brother's child. How could they come from the same family? How could she be my favorite cousin? At that point, she no longer was.

It was unimaginable to me that she could think this way. Here I was guilty of judging her for her mouth as quickly as she had another by the color of his skin.

The death of these two people was a catastrophe, but it was also a lesson for my cousin and me. My cousin lost something that day: me. I lost my cousin.

GHOSTS TALK

The positive that came from that conversation, though, was that I learned not everyone felt as I did. Taking it for granted that everyone loved others as themselves was not true. A horrible lesson it was but one I needed to learn.

The other reason I didn't want to live was because I was afraid of being ridiculed for being who I was. This feeling had been one I had since I was a little girl. After all if someone knew I was a psychic, they might feel the same way about me that my cousin did about the poor souls whose skin color made a difference to her.

Both that dead young man and myself were who we were. We were children of God and as such should be treated with the same respect that every other child of God got.

So I decided that I would take the easy way out in this life. Using the anesthesia as death for me this time, I thought I could control the pain.

The surgery the doctor performed was to take bone from my face because of a bone malformation. During surgery my mouth was wired together. After the surgery was over, my doctor, who was a very nice man, came into my hospital room. Using an expletive, he demanded to know what I was thinking before I went into surgery.

Because I am a very logical person, I needed proof of where I had been and what I had seen.

My guides and I had a conversation about my faith. They reiterated to me that my faith does not come from something I have not seen but rather because I have seen, I have faith. Knowing that there truly is a God and people who are alive on the other side is not faith induced. I have to see it before I believe it.

My faith comes in the knowledge that because I know it is there, I can create abundance in my life just by the very belief it is so.

My doctor found that logical part of me who wanted proof from this side. Until he told me why he wanted to know, I would not tell him what had happened to me.

With my mouth wired together, all my part of the conversation had to be written because I was unable to speak. For a few minutes, there was only one question I wrote and at which I continued to point. It was "Why?"

Not as stubborn as I, the doctor finally gave in first.

Watching his face, I could tell that he was trying to use his logic to understand what he was explaining to me.

He told me this was the first time he had ever had this happen to him. Talking more to himself than to me, he muttered that the surgery was major but should not have caused this.

In a total state of confusion, he kept trying to convince himself that there was a normal reason for what had happened.

He told me that I had my vital signs drop for about fifteen minutes. When he and the team turned to leave me as dead on the operating table, all my signs returned.

Using a curse word once more, he asked again what I had been thinking.

This doctor had just told me that I had died on his table and he was upset with me. He seemed to have the tables turned. Something was terribly wrong here. Because he let me die, I should have been the one upset.

There was no anger. The evidence was there that my near-death experience was real and could be proven by this doctor. This made me more happy than angry.

He repeated, "This just shouldn't have happened. This was major surgery, but it shouldn't have happened."

Feeling about this incident as I felt about the psychic ability in my life, I decided to hide what had happened.

What I did tell him was what I had thought of prior to the surgery. The anesthetic triggered the memory.

It was that I had put my dog, who lived with me for sixteen years, down two years before because she had cancer. Although it hurt me terribly, I did it so that she would no longer feel pain. The way she died under the anesthesia was easier than most deaths I had seen.

The part I didn't tell the doctor was that because that death seemed easier, I had decided to take the coward's way out. The thought that it would be much easier to die than to live went with me into the surgery.

After having been given a drug that morning to make me sleepy before surgery as all doctors do, I assume, I was still wide-awake. When they took me to the surgery suite, my mouth was going ninety to nothing asking questions about everything in the room.

As the anesthesiologist worked at trying to find a vein, she became quite agitated and screamed at everyone in the room to be quiet. We all did. I found it interesting that she had the ability to scream at my doctor and he would listen. Then she looked at the doctor and asked, "Didn't you give her anything?"

He answered, "I gave her enough to knock a cow out and you see her now. She's still going."

Instead of getting bothered by the fact that they were talking about me not with me, their fussing sounded funny to me for some reason.

Telling the anesthesiologist that she hurt me trying to find the vein and that I had asked for a shot to deaden the area before she started, she asked that I be quiet. She also said that it would be a needle too and would hurt anyway. She told me that I was upsetting her more by telling her that she was hurting me. Because I was upsetting her it made it harder for her to find the vein.

As I do most of the time, I started comforting her instead of being worried about myself. "It's okay. Don't worry. Just go ahead and do what you need to. I'll be all right," I told her.

She continued working for a while until she got the needle into the vein and told me that I would have a small burning sensation go up my arm as the medicine traveled. It happened as she said until it got to my nose and I smelled wild onions. Telling her this, I was gone.

When I left my body in the operating room, my body burst out into the warmest yellow-gold-white light in the universe. It was not hot but a loving radiant illumination. I had seen it before on numerous occasions while talking with God.

Instantly, there was supreme understanding. I was aware of everything and everyone. More alive there than I have ever been on this side, I had complete knowledge.

This was home. There was so much love, compassion and understanding because everyone knew everything. No jealousy existed. Everyone and everything was this golden white light. It was God. People were open and accepting. It was wonderful.

Though at the time, I was seeing the whole of God, I knew that there were individuals there making up the whole. Recognizing two spirits who were behind me, I knew they wanted me to go back to the physical. They told me that it wasn't my time.

Knowing I didn't want to go back, I started running as quickly as my legs would take me away from them. At the time I didn't know where I was running, I just knew I had to get away from these two people. Following and calling my name, they were telling me I needed to go back because it wasn't my time to die though they gave me a choice. I knew they really wanted me to go back to the physical world, because there were still pieces of my life that needed completion but I also knew that the choice was ultimately mine to make.

Shaking my head and using my arms to help propel me forward, I continued to run staying just in front of them. I looked down. What I had thought was my arms and legs moving as quickly as possible, were not. My mind still conceived of myself in bodily form but I was a part of the warm yellow light. We were one and the same.

One of the people who was following called my husband's name. "What about Claude," he asked?

The shock of seeing myself without bodily constraints, and hearing my husband's name, got my attention.

I stopped. I remember saying. "That's right, I can't leave him to take care of our three children alone."

The knowledge of how much I loved him came flooding back. Coming back was the logical thing to do.

I know now they could have caught me at any time but they had to give me time to make the decision to come back. It was my choice not theirs. I could have stayed.

If you want to call the place I went "Heaven," you may. I was aware that anything I conceived was real. The warmth and love of that light let me know that if that is what I needed to see, it was what I got. Had I wanted to see a mansion on a hill, then I would have. Anything was possible on the other side. The physical side has its limits but the other side has none.

More than anything else, I was aware that I was not alone. Everything was part of me but I was still an individual with my own thoughts and personality. This reinforced my belief in the ghostly spirits with whom I speak. Though we are all one, we are separate. The soul color of God is the same. It is the outward appearance of the physical that is not.

The two guides, with whom I have worked before, do not appear in any spectacular manner. Instead they come in an earthen looking form. The physical shape is one of ours, but the whole inside of them looks as if it is made of earth. They chose to look this way for my education. We don't have to look alike to make sense of living. We only have to have our own thoughts and personalities.

I did not tell my doctor what I had seen while on the other side. Still hiding from people's views of the psychic, I felt I could not admit what had happened to me. My reluctance to admit to anyone I was psychic stood out like a sore thumb. Also I was not so sure he wouldn't try to have me committed. (In Louisiana, it was very easy. Besides, I hadn't told my husband yet and wasn't sure I would.) It just seemed as if I should hide the near-death experience in the same way I had hidden my psychic ability all my life. Self-preservation made me fearful of telling.

I had only been married for three months. My husband, a wonderful man, most of the time, tries to be there for me but does not let it interfere with the way he believes.

Keeping the fact that I was a psychic from him because I didn't have faith to think he would still love me, I wasn't about to tell him about this experience. I wasn't far wrong. Besides, husbands commit wives to sanitariums every day.

My ex-husband had told me, on numerous occasions, he would put me in a mental institution. The reason he threatened me with this was because I always told him who he had been with and what he had done the night before. Being the helpful teacher he was, he continued to test me with other women on a nightly basis.

Fear had been ingrained in me all my life. My father, without realizing it, had taught me I could use my abilities only in church. Here I was married to a man who could have me institutionalized without conflict from anyone in my family, or so I thought. Not thinking even my father would try to help me; I ran scared of telling anyone.

Since then, I have come to realize that was one of my budding lessons. Part of my being human was to learn this lesson.

Being proud of who I am and making use of my abilities with others is a part of my growth. It didn't matter how hard the lesson was. I had to learn to quit fearing. **Fear is Failure.**

By that I mean, when you are so frightened that you are unable to do what you know you should. Then you have failed. As long as you keep trying and be true to yourself, then you are a success. Not trying because you are afraid is what causes failure.

My Near-Death Experience

I know without a doubt that when we die we go to a place where we can circle the world and more with a thought because I have been there. It is a place of supreme love and understanding. There is no fear. You are in God's love. **You are God's Love.**

Dying in this manner served to teach me more than one lesson. One is that we are able to die just by willing it and another is I saw the other side in a way, which few others have.

Though it was glorious on the Other Side, one should not think of taking the easy way out. Doing that would only cause more concern for the suicide victim once he or she dies. Having to look over their life and see the costs to families and friends is a high enough price to pay but is not enough. The person who commits suicide learns that they have to go through physical life all over again using the same challenges. Until they learn how to overcome and grow from their life situation, they will repeat it.

Although I speak with ghosts all the time, I had never seen the other side from this perspective until I died. There was an instant understanding of **All That Is.**

I was one with everything.

Life goes on in both sides of what we consider reality.

We are all angels on that side, some a little purer maybe than others, but angels nonetheless. For us on the Other Side the degree of learning determines where you reside in the scheme of things, but we are all one with God and because of this we know who we are and what we have done on the physical side of life.

For me, we, on the physical side of life, are only an angel's dream. What I mean is that the reality of the situation is when I was on the near-death side, it is the real part of life. What we consider the physical realm is just an angel's thought. No more, no less.

Have you ever been in a dream state where you felt fear? I have. Sometimes I have been awakened from a dream state feeling as if I were falling or trying to rescue someone in vain. With my heart about to come out of my chest, I awaken.

Dreams appear real. When they can cause a reaction such as this, they are real.

This physical life appears real. Physical life sometimes brings with it pain. We do get tired. It is all we have until we learn better.

GHOSTS TALK

A near-death experience is not necessarily the only way to see the spirit side of life.

There are times when we consciously or unconsciously go out of body. Now that's a frightening thought isn't it? Most people in their right mind do not want to leave their body. Still we do though.

Take this scenario. Comfortably sleeping you go to a place that you perhaps have never been before and speak with people there as if you are old friends. Nothing seems to be out of the ordinary except that you awaken with the feeling that you are falling. Jerking awake, all your senses are heightened. Returning to sleep without thinking further about what happened, you resume your life.

A few days, weeks or months later, you may visit the place you dreamed of and think this seems familiar. Then, upon meeting people who were with you in your dream, you realize that you are replaying a scene. Knowing what will be spoken next, you have a sense of déjà vu.

You were there before in what you considered a dream when in fact it was an out of body experience in what you perceive as real life. In doing this, you saw the future.

Out-of-body experiences and near-death experiences are similar in that the spirit leaves the body. With both, one can experience learning what the higher plane or spiritual world is like.

Both experiences have similar techniques for completion because both take the spirit out of the body but one takes you on the highest spiritual journey. Each time you return to body, but with both you are learning something that can help you on your physical journey in life.

Taking the sum of my experiences up to now is what I hope to teach you in this book. From what I have learned with my ghostly encounters, we all make it to a higher realm, but some of us have to keep on learning more in order to graduate up to the highest spiritual realms. My point to make is that we learn from all and everything. Please try not to think because you are living what you consider to be a spiritual life, that you are any better than anyone else. We are all on our journey and learn from each other.

Each and every one of us is teacher to the other. Learn and accept what you need for your spiritual journey. Leave the rest.

Section Two

GHOSTS

Chapter Six

WHAT IS A GHOST?

Once as I walked into my den, I almost ran over a stranger standing just inside the doorway. In a panic but rapidly weighing my options, I had to decide quickly how to get away from this person, but he was within arms length, in what had been my safe home just a few minutes ago.

Since he was not my husband, there was no reason for him to be there unless he was a burglar or someone who meant to do me harm. Trying to get out of this intruder's way before I ran completely over him and had no chance of escape, I continued to check out this man from his shoes up, because he should not have been in my house.

Having to make a life-altering examination of this man in a split second was critical. My heart was pounding and my breath stuck in my throat. My mind went into overdrive. What is the best method of escape? How do I fight back? Look at his hands and see if they are reaching for me!

He was looking straight ahead with his arms at his sides and

GHOSTS TALK

never even turned to look at me. Beyond any doubt, I knew that he was aware of my presence. Now I had time to investigate a little more but I was still frightened out of my mind.

This man was around six feet tall, wearing brown shoes, jeans and a blue shirt with some green in it. My eyes made it to his neck, where I saw red on it. Following the red stuff up his neck to his head, I saw dried blood, gray matter and matted brown hair where the side of his head should have been. He was a walking corpse.

I could take a breath now because I knew he was dead, a ghost. Like all the stupid, inquisitive times in my life, my first words were, "What do you want?"

"For you to help me catch my killer," he answered.

Immediately, I knew who the killer was. This man's wife had killed him and then sent her children into the house to find their dead father. Knowing it was a lesson to be learned by all did not help because those children were so young.

He stood there quietly waiting for me to receive the impressions he was giving me. While alive, he was not a shy man but was not overly outgoing, either. I had to digest the whole ugly picture in front of me before I could look at him again.

Looking at him the way he was showing himself to me was not easy either but he needed me to see what she had done to him. When a killer who is shorter than the victim walks up behind that person, puts a pistol to his head and pulls the trigger, it is not a pretty picture. One I was not willing to continually look at.

Without trying to hurt his feelings, I told him that I would rather not see him that way again. He was the only ghostly murder victim I'd seen who continued to appear as he did when he was killed. I asked if he would please turn his body to the other side so that I would not have to keep looking at that gory scene.

The police did not talk with me until years later about this murder, and the victim continued for some time to come and see me. He wanted me to tell the police about his killer and how to get her, but I was unable to do it at the time. I do not normally seek out the police or families to work with but wait for them to come to me. No one did.

Years later I met a policeman who worked on two cases that had really stayed with me. I learned that the two were connect-

76

ed, which is something that had not been publicized. He told me that he thought it was the wife, too, but they were unable to indict her. I told him what the ghostly gentleman had told me, and the officer said it fit exactly, but they had been unable to even find the weapon.

The officer told me that he had looked to find the gun precisely where I had told him she threw it, but that it was such a big area that they probably would never find it.

This is just one instance of a ghostly encounter and is meant to illustrate that they do not have to come by conventional means at all but can come in any shape or appearance they choose. The murdered ghost continued to come to see me with his bloodied head so that I could easily identify him and would not forget what his mission was.

Humans have been taught that they should not see ghosts because if they do, then something is terribly wrong. In fact this is not true. Ghosts appear to their human counterparts because either they have a message, or they want the companionship. Sometimes they even appear to physical people out of boredom, because they want a laugh or they want to make us laugh.

A ghost is an individual spirit who never dies. It lives time and again through the means of a mortal body. This entity is part of a Supreme Being but is an individual nonetheless.

Ghosts are people who no longer carry the burden of flesh and blood, who have passed to the other side and are called dead. They still have the personality they had in life but no longer have the body.

Most religions dictate that if the soul was good on earth, then they are in a place of peace, usually called heaven. If not in heaven, then they are in the alternative, a really undesirable place generally called hell.

My belief is that ghosts are learning new experiences with each incarnation and between those lives. These persons are able to communicate, if it is allowed, in much the same way as when they were alive.

A ghost is an entity who has lived in the physical world even though it no longer has a body. Because of this, it can come up with ways for people on the physical side to be able to see, hear, feel, taste or smell them.

They may or may not take a form or shape. Some even appear as three dimensional without the fogginess or transparency that is attributed to most. When they do take form, it is not for their convenience but for the person who is seeing the ghost.

Please understand that ghosts should be treated with the same respect you expect. They have feelings too. Although, they are no longer in this dimension and can see things with a more knowing eye, they are personalities, too.

They come in different sizes, shapes and colors just as we do. Ghosts may be called angels, beings of light, and a few other choice names, but they are capable of love and thought just as we are.

Having a tendency to associate with people like themselves, they seek out people on the physical side who believe as they do. A compassionate person will have a compassionate ghost seek them out.

We on the physical side become friends with people we have things in common with. Our friends usually have some quality we like and one we possess as well.

Ghosts have to find the same qualities in people they hang out with. Otherwise, it is akin to a genius in a room full of ignorant people. For a little while he might feel superior, but that would soon wear off. Then the boredom would begin.

Ghosts have an advantage over those in physical bodies in that they can see not only the dead but the living as well.

Other animals don't feel the restraints in watching ghosts that humans do. Seeing those in spirit comes more easily to them.

Human beings are only ghosts in human clothing called a body.

The physical is supposedly something that can be touched, seen, heard, smelled or tasted. People believe ghosts are not physical, though they can materialize in physical ways.

A way to test this theory is with the following experiment.

Most people know what aspartame is. It usually comes under the name "Equal," a sweetener. If you have a package, open it. Hold it away from you over the sink and let it flow from the package down into the sink. It can be smelled and tasted. Though it never enters the mouth, the taste is there just the same.

When it was smelled it entered your brain, bringing the taste sensation to your mouth. Was it a ghost of a sweetener or was it physical? Whatever it was, it made aspartame physical to you without your ever putting it into your mouth.

What Is A Ghost?

Here's another experiment: close your eyes. See a lemon in your mind's eye. Look at how pretty and yellow it is. Pick it up. Feel its texture. Roll it in your hands. Smell it. Cut it in half. Bring it to your mouth. Taste it. Your mouth puckers, doesn't it?

Although not actually seeing, smelling or tasting the lemon, it was real anyway. Was this a physical reaction?

In some cases, the physical is what you make it.

When I was a child, I could be scared out of my wits by these ghostly persons. Religion had taught me many things, one of which was that a spirit who visited was usually not one of the good guys.

Hollywood, too, likes to teach that old message. People will not usually buy tickets to a "good" ghost flick. They want the movie that has ghosts running rampant, killing everyone around. The moviegoers' senses are heightened, adrenaline is pumping. Their whole body gets into it as if it were real.

Parents and grandparents use this type of experience as an educational tool, too, as my grandmother did. Even though my grandmother and father had mentioned ghosts to me as I was growing up, I had a hard time with those ghosts. Though I lived with ghosts on a daily basis, they did not react with me the way my grandmother said.

The two of them never told me that ghosts were OK or that I should not be frightened of them. As a matter of fact, ghosts were spoken of always in hush-hush tones. All the ghost stories told to me seemed to be of the kind that portrayed a scary lesson.

One of my grandmother's favorite ghost stories started with a woman whose son had died. He decided to come back to see his brother, who was always in trouble.

The dead brother walked in the front door of his mother's home. His live brother, who was standing there, watching him walk in, knew he was dead. Knowing he was seeing a ghost and fearing for his life, he turned and ran.

There was no escaping the ghostly brother. He grabbed the live brother in a bear hug and dragged him outside the house to the water well.

Thinking he was going to be thrown into the well, he fought for his life. Finally, the ghostly brother turned him loose, but he left his calling card. The buttons on the front of the dead brother's overalls had been permanently imprinted into the live brother's chest.

The moral of this story is the live brother straightened up his act after his run-in with the dead brother. He always bore button-down evidence that there is life after death. His being a little frightened that his dead brother might come back and finish what he started brought about a miraculous change in the live brother's life.

Grandmother told me this ghost story because it interested her. It fit her way of life. Most people are interested in this Hollywood-type ghost story, good versus evil.

Perhaps she also knew that I was a psychic and wanted me to be wary of the things I saw. Having a moral that could make someone straighten up his or her act made the story even better, she thought.

It did not occur to me until I was older that only certain ghosts terrified me. They were the kind my grandmother spoke of, even though I had never met one.

Ghostly spirits being with me was a commonplace occurrence. They went about living just as I did. They weren't frightening, just people. I would not have known how to act if I hadn't seen these dead people. Only the ones who looked a little different aroused any quickening of fear, and that was precisely what they wanted to do. It got my attention.

The fact that speaking with ghosts on a daily basis was part of my life never entered the equation. Not one had ever tried to hurt me. As a matter of fact, they always tried to stay out of my space. They came only close enough to get my attention.

We all grow in spirit from the time we are born and beyond. It is one continuous education, though we are usually not aware that we are being schooled. Spirit never dies. It only evolves.

Being spirits in physical bodies, some of us forget that we were spirits without human bodies before we were born. Feeling the physical body with its restraints could be imprisoning for a free spirit. Thus it is a must that most of us lose the knowledge that we were able to roam free of bounds on the astral side.

Those who can remember are allowing themselves to become spiritual channels to the other side in order to help educate all that will listen.

As an educator, I can tell you about my life with other spirits and how to relate to them yourselves.

What Is A Ghost?

Ghosts are a fact of life just as we in the physical are. We are one and the same. The only difference between dead ghosts and live ones is the fact that one of us has lost the physical body we were wearing.

Spirit and body combine to make a human. As a matter of fact, we who are physical have a ghost living within our bodies. We are only ghosts with human bodies. The human body is only here as clothing for a spirit to wear so it can learn human lessons.

Without spirits, physical life would be boring. Everything and everyone would be robots, going through life without actually experiencing it.

Your spirit gives you the impetus to want to learn. Without learning, we are ignorant. In the dark ages, when wars were fought, the victors destroyed the captured libraries and the intellectuals. Keeping their captives ignorant kept them slaves.

Even the slaves in the United States were not permitted to be educated. It was against the law. The thinking was that if slaves were ignorant, then they would not realize that they were being kept captive. Education is of paramount importance to all of us.

Without a spirit, we would be mechanical beings lacking joy in living. Smelling a flower, feeling the wind in your face or hearing a baby cry would have no meaning. Keeping the body alive would be our only reason for existing.

With spirit each person is an individual. Although they are part of the whole, each is separate, with each having his or her individual mind.

You have heard that old story of being conformist. There are those who fight like heck to be labeled non-conformist, when in actuality we are all individuals, capable of making our own decisions. Actually, no one is a conformist.

One person's decision can be to act as others. The non-conformist would act differently. As individuals it doesn't matter. We are all different.

If you don't believe me, try telling a two-year-old they can't have something at a grocery store. Quickly, everyone in the store will find that two-year-old is an individual with a mind of his own. The closest person to the upset child will be glad to offer that child whatever his little heart desires.

Some people think that when you die, you go to heaven or hell. Others think death is the end.

GHOSTS TALK

Death is no more an end than winter is. There is always a spring. Spring is a renewal.

Without the winter, there is no renewal. Sometimes, though, it seems winter takes its sweet time to end. Restless and wanting to be able to go outdoors, you are tired of being cooped up in the house. The time indoors gives you the interval you need to re-evaluate your life and set new goals.

Even though it looks drab and forsaken, a cleansing of the earth is being done. Bear in mind spring is right around the corner.

Spring is the time of rejuvenation, beauty, sweet smells and cool breezes. Finding new growth, feeling the sun on your face, winter is now only vaguely remembered.

Death, like winter, is a cleansing. It is a time of reviewing situations in your prior life so that your soul can further its path toward complete harmony with God.

The way I believe, we are all part of God. This earth is a part of him or her. God is our father and mother, the Creator of all. We are continuously learning throughout our lives. That does not necessarily mean just our life as a mortal here on earth.

Life does not end or begin with the mortal body. As with an atom, it never dies. The atom rests and then changes form.

We, who are in the physical, look as if we die, but we really don't. The body does. Like the atom, the spirit lives on. Spirit is the energy that keeps us from being robots. It gives us the joy of life. We can marvel at the smaller things in life, laugh and cry. Emotions come from the spirit.

All living things have the joy of life, which means they have spirit, too. Look around. If you watch animals, you will see that joy. A newborn colt rolling in the grass, a dog stretching lazily in the sun, and fish nibbling at the top of the lake, show there is joy in life — spirit in all things.

Even in the plant kingdom, there is spirit. A tree seems to laugh as a gentle breeze rustles though it.

On the other hand, take a look at a tree that has gone without water and had insects attack it. It is tired from the fight. The spirit is giving the body up. Yes, trees have bodies too.

When the spirit starts to give up, death is not far behind. Look at the legacy it left, though, all those little acorns to carry on.

The tree's spirit will continue to live on just as every other

What Is A Ghost?

spirit does.

As with birth, death is an opening into a new life. It resides in a different dimension. Scientists have told us there is more than one dimension. This is true, and we are able to cross those dimensions with a single thought.

A mother gets pregnant with a child by sperm uniting with an egg. Sperm and egg look nothing like that child when it is born. (Where is the spirit?)

The child is now in the womb but is not present in this dimension. It is in another world, one that is wet, warm, and cozy, but a different world nonetheless. It could not survive outside that environment for very long until it is fully developed. In essence, it is a form getting ready for a new life.

We who have already been born cannot return to the womb to live. Our bodies will not let us return to that dimension. Obviously, we would drown.

When that baby matures enough, he or she leaves a comfortable world, where they are protected and nurtured, to enter a new world. The entry into that foreign new world is painful, cold and frightening. When the mother gives birth, a child is born into a new dimension.

After living in the new world for a number of years and aging there, that former child leaves the physical life to return to the life he knew before he was conceived. Again, he returns to another dimension.

The spirit is reborn to the freedom it felt before coming to a restricted physical life on earth.

Each place that being has lived is a universe unto itself.

Physicists have not even begun to find all the dimensions of our universe.

If the truth were known, every cell of our body has its own universe. Look around. Become aware. Every leaf on a tree has its own universe. If you look further, each cell within that leaf has a universe of its own.

Now multiply that by your own body and the body of your pet or your children. It is mind-boggling to try to even consider all the origins out there. Each of these universes exists in a dimension unto itself.

People on the physical side of life are frightened of dying because they are afraid of the unknown. The physical side of life is really the unknown.

Most people do not know when they are going to die. They can

GHOSTS TALK

guess at when they are going to grow up, get married, or start a new job, but they cannot say anything for sure. There are many unknowns.

On the other side, everything is known. Allow your consciousness to explore. Nothing ever really dies. Study the atom as scientists have in storm chambers. It doesn't die. It rests for a while and then begins its life over again. The atom is a part of everything, active or inactive.

Everything is made of energy. The atom is energy. It is a part of us, just as it is part of a tree, a coffee table, books, dogs and anything else that exists. This little energy form doesn't worry about dying, because it always transforms.

When it becomes part of something else, its universe changes and new lessons are learned.

There is more than one side to life. There is the physical, which deals with the mechanical parts of life: when do I eat and sleep?

Another side of life, the spiritual, deals with the mental and emotional. It also is concerned with the physical part of life. Without the body, one cannot function properly in the physical realm. Spirit needs the body to gather information about physical life.

The spiritual deals with the higher good for all. This does not mean it is only concerned with humans. All the earth and any universe we touch influence it. As you can see, this has far reaching effects. Every thing is alive, even those rocks we sometimes like to throw at others.

The spirit is alive both in the physical and what we call the afterlife. The two are combined to make a soul that grows more learned with the whole of its existence.

The unknown is frightening. Once you have education, there is no reason to be frightened.

With the knowledge that whatever God creates can neither hurt me nor is evil, I have learned to accept these beings as messengers and friends. Sometimes, though, I must admit that they have taken me by surprise and left me breathless, too.

Like most people, I usually sat as still as possible when ghosts came around. Generally, they came to tell me someone was dead or dying, because that seemed to be the only message of which I would instantly take notice. This does not always lead to making a person feel comfortable with the conveyor of the news.

Ghosts may come in different forms, sizes, shapes, and odors just

What Is A Ghost?

as humans do. There is no set pattern for them.

In order to get people's attention, they will do aggravating things. For instance, they might take something someone is using. There's nothing like working with a screwdriver, putting it down and realizing it's not there when you go to pick it up again. It can make you doubt your sanity.

One young teen-age spirit, who was very shy, taught me how ghosts use smell and thievery to get attention. The boy ghost, whom I met when I was younger, loved to play hide-and-seek with a can.

He lived with my mother, and my stepfather. He never showed himself but was not above spraying spring air freshener, which I hated, throughout the house when we were alone.

He stood almost continually right behind me in my space. The hair on the back of my neck was stiff with the knowledge of him most of the time.

Without acknowledging him, I was constantly closing doors in the house to keep him out of the rooms I was in. My thinking was that he would leave me alone. He repeatedly played tricks — if you want to call it that — to get my attention.

Being the gentleman he was, though, he would not come into the bathroom when I was taking a bath— or rather he didn't let me know if he did. Still, this did not prevent him from spraying that obnoxious air freshener under my bathroom door.

Upon smelling that odor, I would get out of the tub and look for the can throughout the house, finally finding it next to the day-room door. After having this happen for a while, that door should have been the first place I would visit to find the odiferous stuff. The reason I didn't was because I kept hoping I was wrong.

The day-room door could hardly be opened without waking everyone in the house because it was warped and rubbed against the hardwood floors. This door made such a noise when opened that you were able to hear it all through the house. Although I never heard the door open, it would always be standing wide open with the can beside it.

He seemed to prefer leaving by this door more than any of the others. Standing by this door one day I said, "OK, I know you are not trying to hurt me and you want me to know you're here. Now I know, so you can quit using the spray."

GHOSTS TALK

From then on, he and I spent some quality time together. He just wanted the acknowledgment. The spray was put away.

This ghost never let me see him, but I always felt him. Psychic knowledge allowed me to discern his appearance.

His aura invaded the room when he was there. There were no hot or cold spots, only the feeling of someone right behind me. To describe this feeling, it was one of knowing someone was sneaking up behind me, but I was powerless to stop it.

This ghost taught me patience. It took him a long time to get acknowledgement from me, but he finally did. He also taught me that we all need a little love and attention. There was a need for the both of us at the time. Mine was to get him to stop spraying that air-freshener; he needed me to acknowledge him. Together, we filled each other's need.

Most of the time, ghosts tend to come in a form that does not alarm people. There are times they forget, though, and that can be a harrowing experience. These ghostly people usually do not want to upset a person, because they need that person to acknowledge them. By showing themselves in a way that startles someone, they can get their attention much quicker, if there is a need.

For instance, when you meet a stranger, you are usually unafraid of that person even though you might be wary of him. If that stranger was a streak of smoke drifting over to and speaking to you, it might be a cause for concern. This is why ghosts usually try not to scare people they want to communicate with. Sometimes they do scare a person, but it is usually for the person's safety.

If a person were about to walk off a cliff in the next couple of steps, that person would probably welcome the materialization of a ghost in front of him. It would frighten him so much that he would turn and run the other way. Not only does this keep the person from harms way, but it also becomes a very distinct memory for him, one he can never shake.

When asked, "Have you ever seen a ghost?" he can then answer with certainty, "Yes, I have. It scared the holy *!*! out of me!"

One such entity wanted me to know that he had not committed a crime he was accused of and allowed me to see him as he was. Later, he helped me to teach others what a ghost is.

After moving to Texas, I met this very special man, although he

What Is A Ghost?

didn't seem so special the first time I met him. He scared me literally senseless when I first saw him.

Our two-story house had an upstairs utility room. While washing clothes one day, I glanced over to my left. At the top of my stairs, not ten feet from me, stood a man staring at me as if he could go through me.

The knowledge that I had what appeared to be a physical intruder in the house frightened me more than I can say. He had the stairs blocked and was only a few feet from me. I had no chance of escape.

Instead of preparing for the fight of my life, with my heart beating furiously, I closed my eyes and begged God to make him go away. Maybe the subconscious psychic part of me knew he was a ghostly entity.

Opening my eyes, I noticed he was still in the same place watching me. I closed them again with the same prayer. No luck when I opened them. Then I noticed that the man was not dressed in modern-day clothes. Finally, I realized that he was not of this dimension or era.

Once I decided he was a ghost, I was able to listen to him. Until then, he was just an unwanted intruder in my home.

The reason he had come to see me, he explained, was because he wanted the record set straight with someone. This man had been hanged as a thief because he was in love with a married woman, and she with him. He became a good friend and visits me occasionally.

As a matter of fact, he helped me give a lecture once. It was for a very nice new-comers club in Arlington, Texas. The women in this club had asked me to come to a house and do a psychic lecture.

During the lecture, I noticed that the smoke alarm had been taken from the wall, disconnected and laid on the bookcase. It gave me the idea to tell these women about my ghost friend who liked to antagonize my husband.

Ladies were sitting on the curved stairs of this beautiful home as well as in chairs. They listened with rapt attention as I told them about the ghost who had frightened me in the upstairs utility room.

Then I told them about my husband hearing the ghost's footsteps on many occasions. He would go through the house to see who was there, though I told him each time that it was only Jason. He never believed me until he searched the house.

One night my husband was lying on the couch, reading a book.

GHOSTS TALK

He looked around at me and said, "You know, we haven't heard from Jason in a while."

On cue the smoke alarm went off. There was no smoke in the house. Claude looked at me and said, "What was that?"

I replied, "You know what it was. It was Jason."

Sitting up, he put his hands on his hips and in a mocking voice said, "Well if it was Jason, let him do it again now."

Jason did, both for my husband and for the ladies, because just as I was ending the story at the new-comer's meeting, the detached smoke alarm went off.

The ladies had to be calmed down. They were leaving those chairs and the wonderful curved steps as quickly as they could. Thinking they had enjoyed the lecture and the sound effects, I knew I would probably be asked back to lecture again. Those ladies, however, had other ideas. They never asked me back.

Jason's lady friend, Elizabeth, had been in the house on numerous occasions before this, leaving a jasmine odor anywhere she stood. She liked to open the attic door, which like the door in my mother's house needed adjusting, even though this house was only a couple of years old. (If you didn't know better you might think ghosts like to make noises, when actually they are only trying to get attention.)

This ghost had a real sense of humor. Elizabeth liked to tell us when our teen-age son came home. In the dark, down the hall, through the library, sneaking downstairs, he would get a plate of food to take back upstairs to his room.

While he was downstairs, she would close the door to the library so that when he came back upstairs in the dark he would run into the door and drop his plate on the floor. All that noise would wake up the dog, and she would tell on him.

One time before I came out of the psychic closet, my children, my husband and I were eating dinner when we heard footsteps right above us in the library. Looking at me, my husband asked, "What is that?"

Without hesitation, I answered in unison with my children. "It's the ghost." To my knowledge at the time, I did not know my children knew she was there, but they did. We all looked at each other as if we had told a deep, dark secret.

Our oldest son, Randy, liked to burn incense. My husband did-

What Is A Ghost?

n't like it because he associated it with the kinds of things kids shouldn't be doing. One day Claude smelled it by our bedroom door coming down the stairs.

Up the stairs he bounded. Flinging open Randy's door, he yelled, "What are you burning up here?"

Randy looked at him and said, "It's not me. It's her."

When she entered a room, her sweet odor permeated a two by two foot square about head high. As Claude bounded up the stairs, she stayed with him all the way to my son's room.

Ghosts can also use cold in localized areas to communicate their presence. Since they no longer have constraints of body, they can form themselves as they please, and they'll do whatever they can to get your attention. Like a mischievous child, if they don't succeed the first time, they'll continue to try.

They use this ability to provide evidence as to their specific identity, too. I don't smoke, and no one in the house smoked. One day after my husband's uncle died, though, my car was full of cigarette smoke.

I was not the only one who got to breathe his second-hand smoke. A friend came over one day and was standing outside on our back deck. He announced to my husband and me that he was standing in some rancid smoke. The smoke stayed about his head high in a two-foot by two-foot range. We told him not to be alarmed, that it was only my husband's uncle.

When I told my husband what his uncle looked like and how he dressed and walked, even though I had never met him, and how the cigarettes he smoked were getting to me, Claude knew immediately whom I was talking about.

Ghosts give you information you can use, if you only give them a chance. They are not trying to do you a disservice. Instead they only want the acknowledgement that you can see them. Then they can either give you a message or just be content with the fact that their presence is known by people they care for.

People, who have never seen a spirit before, ask me how they can see one. They do not believe how easy it is. Really it is very simple.

All ghosts need is an invitation if you want to see, hear, feel, taste or smell them. It's that easy.

Give yourself permission. They do the rest. Be prepared though, it can sometimes be exciting.

When you were a baby, you could see people from other dimensions as easily as you saw physical forms. As you grew older, you were talked out of believing that you saw spirits. Your parents wanted you to fit into society, and society dictates that dead people are no longer physical and therefore cannot be seen.

Parents tell their children that their imaginary friend is not real, only their imagination. "Don't lie to us!" they say.

Seeing something from the meta-physical world has a tendency to scare most people. Frightened by the unknown, they would rather believe there is no such thing.

If it is not what humanity considers real, then it does not exist. Just like prejudice, it is not tangible but can be felt just the same.

When you give yourself permission to see ghosts again, anything can happen. A friend with whom I do television and radio asked that he be able to see ghosts. I told him that he could and would shortly. Not believing me, he went on with his life. But still he had asked, and they are here to oblige. He heard them, but it frightened him so badly that he would often wake me in the middle of the night when it happened.

Footsteps were echoing off his attic floor and kept him up most of the night. There was no doubt that it was footsteps and not some wild rodent. After a few ghostly visits, he decided to wait until the next day to let me know of his experience.

Incidents kept escalating, until he finally saw a light coming under his bedroom door when there were no lights on and none could come into his bedroom like that without assistance. He now believes in ghosts and his ability to see them.

Once ghosts know people can see them, they congregate close to those people. Like moths drawn to a flame, they search them out. Like attracts like. Good people attract good ghosts.

After loved ones die, they come back to see and talk with the ones they loved. People have told me they could feel, hear and smell a dead relative in their homes. They were right.

Ghosts sometimes show themselves in what people may consider funny ways. Most of the time, their intent is not to alarm people. They only try to alarm when they need your attention quickly.

Many people have seen someone standing or walking close to

What Is A Ghost?

them in their peripheral vision. Upon turning to check, there was no one there. That was a ghostly encounter. Normally, the person having this experience can describe the person they saw in detail if asked. Unless asked though, they don't take the time to realize that they can describe their ghostly meeting.

A person might also hear his or her name called when no one is around. Perhaps the person is driving along, so focused on what he's doing that when someone whispers his name he instantly responds to the call. It's often easier for ghosts to get someone's attention when the person is concentrating on something else.

Ghosts sometimes speak to people in this manner to avert disaster. Most people have a tendency to look up quickly when they hear their name called. A person having his name called warrants special attention, especially when there is no one around that could have spoken. The person who had his named called has his body go on full alert.

Sometimes, though, it is only a way to get your attention. This happened to me when I visited a little town close by to do research for a novel I am writing. A psychic friend and I were sitting in a small restaurant. When we were seated, I heard, "Da Juana, we are glad you are back."

Ordinarily that would have been fine, except that I had never been to this place before, nor was there one live person nearby who could have said those words to me. Looking around to be sure, I turned back to my psychic friend and asked, "Did you hear that?"

"Yes," she replied. Then she began to repeat the exact words I had heard.

Some psychics are accustomed to hearing from the other side, but occasionally it even surprises us. This was a little disconcerting because the voice said they were glad I was back, especially since I had never stopped in that restaurant before in this life.

Ghosts can show up wearing what looks like a human body or can be a mist. One ghost that has appeared to me comes with half his body from head to toe totally human looking and the other half looking like static snow when the television station goes off the air. They sometimes appear as light or color and then speak with a voice you recognize. The point I am trying to make is that there is no tried-and-true method to what appearance a ghostly spirit may take.

GHOSTS TALK

They may even set the stage in a theatrical manner. The old adage of the whole world being a stage is true with ghosts. It appears that they use every opportunity to get their points across, as this next experience from my childhood will relate.

Except for the little bit of light from the stars stealing its way into the window, the night was dark. It was hard to breathe. There was someone entering the room.

Holding the covers as close around my throat as possible, I watched in horror as the white sheet of fabric floated in through my bedroom door and hovered above me. It was so close. I could have reached up and touched it, but I dared not.

Too frightened to move, I watched, frozen, unable to speak, as the wind in the room touched only this piece of cloth, moving it gently in soft waves.

It seemed as if she hovered above me for an eternity, when in fact it only lasted a few moments.

How did I know it was a she? Instinctively, I knew who she was. Although there was no similarity to any human being floating above me in cloth form as she did, I knew what she looked like and who she was.

Recognizing her as an aunt who had been sick with cancer, I was not happy to see her even though I loved her very much. She was, after all, now a sheet being gently fanned by air coming from nowhere physical. She finally dissolved before my eyes.

At that moment I knew: an aunt I loved was dead. This was a very sobering sensation for a child. It felt foreign somehow. I would have thought she would have appeared to me as she looked while alive. Instead she showed me this ghostly image of her. Only now have I discovered that she was telling me she was finally free of the earthly bindings of cancer. She could take any form or go anywhere she wanted.

Even at the time, I knew she was happy. With new freedom, she gave me the news that she was dead.

Thinking that she should have told her immediate family first, in my child's mind, it did not occur to me that they could not see her after death.

Finally, I slept. The next morning while walking to the kitchen, the phone rang. As my father walked to the phone, I told him they were calling to tell us my aunt was dead.

Daddy picked up the phone and learned she was indeed dead.

What Is A Ghost?

People on their deathbeds will sometimes tell their loved ones that they see a loved one who has previously died standing close by. Generally that departed loved one comes to greet the person and take him or her to the other side.

This makes an easier transition for the person who is dying, but the person who is living is left to wonder if the relative was actually seeing the dead loved one or was only hallucinating. The other alternative in the loved one's mind is that ghosts only come when someone is going to die, which is far from true.

Death is like birth: we are only stepping from one dimension to the next. If someone who loves a person can make it easier for him or her to go to the other side, then we who are living should be grateful that they do.

Having heard the stories of a dead person coming for a live one is probably one of the reasons some people tend to be frightened of ghosts. Not every spirit one sees is coming to help a person get to the other side. If that were the case, I would be in big trouble.

Some are here to further your spiritual education. Others come to help prevent some bodily disaster from befalling people.

A case in point is my Aunt Rosie. She had a best friend, Gayle. Being closer than most sisters, they did everything together. There were no secrets between the two of them.

Gayle developed that terrible disease called cancer. She died after a valiant struggle. My aunt helped her every step of the way and was heartbroken when she finally died.

Years later, after I had come out of the psychic closet and was talking with my aunt, my ghostly guides told me that my aunt had seen two ghosts. The first was her brother, and the other was Gayle.

Telling her what I had heard, I added that she was frightened of Gayle for no reason. Gayle told me and I conveyed to my aunt that my aunt had hurt Gayle's feelings but that she truly understood my aunt's reason.

My aunt was dumbfounded but told me I was right. She had seen Gayle after she had died. Gayle came to her bedroom window, knocked on it, and said, "Let me in. "

Thinking Gayle was there to take her to the other side, my sweet aunt told her to go away. She said the reason she told her friend to leave

GHOSTS TALK

was because she was frightened. Being as close as they were, each made a pact with the other that the one who died first would come back for the other.

My aunt's first thought, mistakenly, was that Gayle had come back to take my aunt to the other side.

The fact was Gayle missed her and just wanted to see her. She also wanted my aunt to know there truly is life after death.

All those years my aunt knew there was life after death, but she was frightened of a friend. Just think, she could have enjoyed being with Gayle even after her friend had left the physical side.

It is really very simple to get rid of the unwanted advances of some ghostly visitors. All one has to do to free themselves of some otherworldly presence's is to ask them to leave.

This may sound too simplistic, but it is not. Most people want pomp and ceremony in their religious encounters and also in ridding themselves of ghosts.

Some psychics and ministers are called upon to exorcise a home. My solution is much simpler. All you have to do is stand in the room or area that you most often see the specter and ask that it leave your home.

In my experience, this is all that it has taken to be rid of your noisy roommates.

They may not truly leave the house but they will try to leave you alone so that they may enjoy your company without your knowledge. Most ghosts are not ungrateful creatures.

With specific personalities, they too may enjoy a little people watching. It may be just a little inconvenient for the physical person who is targeted.

The only cases in which I have not seen this type of exorcism work were when one of the members of the haunted property was stretching his psychic wings. Outwardly, he may have agreed with the other people in the household that he wanted the ghostly visitor gone but inwardly, he was enjoying the visits. As long as one person asks them to stay, they will.

A few years ago, some very nice people called me to investigate the haunting of their house. They told me that they had ghosts in the house and didn't know what to do with them.

The only bad things the ghosts had done were to hide one shoe

What Is A Ghost?

each of several pairs of shoes and a hammer. The owners were not to the point of wanting to leave their home to the ghosts but were having a hard time with the items being taken. One moment, the needed items were there, the next they were gone. It was frustrating.

Upon visiting the house, I came to realize quickly that this was a nice house for ghosts to visit. The daughter who lived there was quite an artist in more ways than one. She was so gifted psychically that it was even hard for her to fathom. Most of the ghostly entities were around her age.

Focusing on her, I told her that if she wished the ghosts to leave, all she had to do was to tell them to go. Finally she confessed in front of her astonished parents that she did not want them to go. She rather enjoyed the ghostly company.

The girl did ask that the items that were taken be returned. Except for the hammer, they were returned overnight and found the next day in the middle of the living-room floor. The hammer was found under the father's side of the mattress that night.

Innocently, the teenaged artist told her mother that she would like to go to the beach for a sand dollar because she would like to paint the doves inside. The next morning a sand dollar had been left on the living room floor exactly where the other returned items had been placed. It was cracked open with the doves flying from it. None of the physical occupants of the home had a sand dollar in the house.

The artistic psychic continued to bloom with her abilities and asked the ghosts to tone it down a little so that they would not bother her parents. Everyone was happy then.

Psychics' gifts of communication allow them to relate more freely with ghostly entities and entreat them to stay, even if it is done on a subconscious level.

As long as they ask the ghostly presence to stay, it will. Many budding psychics do this without their own conscious knowledge. Those psychics are not always adults. A child in the house may keep the visitor there too.

In order to purge the haunted area, all physical people must think the same about the unwanted spirit. It must be a group consciousness that asks the uninvited guest to leave. If this is done, generally the ghostly presence is no longer felt.

GHOSTS TALK

People would do well to remember that most every place is a possible haunt. There are just too many ghosts around for this not to be the fact. Whether they communicate with physical entities or not, they are still there. Sometimes they are only passing through. At other times, they stay awhile.

Having a physical home gives a person the right to have only the visitors they want. The people who live in the residence make the choice as to whether they want to acknowledge the ghostly manifestation or have them leave. It is their choice.

Chapter Seven

ANGELS

Angels may or may not have
been born to a physical body. They may appear as ghost or as a physical person because they have the ability to show themselves in either guise just as any spirit does.

Ghosts are guardian angels, although not all ghosts are what we consider angels. Angels are ghosts in a little higher degree. They are more educated in the Supreme Being's manner.

Angelic persons give the gift of tenderness when they appear to a person. Even if that person cannot see them, their presence is felt as warmth and love. Their soul tends to interface, tenderly, with any individual they choose.

Compassion, when in the company of these beings, is overwhelming, almost to the point of tears. People have told me that they felt inundated by love when they encountered these saintly persons. They were sometimes unable to control their emotions.

In my visits with them, they have brought me extreme joy. They lightened up my day and eased whatever distress I felt. Like shining lights to my soul, I felt I was in spiritual company.

Having lived more spiritual lives than some, they have become more God-like. Because angels have learned the lesson of knowing we are all one, they show no partiality in loving. Not always appearing in the way one would expect, they come in many shapes and sizes.

Angels have been able to overcome some of the loathsome ways of mortals, though they may never have been on earth in the physical sense.

Usually angels become visible to me in a blue white or golden white light. That is my distinction between them and other beings I encounter. In this way, I know immediately who they are.

They may appear to others in a different way. It does not matter how they show themselves. All that matters is that they do.

Angels have bounced, with utter abandon, all over my bedroom in little balls of blue-white light. Looking like little glistening fairies, they gave me comfort at a time I needed it. They acted as though they knew they were bringing joy simply by their actions. When an entity has that much lightheartedness in its soul, it infects others positively.

There are light beings I call angels. They actually have a form, which looks much like us on the exterior, but they are entirely made of light. All features are part of the light such as eyes, noses and ears. The person seeing the light being knows what those appendages look like even though they are not outwardly apparent.

These beings wear no clothing but have no need to cover themselves. Human beings can tell at a glance whether they are male or female, but there is no physical sign of either. This comes as instant knowledge even though ghosts and angels can assume the sexual identity they want to.

There are angels, appearing as both men and women, who have the most beautiful complexions and dress in long, flowing, robes. These ethereal individuals do not command adoration. Instead, they enjoy having people see them. Even angels have a sense of humor and drama. They are individual personalities who enjoy life in all respects.

They seem to want people to believe there is an energy being higher than all of us. Their message is correct; God is everything, but we are all part of God. As a part of the Supreme Being, we are able to access that higher energy, though we may not be aware we can. Angels

Angels

tend to give us something to aspire too.

Some appear wearing clothes just as we might dress today. Having all the physical attributes of your next-door neighbor, they come into your life for a few precious moments and leave a useful message behind.

In a town in Arizona, I met an angel who appeared as a physical man. This Native American came to my motor home and asked for money. My usual answer would have been to give him a little bit of money or say I'm sorry, but this time something stopped me.

Through the dirt on his body, I saw an Angel's eyes. It helped to hear a voice reinforce my thoughts by saying, "This is an angel you are turning away."

Stopping myself from the usual cliché answers, I asked, "Would you take a sandwich instead?"

"Yes, ma'am, I would."

Going inside the motor home, I told my husband I needed to make this man sandwiches. After doing so, I brought them out to him. He said thanks and left.

My husband and I drove over to an automotive supply store across the street. While my husband was in the store, I saw the man again. He sat down on a stone wall next to another man who looked worse off than he did and offered him a sandwich too.

As I sat there watching, I knew without a doubt I met an angel that day. He had a human face and the ragged clothes of a beggar, but he had the heart of an angel.

Ethereal beings don't always have a form. They can make their presence known in other ways.

Angels sometimes come in the form of music. There is none like it on earth. It has a tinkling, otherworldly sound that seems as if it were sent from many miles away. With no way to describe it, the closest thing to their music I have heard is an instrument made of leaden glass. Although that instrument has a wonderful sound, it cannot compare to the angelic music played for me.

Heavenly entities, like ghosts, will appear on occasion to warn people of impending disaster. Sometimes they ease into the situation. At other times they seem to appear from nowhere. This happened with a friend of mine.

GHOSTS TALK

As she was on her way to work at about five a.m., she had a flat tire. This was not a desirable area in which to have car trouble at any time, much less the time of morning she did. While changing her tire, a car slowed and came to a stop beside her.

My friend stood up to greet the other person but felt very uncomfortable in doing so. She could not decide what to do. There were no houses close by, only a lonely stretch of land. She told me she was frightened out of her mind, and was unable to decide what to do next.

As the man stepped from his car, a man stepped out of the bushes beside my friend's automobile. Without hesitating, he told the man from the other car that they did not need his help. With that the man got back into his car and left.

My friend was in a state of shock. She didn't know whom to trust. First a car stops, then a man she had no idea was there steps from the bushes. Her instincts told her that something was wrong. She was right.

Subsequent to the car leaving, my friend turned to the man who had stepped from the bushes. Wondering where he had come from and why he decided to step out at the moment he did, she realized she had no reason to fear him. He was gone.

My friend told me later that she knew an angel had come to help her. When she had felt frightened of the man who drove up, as she stood up from changing the tire, she begged God for help. He sent it. An angel came.

She could describe this angelic man, who looked nothing like an angel, in detail. Though he had no wings, he helped a person who was in dire need that morning.

My friend told me this story with trepidation because she wondered if I would believe her. When she found out I did, she said she was never so glad to see another person, especially the one she had that morning.

Muffin, my puppy friend and companion for many years, was an angel to me. She taught me many spiritual lessons after her death. Refreshing my memory, she brought back some of those philosophies I sometimes forget and expounded upon them.

The day she died, angels sent me a message that she was all right. Another friend had come to our home because she knew my husband and I were grieving. My friend insisted that she and I go out and pick up something to eat. With pressure from both my husband and her, I

Angels

decided to go.

While she drove, we talked. Her radio was turned down so that we could not hear the music playing. Hearing a tune I recognized as one I sang to Muffin every morning, I asked, "Is your radio off?"

"No," she answered, "but it's turned down so much that you can't hear it. Why? Do you want me to turn it up?"

"Yes," I answered, "Because I hear 'You Are My Sunshine' playing. That is what I always sang to Muffin."

She reached over and turned the radio up. "You Are My Sunshine," by Jimmy Davis, former Louisiana governor, was playing on a station that would not ordinarily have played that song, especially in 1993. That song is played very rarely, but it was playing the day Muffin died to let me know she was still able to communicate.

Angels help us with needed lessons and assists our minds to evolve.

John, my guide and friend, was an angel in his own right. He too, helped me to remember both spiritual and mundane ideas. His most important lesson for me, and one he kept pounding home, was that I was never to manipulate another. My friend always let me see life from the other person's point of view. He wanted me to understand that others had feelings just as I did. Anyone who teaches this has to be an angel.

Angels can come back to people in the form of lost loved ones. They may be there to help with a problem or to welcome a new experience in the person's life.

When we call upon a lost love, then that spirit will try to help us with any problem we may have. The thing we humans need to remember is that angelic souls are intelligent beings too. They love to help but have their own life's business to deal with, too. It is in their nature to want to help us, but it is not their only job.

The Biblical stories that speak of avenging angels is not what I have found to be true. If anything, it is just the opposite. They always try to be loving, even though they may appear a little cross at times. This outward show is only to get your attention.

Human beings have a tendency not to acknowledge a person who is always nice to them. Let a person speak or look at others with malice, and they have their undivided attention.

Without giving one thought to the consequences of our actions, we humans run at a rapid pace chasing our rainbows. Unaware of our safety in these times, we will only take notice of someone who looks malevolently at us. That person gets our attention much more quickly and can divert us from whatever may hurt us at the time.

Malicious looks from angelic people who want to help us might be where the stories of angels seeking retribution came from in the Bible.

Sometimes angelic spirits don't even acknowledge your presence.

This happened to me some years ago. My husband and I were sitting at our table discussing a particularly unsettling time in our lives. Both of us were quite distraught. Claude's father was ill and not expected to live much longer. We had some other problems as well. That time in our life was very stressful, to say the least.

As we talked, I glanced out the window and saw a Native American male dressed in white from head to toe, standing and facing north. He had some adornments of turquoise and other colors on his belt and headband. He wore a white feather headdress from his head to his ankles.

He was one of the most gorgeous people I have ever seen. He never acknowledged my presence, but he had a golden glow around his body, which made me immediately understand he knew I was there. Peace washed over me instantly. Knowing everything would be all right, I explained what I had seen to my husband.

Later, with the vision of this man still fresh, I spoke with someone who knows something about Native American lore and told her my story. She said this man was Sweet Medicine and is equivalent in their beliefs to Jesus in the Christian religion.

According to her, he is the teacher of peace. He certainly felt that way to me. She said that he is the highest medicine person in most Native American tribes and that the Lakota Sioux and Osage have particularly high reverence for him.

Why this man decided to come to me at this time of need, I don't know. Maybe he was giving me not only that sense of peace I so desperately needed, but he was also letting me know that it could come from a source of which I had no knowledge.

The woman I spoke with also told me that seeing Sweet Medicine looking toward the north meant that a resolution to my dilemma was at hand. At the time I saw him, it stuck in my mind that

Angels

he was facing north and never once looked my way. After relating it to her, she confirmed what I had sensed from his presence.

Sometimes angelic beings use other human beings to teach and bring messages.

When I was a child there was a family who rented a three-room house next door to us. These people didn't have much, but they had love and, undoubtedly, understanding of the needs of others.

The family consisted of a father, mother and three daughters. Two of the daughters were close to my age, and we spent some time together.

Their mother would always set another plate for anyone hungry, even though it was only turtle soup. Her turtle soup was wonderful though.

They allowed a Native American man to stay with them for a while. My father warned me to stay away from him, but I couldn't. While he was there, I went to their house as quickly as was possible to sit on his knee.

There I spent my ninth year of summer days drawing butterflies on one side of a notebook as he taught me how the butterfly went from worm to flying loveliness and what each dot and line meant on those beautiful insects.

"You are a special child," he would say. At the time I didn't understand what he meant, but his patience, teaching, and encouragement meant a lot that summer.

My parents were divorced, and my father was frightened of the man because he said the man was a drunk. Perhaps he was, but he gave me good memories that can never be forgotten.

Now I know that my father thought the man might have been a child molester, too. This man never asked anything of me but to listen and let him teach me. He was an angel who gave of his time, unselfishly, to a little girl.

Angelic spirits are always ready to assist anyone who needs them. Making those in need feel better for having been in their presence is part of their mission. Their loving warmth gives people knowledge of what the afterlife can be.

Chapter Eight

ANIMAL GHOSTS

Fig or those of you who believe animals are on the other side, and even for those of you who don't, well, it is true. Also, there are trees and all sorts of plants. Anything you see on the physical side is on the other side.

The way I found out there were ghost animals was quite innocent.

My father used to take me to places he knew were haunted. Being a fisherman, it was even better for him when these remote places had fishing.

As ghostly events would occur, he would ask me what had happened. This was an accepted part of my life. He wanted me to tell him what I had seen. Later, I was to find out that he was testing my ability.

Anyway, on one camping expedition he took me to a camping area that was supposed to be haunted by a man and a horse. He told me nothing about the ghosts.

This camp was a small Louisiana State Park by the Ouachita River. People rarely went to that park because it was relatively unknown. It had only a few picnic tables and was located deep in the woods close to a bluff above the river.

We built a campfire and did all the things that campers do. My little Spotty dog was very restless and would not venture far from us. When it was dark, he would not move out of the campfire light, but he continued to circle the camp, apparently to protect us.

Not wanting to sleep with snakes or bugs, I made my bed on a picnic table where I felt safe. My two brothers and my father slept on the ground. Sleep came even though I was lying on an uncomfortable concrete picnic table.

In the middle of the night, I was awakened by something jabbing me in the stomach. Before I opened my eyes, I heard a snorting nose.

Having been awakened in an unfamiliar place with that kind of noise, my adrenaline was flowing. My heart was pounding, and my breath was stuck in my throat.

Here I thought I would be safe up on that table. Now I find someone is nudging me in the stomach and making all sorts of noise.

When I finally got brave enough to open my eyes and look up, I saw the most beautiful black horse I have ever seen. The white star above and between his eyes bobbed with his head, up and down. Snorting, as horses will, he waited until he was sure I was awake and then he backed away from me.

Sitting up, I looked him over. The only other white marking on him was a stocking on his right back leg.

This horse knew he was beautiful and wanted to let me know he thought so. Standing quietly for a few minutes, he let me admire every inch of him. Then he turned, raised his tail and pranced off. When he had taken a few steps, he disappeared.

The next morning after breakfast, while my brothers were off playing, my father asked me if I had seen anything unusual the night before. At the time, his questions did not seem unusual to me because he was always asking me questions about psychic things.

Telling him how I had been awakened, he asked me what the horse looked like. Upon relating what I saw, he informed me he had seen the same one swim out into the river, come back and disappear, some years before.

He told me the story he had heard about the place. A middle-

Animal Ghosts

aged man had lived alone with that horse. Thieves looking for the man's money had killed them at the same time. The robbers had dug six-feet pits all over the property searching for riches.

Animal ghosts don't always visit a place because of circumstance surrounding their deaths. Sometimes they just come to visit or to make a point.

One day while in my living room, I saw a pretty little bunny rabbit. Sitting in front of my television cabinet, he seemed to be thoroughly enjoying himself. Without addressing the bunny or thinking, I silently asked my guides, "What is he doing here?"

With no hesitancy, I heard these words coming from somewhere in the room. "He's food for the snake."

As soon as I heard those words, I saw a snake lying right in front of my couch. It was about as long as my couch and was looking at the rabbit. Ordinarily, this would not have been a thought I would think. Bunny rabbits are pretty little animals to be enjoyed, not food for snakes, but they were both there in my living room.

Of course the snake did not eat that bunny rabbit in my living room. They appeared and disappeared as quickly to let me know that there are more animals on the other side than just the cute and cuddly.

I have seen several animal apparitions, but the one I loved most was my dog, Ms. Muffin Byrd. Her death was very hard for me. She was such a big part of my life.

In telling you we are all one and the same spirits but separate individuals, I mean God is everything. He is the whole while being separate in personalities. Muffin was part of me.

People who never knew I was a psychic said we read each other's mind. They were right.

My Muffin got diabetes, a horrible disease. She had to take insulin for about a year and a half before her death. This beautiful little dog went blind about four months after our finding out she had diabetes. We had surgery to restore her sight. My husband and I wanted her to have sight, even if it were only for a few minutes.

Muffin loved seeing. She drank up nature as if there were no tomorrow. A seasoned traveler, she taught me new ways to see. I was allowed to see through her eyes. My little dog did not miss a thing.

Once, about two years before her diabetes, she stood precariously

GHOSTS TALK

close to the edge of one of the highest mountaintops in Colorado. I watched as she surveyed the valley below. Absorbing everything she saw, Muffin didn't just glance at something, she reveled in it. Using all her senses, she enjoyed what she was doing to the fullest.

On that mountaintop, I could see and hear her thanking God for something so precious as the gift of seeing his miracles. Tears of wonder sprang to my eyes.

Muffin was a constant inspiration to me. Watching her made me more aware of my surroundings and the wonder in which they were made. Learning to enjoy those surroundings came from my taking the time to become aware of them. She had such a zest for life; it was hard not to see what she saw.

She was a proud miniature Schnauzer, gray as my husband's hair, and she knew everyone in the neighborhood. If I told her we were going to a certain neighbor's house, she beat me there and barked at the door until the neighbor opened it.

Most people who met her loved this arrogant little animal, which stopped to smell every flower she came across. When she died we received sympathy cards from so many wonderful souls who told us how much they missed her, too.

On June 2, 1993, my little girl, who had been up all night, asked to go outside. After doing her business, I carried her back inside. She asked if she could lay and watch the sun come up through the French doors. I lay on the floor beside her, and we both watched the dawn.

Within five minutes, the wind came up. The trees started blowing. As we both noticed the wind we turned to look at each other. "God's doing this for you, baby," I said.

With all the strength she could muster, she tried to get to the door. She waited for the next three or four hours outside until we could get her back to the veterinarian's office.

Though I knew this was the day, I was not really prepared for it.

Since the day I had told my husband I thought she had diabetes, without knowing a dog could get such a disease, I knew when she would die. It's not always easy to live with that kind of knowledge, but I would rather know than not know.

We had her put to sleep around 11:45 that morning. According to the weather, the cold set a record that day. God marked that day with the

Animal Ghosts

cold wind because He knew how much it was going to hurt all of us.

It's hard to lose someone physical to the other side, but it is a part of our own growth here. It serves to give knowledge to both the dying and the ones left to live a physical life without them.

While the veterinarian was injecting the drug to take her life, she was looking into my eyes. I kissed my little angel good-bye to the corporal body and did not cry. My crying was done later.

Watching her while she was given the injection, I could hear someone saying "Mother" over and over again. The words kept getting fainter as I saw her floating away from me. Even though I did not realize at the time that it was her calling me as she left the physical body, I knew she was dead before the veterinarian. Looking at her doctor, I said, "She is gone."

The vet replied, "I haven't finished with the shot. She isn't dead yet."

"Yes, she is. I saw her leave."

She checked her heart and said, "You're right."

"I know. I saw her leave." Looking at the clock, I touched her hair again.

Having made prior arrangements for the doctor to keep the body for science, I looked at her one more time. Then a few tears came.

While touching her, I was suddenly aware of a small black and brown puppy circling my feet. I heard the words, "Momma, I am not there." The puppy continued at my feet.

Then and there the realization hit me that Muffin was speaking with an audible voice. My brain is taking this all into consideration because my Muffin was a beautiful color of gray not the color of that puppy.

As I watched, the insight became clearer. Looking down at her, I watched her change into a gorgeous eagle and fly away. Her words were simply; "I can fly now."

In some ways this gave me relief, but at the time I was lost in my grief at the loss of a friend with whom I could share anything. She loved me no matter what I looked like, how much we had or whether I was psychic or not.

Waiting until my husband and I got home, I told him about the little puppy around my feet, how it looked and the fact that it flew off as a bird.

Her color bothered me, and I told him so because she was not that color.

Walking upstairs to my office, I glanced at a picture of my baby on the wall. Calling my husband to where I was, we stared at the picture of a little black and brown puppy playing with my husband. It was Muffin when she was small. I had completely forgotten about that.

An answer had come. Looking at my husband, I asked, "Why do you think she showed herself in that way?"

Instantly I heard, "Because I was born again."

At that moment she answered a few questions for me. When she died physically, she became new again, a baby as such. She was starting life over again. Then she changed form into one of the things she loved most in this world, a bird. The added emphasis that this also happened to be her last name had eluded me until that time.

Muffin always had a thing for birds. She followed them around watching everything they did. My husband and I put up a bird feeder for her because she loved watching them so much.

Ms. Muffin Byrd didn't hurt anything. She hurt a bird once, by putting her mouth on it without biting, but I told her we didn't do things like that. From then on she watched everything and reveled in its life as much as her own.

Observing her convinced me she was better at life than I was. She lived it fully.

While meditating one day, I saw Muffin's heaven. Spellbound, I watched.

It was a wall of energy. That wall was God. In this wall, which I liken to a piece of plastic with a regenerative feature, I saw many people. Standing behind this wall, they all appeared to press their bodies against the plastic. Jamming themselves into the plastic so that I could see each of them, I realized they were all one yet still separate individuals.

Then one of the individuals stepped through. It was Muffin. As soon as she came through, the plastic closed behind her as if she had never been in the wall, but I knew she could re-enter at any time and become one with it again.

Muffin and God wanted me to understand that we all come from one source. There are individuals, but they are encompassed in the whole. When we begin to realize we are not alone, that we all touch each other be it animal, plant or rock, then we learn more of God's understanding ways.

Human beings think that they have dominion over all without any regard for themselves or others. With this dominion comes a responsibility. In hurting another, you hurt yourself. It may take a lifetime, or several, but there is a day of reckoning.

My puppy not only taught me to enjoy the earth, while alive, but she also made me remember what God was truly like.

She came back to see me several times afterward. Cooking dinner for my husband one night, without any thought of her in my mind, I heard her voice trailing from the kitchen to the back door saying, "Daddy's home."

She had always run to the door when she was alive to let me know he was home before the garage door raised.

Knowing it was not time for him to be home yet and without thinking, I responded, "No, he's not."

She was right. Within seconds, the garage door opened. Daddy was home.

Another time, I walked through the hall to the front door. There she was lying in the dining room under the table. That was the spot she always lay when she wanted everyone to leave her alone. It was her time-out spot, and when she was there you really needed to leave her alone.

Not expecting her to be there, it took me by surprise. I asked, "What are you doing here?"

"I needed a time out," she explained. Psychically knowing why and being glad she could still come home, I left her to rest.

Other ghostly animals have visited me over the years, but as with other human ghosts I have a tendency to ignore them just as one would anyone while standing in a crowd unless someone in that crowd initiates conversation. At that point, I would speak to the animal entity to find out the purpose for the visit.

So if someone tells you there are no animals in heaven, that person is wrong. Heaven is only the spiritual dimension, and as such has all we have on earth and more.

Ghosts are alive just as we are, but they are in another dimension. Seeing and speaking with ghosts has proven to me that there is truly life after death. This applies not only to humans but to animals as well. That is why I try to do unto everything as I would have it done unto me.

Chapter Nine

THE EDUCATION
OF GHOSTS

The education of ghosts or spirits is the entire reason for living a physical life on earth and for dying in that life. Living and dying portray earthly dramas that allow the spirit great chances for evolution of the soul. Humans are only ghosts in physical form. A ghost is a spirit. The spirit resides in the human body.

Not only do ghosts learn on the physical side of life, but they also learn after they die. Our education continues through each phase of life. All of life's experiences are lessons to be learned. The cycle of life, death, life, death is one continuous education. There is no time one is not learning.

People who are on the lower rungs of development are being educated by what they do in life. Murderers, for instance, are lower entities but could rise to a different plane by simply changing their belief patterns either here on earth or after death.

Human beings, and even ghosts, have a tendency to change slowly. Life may not be everything we want it to be, but we seem to be content with it or at least, like the battered wife, stay with the abuser because we know what we have. This is only because we feel comfortable when our lives take on familiar patterns. We continue with the same patterns over and over, sometimes not so merrily. We take the path of least resistance and are therefore resistant to change.

Those patterns are learned behavior. They are habit. It takes a month of continuous resistance to those habits to break the cycle. This is not an easy experience for most, so they do not take the time or trouble to break a habit but continue to live the same cycle over and over.

Ghosts carry their personalities to the next dimension. With their very human behavior, they like the comfort of behaving as they did in the physical.

Without thinking of the consequences, they continue on with their way of doing the same things they did while alive. Usually there is no chance for change until that soul matures. Maturity comes with education. Education comes with experience.

Life teaches us by allowing experiences, both on the physical and astral side. When one dies physically, he can continue to learn by helping and watching human beings. Even death is an experience that teaches all those concerned with the dying person.

Some spirits are guides. Others are watchers. On the Other Side, there are those who know they can interact with physical human souls, and those who have not learned this yet.

The guides or angels who have learned they can interact with humans help people with our earthly education and thus aid themselves. Knowledge is experience. They experience the things that humans do when they are helping them to learn in the mundane world. This is so that both the human they are helping and the ghostly entity become more spiritual.

Of course, some of those ghosts are murderers who have died. They may find themselves able to interact with others, too. As guides now, they continue on the same path they had while alive in helping the people who have chosen someone like them for assistance.

Most guides can see the whole picture. They know before an action is taken what the outcome will be. The murderous guides either do not use this ability or prefer not to look most of the time.

In one of their lifetimes, they find they no longer need to be all-powerful control freaks themselves. Thus they learn to become more spiritual and open to receiving God's answers.

This is where the church's notion of good and evil spirits comes into play. The consequences of what we do affect everyone and everything. Our actions have no limitations. Newton's law is at work: "For every action, there is an equal and opposite reaction."

Take a pebble and throw it into a pond. The rings of water it causes start small but get larger the farther from the pebble they are until the whole pond has been touched by it. As with that pebble, our actions create larger reactions as they move away from us and affect many more souls than we sometimes anticipate.

Remember that birds of a feather flock together. Do not be afraid that a killer will become your guide. Only another killer can attract that sort of guide.

Many ghostly spirits have come to my metaphysical classes. Are they learning from me, or am I learning from them? Not only is it comforting to have them in my classes, but my students get the benefit of seeing them there as well.

Part of the education value is watching my class see these entities for the first time. They have the opportunity to learn that all they have to do is open their spiritual eyes.

One particular class was given in a huge room without windows. Throughout the whole class, I had watched some blue-white light forms do calisthenics in the back of the room.

At the end of the class, I asked all of my students to turn towards the back of the room. A student went back and turned off the lights, as I requested.

When the lights went off, gasps, oohs and ahs started. Without my calling any attention to the spirits, there was no doubt my class saw them. People began talking as quickly as the lights went out about how certain entities were doing different things, such as rising in the air and turning somersaults. It was amazing to them that they could see the ghostly forms.

All I did was have the lights turned off so the class could see them more easily. They were able to see these ghostly people all along but without the aid of my being there and simply turning off the lights, they would not have allowed themselves the opportunity to really acknowledge their presence.

This reminds me of the parable in the Bible that speaks of two or three souls gathered together in one accord. If they have only the faith of a grain of mustard seed, then they can move mountains.

The only difference between this parable and my class was that I never told them there were ghosts back there. Telling them only to face the back of the room while someone turned off the light gave them the option of granting themselves permission to see a fantastic sight. They now had proof of paranormal activity.

My friends, the ghostly acrobats, did not have to come to the class, but they were there to teach and learn. Doing so in the manner they did caused fewer problems with acceptance from the physical students in the room. Who could have a problem with comedians who were only trying to make them laugh?

Spirits usually frighten the living because we fear the unknown. These acrobatic spirits came in such a way as not to alarm my students. Taking the time to play for their earthly classmates let them teach in a less distressing way. Because we are all spirits, we should not be scared of other spirits, but we are.

According to the Bible, when God made man and said He made us in His own image, it was the spirit rather than the physical I think He meant. Even with that thought, though, most people are still terrified of ghostly spirits.

Taking that thought to heart, I can't see why we have to fight with each other over the color of our skins, cultural lines, or religion. These things have nothing to do with the image God made. The spirit does. It never dies; it only changes appearance, like the atom.

Be careful at whom you throw stones because of the color of their skin, culture, or religion. You, as a spirit, may return in just that hue. Karma requires it. Seeing those same stones flying back at you in another life will make you appreciate the lives of others more.

The spirit's life is made up of many births and deaths. With each living and dying, the spirit learns a spiritual lesson, no matter how insignificant the life may seem. Some lives are lived to expound on what the spirit has already learned.

In essence, you never really die. Going from death to life to death is one continuous life, rather than more than one.

The Education of Ghosts

For our linear way of thinking we need our lives and deaths so that we can put a timetable on our spiritual beings.

Both the physical and the emotional manifest the spiritual. The spirit never dies; it only continues learning.

Part of the learning process starts on the other side. Usually one spirit decides to visit earth with a group of entities like themselves in order to learn.

If you recall, we had all the great composers, painters, philosophers, and mathematicians born in groups at certain times in history. I believe that while they were on the other side, they chose the time to come to earth to help further man's development.

You, as an individual, have a tendency to do the same thing. We like to live our lives in the company of those we know and feel comfortable with.

Maybe some of you feel there are a few people in your circles you certainly would not choose to be around. My belief is that you did choose those people to be around you because that is a part of learning, too. Though they have a tendency to rub you the wrong way in this life, they could have been lovers, parents, or siblings with you in another life.

That's a refreshing thought isn't it? It could lead to explanations of why there are some that have incestuous relationships. This is not to condone such behavior but could explain why that type of horrible incident occurs.

As our own creators, we have decisions to make regarding our lives. Conscious choice is the product of living this life. We always have a choice.

Those adults who push an incestuous relationship upon their children are learning lessons in their lives. The children are learning, too, even though they are being hurt as children. Pain is a growing tool no matter how horrendous it may be.

I cite this as an example because even though it is only a lesson to be learned, by all that are participating in these roles, it is a horrible one. Those on the physical side of life are not prone to wish to participate in these type lessons. No one in his or her right mind would want this type education, but it does happen.

Hypnosis and meditation can explain prior lives and give us

GHOSTS TALK

meanings as to why we are living the life we are in now. These two methods of accessing past lives are only educational tools.

Under hypnosis, someone I know learned she had a lover in another life. When she came out of the hypnosis, she realized the lover she had then was now her father. She was highly distressed because she felt as if she had participated in some sort of incestuous relationship in her past life. She hadn't. The life she lived then and the one she was living now were two separate and distinct lives, though the spirit was one in both.

Spirits returning in many physical lives can be disconcerting for those living under the boundaries of society. Society dictates rules that must be followed in each life so that we may co-exist on earth with each other. These rules have changed with the times. Some have become more stringent, while others have relaxed. Spirit has no limitations, while we under societal law need limits that grow with the times.

Generally, most come back with the same group of people because we have chosen to live and manifest experiences with that group. On occasion, we may add other spirits to the group.

Thus, the people within the spirit group may be a father or mother in one life and a lover in another. Usually, those other lives are not remembered while in another physical life, so it does not interfere with the life you are living now. That is, not until you start to question the spiritual meaning of life. Then those lives may catch you unaware.

We are all given freedom of choice. This means we have the freedom to create our own images in the likeness of God. The choices we make here were thought of on the other side. Lessons were created when we were on the death side of life so that we could make choices influenced by environment, other people, and ourselves on the physical side of life.

In other words, we set up situations, with the full approval of those involved, while on death's side. When we come to the physical side, we are able to make conscious choices. No decision is wrong. It only takes us down a different learning path.

For instance, I was born to a family with a father who was thirteen years older than my sixteen-year-old mother. My father, a minister, chose to be father to me, two brothers and my mother. She grew up and divorced him, leaving me to take care of my father and two

118

brothers when I was seven years old.

Now in looking at those choices, my father didn't have to look at a fourteen-year-old girl when he was twenty-seven. She didn't have to return his gaze, but she did.

My father could have looked at my mother as an equal rather than a child, but he didn't. That meant she had to grow up and decide whether she wanted to stay with him and continue the family. She didn't stay.

We three children had a choice as to whom we wanted for a father and a mother before we came to the earthly lives. We chose them. Once we did decide, we knew that as physical children we gave our choice of living situations to the adults until we were old enough to care for ourselves. The choices made by us, the children, in dealing with this environment formed the adult behavior we were to exhibit. It was our choice how we individually handled our own situations.

We put the lessons out there and then made the choices on the physical side as to how to proceed with our lives.

We have the complete freedom of choice. Nothing is predestined.

Coming back to earth is not an easy issue to deal with but is something each soul must do. Giving complete control of their bodies as children to another's whim is hard. As a spirit it seems easier when we know the other souls we are dealing with, but as a human we struggle for control.

A baby comes here struggling to be free of its mother and thus in control of its own life. Of course, that takes some time, but that is what earth life is for.

The group we associate ourselves with on the death side decides what kind of outline the physical life needs. Once we are born to the physical side, we add the superfluous material. Still, conscious choice is there.

Because you have chosen to come here with a particular group of people to learn certain lessons, you need the body for as long as you are a part of those lessons. Consequently, you need to take care of it.

When you no longer need to use the body, then you pass to the other side. There, you will continue to learn and be of help to other souls on both sides.

As a ghost, you can become a guide or guardian angel to those you love on the physical side. In physical form, you can be a guide and help those on the spirit side as well as the physical side.

Other humans are constantly rating humans by their capacity to help others. How many times have you heard someone say, "Oh, she is just the most wonderful person? She helps anyone who needs her." Conscious effort by either being sweet or by being well known is a couple of the ways to guide human beings, but there are other ways to assist others, too.

While in the physical body, you can go out-of-body to help anyone who needs you. Meditations, out-of-body experiences, daydreaming, and even worry are other methods for assisting those we love. The person who is out helping needy people rarely remembers doing it. This is because it is done on a spiritual plane rather than an earthly one.

Worrying is one of the quickest ways to allow part of your spirit to go out to help others, without your ever being aware it is happening.

For instance, a mother has a bad feeling about her child who is not at home. When she starts to worry, part of the soul goes to wherever the child is to find out if they are all right.

I have heard children say that the reason they quit doing something they knew they shouldn't do was because they saw their mother's face looking at them. They knew she was alive and nowhere around, but they saw her face. This is enough to change even the most hardened offender.

Dream states can offer workshops to help others both living and dead. Ghostly beings can come to humans in a dream and tell them whatever needs to be said without the fear most people feel in talking with a ghost.

Those we have known and loved can be our guardian angels. We can be theirs when they return to physical life and we are considered dead. The spirit of that guardian angel exists in most of us. Taking turns, we care for our loved ones and thus encourage learning on everyone's part.

Chapter Ten

GHOSTS AND HAUNTING

Most people have heard of places or houses that are haunted. Some of those people are terrified, others are intrigued, and others hunt ghosts. There are many reasons for a place to be haunted.

Ghosts sometimes show up where they are expected. Those old tales of ghosts who haunt certain places could be fantasy made reality by some well-meaning people who have passed on.

Ghosts also have a sense of humor and therefore haunt for the fun of it. For physical people it can be less than fun, but for some otherworldly entities it can be a knee-slapping good time.

People on this side tend to think that when they go to the other side, life as they know it stops. Having heard so many describe heaven as pearly gates without a care in the world, one could see why it might be alarming to think that a ghost would want to return to visit.

Living without a care in the world would truly be boring. Besides, it's not what the ghostly entities I have spoken with have told me exists

GHOSTS TALK

on the other side. Heaven for them is a place of learning.

All they have to do on the other side is to think something and it happens.

That doesn't mean they sit around playing harps all day and walking streets of gold. These people have other things to do. They are in the process of getting on with life.

Some ghosts are purely theatrical. Others find ways of "getting our ghosts," as it were. Given the chance to do both, they will have fun doing it. Just like some people on the physical side, they like to kid around and cut up, too.

Here is a prime example of what I mean.

When I was a senior in high school, I heard about a ghost who was seen repeatedly at a railroad crossing in Crossett, Arkansas. My mother, a friend of hers named Margaret and I went to investigate.

An uncle, who was about six feet tall, over two hundred pounds and afraid of nothing, had seen this same ghost. He told us he would never go back to that crossing again because the ghost had gotten between him and his car. When he finally decided to give the ghost his car and run for his life, the apparition disappeared.

One fall night months later, the three of us drove up to Crossett and asked directions at a local service station because we had not gotten them from my uncle. Of course, the attendant knew exactly where the ghost had been seen and who he was when alive. When we arrived at the crossing, we parked the car on the south side of the track, got out and waited.

We waited and watched down the track for what seemed an eternity, but it was really only about thirty minutes. Apparently, the ghost was setting the stage. A crowd who had to wait on him would appreciate him more.

I was between Margaret and my mother. Out of nowhere, something appeared about two hundred yards down the track.

When I saw the specter appear, Margaret uttered a sound of pure fright. As quickly as I possibly could, I told her to hush and be still. Even though she was shaking like a leaf, I warned her not to move or say another word.

What we saw was something that shot straight up from the railroad track to the height of about six feet and rolled into a body with a

Ghosts and Haunting

lantern or light in his right hand. Floating towards us was a ghost made of a foggy mist.

Again I warned mother and Margaret not to move or say anything, no matter what happened. I wanted to see how close it would come, and I was even braver because I had two people with me who were frightened enough for all of us.

It continued slowly down the railroad track, building the suspense in Margaret and Mother, until it was about ten feet from us. At this point, Margaret could no longer contain her fright. She screamed, and it disappeared before she had finished. It seemed as though she frightened him.

According to the service station attendant, this man had been a lantern worker on the railroad and for some reason had gotten off the train to do something. The train had rolled over him cutting off his head. The ghost we saw did not show up without his head.

Maybe it was one of those ghosts whose sense of humor made him want to give us what we were looking for. In other words, if we wanted to see a ghost at the railroad crossing, then a very accommodating ghost filled in.

Some haunting ghosts are just psychic impressions left on the landscapes. The image continues to do a certain task, such as walking through a room. Without acknowledging you, they keep right on going, retracing the same path over and over again. They never vary their routines.

When they are repeating this behavior, a person could walk right through them. The ghostly apparitions would never acknowledge it. It appears they have no knowledge that the person is anywhere close. The person, on the other hand, would get a definite buzz, a little sweating, maybe a cold spot or two, but nothing that could injure him. Ghosts are not in the habit of hurting people. We hurt ourselves trying to get away from them.

These apparitions continue on their way as if nothing has happened because they are like reflections rather than a ghost who has a mind of its own. They have no will of their own. Like short movie reels, they replay the features over and over and allow a person to walk through their projections without interrupting the action.

They are not truly ghosts. I believe they are energy fields left by ghosts that continue to repeat the same gesture over and over again. They do have something in common with other ghosts though — the ability to scare the bejeebers out of you.

Being creators, ghosts can manifest images to continue doing whatever they want for eternity. After all, there is no time limitation for them.

This continuing image is something like a screen saver on your computer. The only difference is that the manifestation serves no purpose but to make physical people realize there are ghosts.

A real ghostly spirit will acknowledge human presence. It will even seek humans out. Sometimes a spirit will stand and move in front of a person so that you know it is alive and has free will, too. If they can move to stand in front of the person regardless of where he turns, this shows they have free will.

This is not to upset people. Most of the time it is to let people know that they are in the presence of a ghost who is capable of thought. The ghosts are telling people, in essence, that the person is psychic enough to recognize ghosts.

One such ethereal encounter with a ghostly reflection happened when a psychic friend and I went camping in our motor home. We were enjoying doing normal things a vacationing psychic does.

She and I were playing with tarot cards, giving each other readings. Normally neither of us uses cards but that night we were playing with them nonetheless.

Looking up, I saw a man dressed in a nightshirt and carrying a candle literally walk through the motor home door (which happened to be closed at the time). He continued out through the bathroom door, a few steps away. It was obvious what he was doing. His one objective was to find a potty in the middle of the night. Looking neither right nor left, he had one thing in mind. We were of no consequence to him.

He was going to the outhouse in the middle of the night just as he had done while he was alive.

The psychic I was with had told me that she could not see ghosts, so I wasn't going to mention it. After seeing the apparition she and I turned to look at each other at the same time and burst out laughing.

"Did you see that," she asked?

"What," I replied?

Ghosts and Haunting

Wanting to know whether she had really seen what I had seen, I asked her to give me a description of the man. She did, and we laughed for a while at this man's comedic efforts.

This mirror image would continue to go to the toilet on a nightly basis, providing a little laughter for all those lucky enough to see him. The ghost who made him had a nice sense of humor.

Happiness and fear are two of the most powerful emotions and can manifest themselves more quickly than others can. Also, if you've ever noticed, those feelings are infectious.

Fear gets the adrenaline going. Happiness or joy brings on the endorphins. Both of these chemicals cause physical changes that affect emotions.

A ghost leaves traces of himself much the same way. If he died a horrible death, he might stay at the scene for a while replaying the death scene. This can be good for those of us in the physical world, because it serves as a warning of danger that we might not ordinarily see. With our adrenaline pumping after having seen such an entity, we are more aware of our surroundings and thus more careful.

In the same vein, if a ghostly person loved the place where he lived and felt life there was wonderful, he might stay for a while to enjoy it after he dies. Physical humans would find that area was haunted. These ghostly people do not want to hurt anyone. They only want to enjoy their home and to check out the people now living there.

Because ghosts have free will like us, they do not have to stay at a certain place. They have the freedom of choice. Actually, they have more freedom than we on the physical side have. They are able to go anywhere or do anything with a thought, while we can only sit and dream of such abilities. Conscious choice also keeps us in the confines of some relationships and other choices that restrain us.

Haunting occurs all around us. We usually go through life unaware that the place is being visited until we open that psychic sense we all have.

Upon the opening of that sense, we realize that people from the other side have been here all along.

Another type of activity normally attributed to ghosts is manifestation. When there are young people, emotionally tormented people, or budding psychics in a house, a person can find demonstrations of this phenomenon.

GHOSTS TALK

A manifestation is thought and emotion combining to create an activity that appears abnormal.

Poltergeists are one form of manifestation. These supposed ghosts might fling one's property across the room as if they are trying to impose judgment on an offending member of the household.

At other times, the manifestation may materialize as something so simple as what appears to be blood on a wall.

Others might occur with the lights in the home. They may go off and on without any intervention. All these things can be causes of concern for people living with them, but they can be explained.

Manifestations occur generally when there are children, psychics or adults who are emotionally disturbed.

When an adult is upset over one of life's dramas, his psychic energy manifests an occurrence that even he may not know he is capable of. The subconscious doesn't care if the conscious knows, so it goes to work with its own agenda and creates sources to vent this destructive energy.

In our house, we keep plenty of lights on. They have a tendency to blow out when I am upset. My husband has threatened to make me change them because they apparently don't live long when my energy is in a volatile state. This occurs more times than is acceptable. Any time I am nervous or upset, out go the lights.

A doctor who was doing minor surgery with a local anesthetic found out about this ability. Not only did I bring my raging blood pressure down before his eyes, but I also broke his automatic blood pressure machine.

Going in for surgery, even though it was elective, did not calm my fears. By the time I got into his office, he explained he would not be able to do the surgery because I had such an elevated blood pressure. The doctor was not accustomed to a patient saying she could bring her blood pressure down in the next ten minutes or so. He attached the blood-pressure cuff to my left arm and waited.

Within ten minutes he was starting the surgery with the help of his wife, who was also his nurse. My eyes were closed because I did not want to watch, and we talked as they worked.

When he was almost finished, I had had about as much of that blood pressure machine as I could stand with its constant whining as it filled up with air and then deflated. It seemed to me that it was staying inflated more than it was deflated. When I decided to myself I had had enough, with intense emotion, I thought to myself, "I wish that machine would stop."

The instant the thought left my mind, the blood pressure machine stopped. My doctor commented to his wife that the machine had broken and he couldn't understand why. He didn't ask me, and I didn't volunteer any information. You learn to keep quiet about such matters when you display your abilities as I sometimes do. Besides, it could have just been some type technical difficulty that happened at the precise time I thought about that machine stopping.

Another manifestation occurred with a woman who did not like her husband going out of town so often on his job. She and everyone who lived close to her were very upset when her wall started bleeding.

After finding that there was no organic cause for the red substance, it was finally found that she was angry at being left alone. This phenomenon only occurred when her husband left town. Once she learned she was the cause; she could control her emotions so that this did not happen again.

Children are usually the main culprits when manifestations occur. Most have not learned to control their emotions, and when they are very unhappy, they can use this ability in some very destructive ways, such as by making objects fly.

Other kinds of kinetic energy may include a phone ringing incessantly. This can frustrate the adults in the house and does not lend itself to a wonderful home life.

Most children do not recognize they have this ability. The causes of their anger have to be isolated so they can learn how to use their abilities.

Mentally ill people can also manifest spirit. Many psychics have been considered mentally ill because of their ability to see and speak with spirits. Some of these people are so troubled by the fact that they can see metaphysical things, because they have been taught that psychic ability is bad, that they create a ghostly apparition to haunt and physically abuse them for their supposed sins.

One such case involved a small group of people, a therapist, another psychic, a patient and me. When I first came out of the psychic closet, I was talking to a psychic about something I saw in her life. This troubled me because I had never seen anything like this before. In all my years of speaking with and seeing ghosts, I had never had occasion to have one of these things near me.

After having told the psychic what I saw around her she became very upset and told me to leave it alone, but it was too late. The thing I saw was a woman who was being bitten, beaten, and thoroughly abused by what seemed to be a malevolent spirit.

Since I had just come out of the psychic closet, and was yet unsure what was expected of me, this was a pretty terrible scene. Thus the mature psychic told me to leave it alone. She was worried that I might not be able to handle the situation.

Because this was one of the most horrid visions I had ever had, it just wouldn't seem to leave me alone. Looking back I can say now that I know why it sought me out, but at the time, it was not funny.

Every time this monster perpetrated an attack on the poor woman, I was aware of it. The mature psychic and I would be talking with each other, and I would find that I was right. It went so far that I traveled out of body to the institution that the unfortunate woman was in to watch her. Standing on the other side of the wall, I was able to see through the wall as if it were glass. I watched as she and other patients spoke of what was happening to them. Fear gripped the room.

All of a sudden I saw a shape leave the woman with lightening speed, and carrying a considerable wind, it headed straight for me. Thinking I was hidden behind the wall, I felt safe until this monster made my hiding place unsafe by coming through the wall right up to my face. His face was hideous.

Turning on my astral legs, I ran with him chasing me as fast as I could go back to the safety of my own bed. Looking down upon my husband before I entered my body again, I screamed his name. "Claude," I said, "wake me up now!"

Fear gripped me more than I think it ever has except for the occasional close encounter with a snake. Claude flew straight up when he heard me call him and grabbed me. The monster was gone.

Claude didn't have it easy those first few months that I came out of the psychic closet. My dependency on him as a safety anchor was great. He was my rock after John left.

In the cold light of day, I went over and over what had happened the night before. The feeling of apprehension was enormous. This thing had struck out at me during the night when I was afraid of the dark, too. Now he had my address because he most assuredly had followed me home.

With trepidation upon going to bed the next night, I decided again that whatever God had made could not hurt me. Falling into a deep sleep as soon as I hit the bed, I felt strange. At two-thirty in the morning, I sat straight up in the bed. Thinking that since I was already awake I would just go on to the bathroom, I went. As soon as I deposited myself on the commode, I heard the rumble of wind and saw his face coming in my direction.

He stopped two inches from my nose. Now, I was mad. "Get away from me," I growled in a low voice. "You don't bother me, because you are not real." Instantly, he disappeared.

Speaking later with my psychic friend, I told her that the woman manifested her own ogre because she was a psychic and needed to punish herself for having a gift in which she didn't believe. My friend told me that I was right and that she and the therapist had decided this was the patient's problem. After making the patient understand this, her monster left.

Guilt can also create spirit monsters, and they appear all too real. As creators ourselves, we are able to construct anything we want. We need to be aware of our creations and do it on a conscious level.

Everything we touch has to do with our spiritual growth, and those experiences teach us. They may not always be fun— as the case of the patient demonstrated — but we learn from them even so. Learning from those situations helps you to help others who might have the same problem.

Manifestations are troubled spirits, in a way. The only difference is that some of these spirits wear human bodies. They are not your usual ghostly phenomena, though they can create some concern.

Most created manifestations are not nearly as nasty as the patient's ogre, but some can leave something to be desired. When I first started to consciously spread my psychic wings, I was coerced into inviting three women to my house whom I barely knew. They had watched me when I met other psychics at a lecture given by a famous psychic. When I asked the famous psychic a question, people in the crowd started asking me how I did what I did. Looking for a teacher, I inadvertently had become the teacher.

These women must have thought that I was a very gifted psychic who knew all there was to know about that ability. In truth I was still learning then, just as I am now. Needing help from my guides, both living and dead, I listen to all the information and decide what I think is right for me, which is what I am asking you to do.

We were upstairs in my study at the time, holding hands, making a psychic circle as one of them had suggested. After my little monster guest had visited me, I had nothing to be terrified of, so I was open to possibilities. I was unaware of what I had let myself in for. The women wanted to contact ghosts, something I had been doing all my life without the use of a psychic circle.

After quietly asking for ghostly visitors to show themselves, we waited. We didn't have to wait for long. The lady sitting directly across from me presented one of the weirdest phenomena I have ever seen. This ghostly creation rose out of her head, with about half his body showing at first. It was different, to say the least. Then he settled back down into her. It seemed that when she breathed he would expand himself and then retract back inside her when she exhaled.

Watching this behavior did not ease my tension, but being a hospitable sort — not to mention curious — I was not going to chase the three of them out of my house until I found out what was going on. As I have said, I believe that we are all here to learn, and this was one of those learning opportunities.

When the entity rose out of her, I saw a man with brown hair, a beard and moustache, wearing no shirt and with a hairy chest. That was all right in my book, but the small nubbin horns right above his forehead were a surprise and a cause for wonder. For instance, was I seeing things? Could this really be happening? There is no such thing, but there it was in front of me in living color.

As he retracted back inside the woman, he would throw back his head and laugh as if the world had made a funny joke and he was the only one privy to it. But this was no laughing matter to me. Finally, he showed three-quarters of his body. Now I was sure. This was the mythological creature Pan. This lady seemed to be possessed by him.

We stopped our little psychic circle right then and there. Telling the lady what I had seen, she informed me that she had been to a lecture where a man had channeled Pan and that when he had stopped, she had asked the mythological creature to come into her.

Explaining to her that I thought she was manifesting this creature and needed to tell herself and Pan to stop, she said she might. The woman actually enjoyed having this manifestation with her. Later, I found that she was studying the black arts and had a need to manipulate. In coming to me, she found out that what she had done had worked. What she had wanted from me was confirmation. She had no intention of getting rid of this playful manifestation.

This was not something that I condoned, neither the manifestation nor the black arts. Needless to say, she never came to my home again. In a way though, I feel sorry for her because she needed to have this presence inside her to feel as though she were a part of the paranormal. In truth, the act of living involves the paranormal. Her soul should have been enough to occupy her body without inviting something she created to live with her.

Manifestations are creations of the psyche, no matter how you look at it. Some are monstrous, while others are a little more benign, but regardless, they are manufactured.

Ghostly spirits, on the other hand, will try to accommodate you in the manner you wish to see or hear them. Never wanting to panic people, ghosts appear in the least startling manner. Spirit people are very thoughtful. They will also speak in the voices that people attribute to them. For instance, if Shakespeare appeared to a person, then he would use the speech of his time so that people could recognize him. Never mind that he has had three lives on earth since then. Remember, we are all spirits, and as spirits we are the same as those ghostly entities.

Spirits are always eager to please, and despite what some religions teach, they are not of the devil because they try to please the person they are with. My father used to tell me that Satan was the Angel of Light. Saying that the devil would come to me in other forms to mislead me, he told me to be very aware that anyone appearing as a Light Being could be the devil.

In my opinion, fear motivated my father to believe that he could be deceived by anyone dead. Most humans are afraid of ghosts. They have an innate fear of the unknown. For them death is a mysterious state they don't want to contemplate. Therefore, they panic when they meet anyone who does not appear as they do.

Instead of being deceitful and trying to steal your soul, a ghost will try to appear in the way one wants him too so that he can teach you some lessons. There is no right or wrong way for a spirit to appear to us, as I learned early on.

Right after I decided to try to make my psychic ability grow, I went to a numerologist's house for a reading. She lived in a very nice house with two or three cats. These cats greeted me at the front door so I knew they were there.

In her living room, the numerologist was sitting across from me. I had a view of her utility room, hall, and kitchen. A beautiful staircase was on her left. Taking it all in, I noticed how clean she kept the house, especially with all those cats.

At that moment, I saw what looked like a little man about two feet tall skitter across her hall from one side to the other and look around the door at me. Being ever the logical person, I wasn't going to mention it. Trying to make sense of it all, I decided it had to be one of the cats. Two were sitting with her.

She kept talking with me. There went another one again. And again this one peered around the door at me. Another was peering from the other side, too. This was becoming a little weird. "Ignore it," I thought. "It's just the other cat." No, there it was again. I could hear them talking to each other. Then the parting shot: while the little man was watching me, I sensed motion on the staircase. There stood her other cat.

One of the men was still staring at me. He looked like a little gnome standing in the hallway, very proud of himself and quite the little spirit. They all looked similar. With bewilderment, I looked at her and said, "There is a little person in your hall."

Nodding yes, she answered, "They are here all the time."

Now, that didn't make me comfortable. I might have Irish and English blood in my veins, but I surely didn't believe in that. She had little people in her house. I'm open to all kinds of possibilities, but this was a little too much, and I wasn't going to call her crazy in her own house. After all, I had just seen them.

It took some time for me to listen to my guides and to figure out what was happening. I tried to put it out of my mind because my intel-

Ghosts and Haunting

lect wouldn't let me believe that something like that existed, so I set the incident on the back burner for a while.

When I finally let myself look at the situation, I realized that she wasn't capable of looking at a large-as-life ghost. She needed the friendly, elfish little people who would not threaten her, and her spirits came in just that fashion. The ghosts were accommodating her wishes.

Other ghosts may appear to someone because they feel comfortable in that person's home and feel any visitor will welcome them just as the homeowner does. My father became quite agitated at my home because he saw a ghost who frightened him. In his eyes, this was a haunting, even though it was in my house and condoned by me.

He wanted to believe my stepmother was walking downstairs in the dining room, but she wasn't. She was upstairs getting dressed and had not even been downstairs in quite some time.

Daddy, Claude and I were sitting in the den watching television, but Daddy was not giving it his full attention. All of a sudden, he started calling my stepmother. Knowing he was upset, I asked him what was wrong. He ignored me and called her again.

"She's upstairs," I told him.

He said she couldn't be because he just saw her walk through the hall into the dining room.

Smiling, I said, "No you didn't. Who did you see?"

Without answering me and quite irritated, he got up and walked upstairs to confront her.

My stepmother told him she had been upstairs the whole time getting dressed and had not ventured downstairs once since breakfast.

When he came back downstairs, I couldn't leave it alone because I knew what he had seen. Again I brought it up. He said he just saw something.

After my father and stepmother went home, I spoke with my younger brother, who lives close to my father in another state. He told me that Daddy was so unnerved by the incident that he didn't want to talk with me, but he did want to tell someone. He described the man in detail to my brother.

What he described was funny to me because the man he had seen had been showing himself to me quite often in the few weeks before my father came to visit.

GHOSTS TALK

He wore overalls with a plaid shirt, and when he was alive he was a large man — tall and stout, but not fat. There was only one problem, and this is what really got to my father. The ghost had no head. Other than that, he was quite neatly dressed and looked perfectly normal.

There was no reason for this man to be visiting our house other than that he knew we welcomed him and could see him. Others were welcomed in our home as well.

Ghosts do have a sense of humor. My guides show it to me quite frequently.

Daddy didn't think it was funny, though. He didn't tell my stepmother he thought she was a man with no head. The comparison might have upset her quite a bit.

Another ghostly communication that my father participated in at our house involved Claude's uncle. Knowing that he was welcomed in our house, he came and went as he wished. He could always call our house his home.

Daddy and I had a habit of getting up earlier than the others in the house and drinking coffee together and talking. This was something I always appreciated because I didn't get to see my father often, and we got those moments to ourselves before the rest of the house awakened.

While drinking coffee, Daddy told me that he had rid the house of a ghost the night before. He said he had told the ghost to leave and was astonished when the ghost retorted that it was cold outside. But Daddy said, "I told him to leave anyway."

I asked my father if the ghost was wearing tan pants and a hat, and he said he was.

"Daddy," I explained, "you asked Claude's uncle to leave. Now let me tell you who you thought you threw out of our house."

My father got just a touch defensive because he thought that he had cast out a demon. Instead, he learned that it was just a very frightened man. At least he was open-minded enough to listen.

I told my father that Claude's Uncle S. T. had been in World War II, just as my father had, been injured and come back from the war shell-shocked. Because of this, he decided not to marry his fiancé, whom he really loved. She went on to marry another man.

Claude's uncle spent his life alone pining for his lost love until

Ghosts and Haunting

one day, years later, when she came back and told him that she had never been happy and still wanted him. They planned to get back together. But after a few weeks, Claude's uncle thought it over again and explained to her that he would not be able to marry her. Still unsure of his mental state, he was afraid that he would not be a good husband. Shortly thereafter, he died.

Until he came to our home as a ghost, I had never met him. Seeing him pacing the fence outside our house and appearing very lonely, I invited him in. After I found out who he was, I told him that he was welcome in our home for as long as he liked.

His gentle nature was one of the most beautiful I had ever felt. This man I had never met while he was in an earthly body was such a comfort to me after his death.

Upon finishing the uncle's story, my father said he didn't know and that he was sorry for trying to send him back outside. I told him that he should ask the ghostly visitor first who he was before he exorcised him. That was a lesson daddy needed to learn.

Of course, the uncle knew that he had an open invitation from Claude and me to live with us. He visited with us until he decided to return to earth in a physical body. While he stayed with us, he was one of the most conscientious guests we ever had.

On occasion, I have had a ghost appear to be frightened of me, as if I were the one haunting the house or he didn't expect to see me.

Once, quite a few ghosts had been playing around in my den for a few days. It's not unusual for them to be in my home, but at this particular time it was as if we were having a ghost convention.

Suddenly, one of them, who was wearing an unusual black hat, stuck his head through my ceiling. After jamming himself through the ceiling, up side down, all the way to his waist, he saw me below him. The look of fright on his face told me he did not expect to see me there. I was the apparition.

As quickly as he appeared, he lifted himself back through the ceiling and was gone.

This brings up another question. If they are ghosts to us, are we ghosts to them? The answer most definitely is yes. Our spirits are just a bit coarser in vibration because we are earthbound in these physical bodies. That is why, when people see ghosts, they usually find that their mouths are dry and they are very thirsty. Sometimes they will even become overheated while in a very cool area, or cold in a hot area.

Ghostly visitations affect us in different ways. As I have said, ghosts do whatever they need to do to get our attention, whether it is to teach us or to warn us. You can recognize a ghostly entity through such sensations as the hair on your neck or arms standing on end, localized chill bumps, or having someone you can't see touch you.

An area is haunted when a ghost decides to show himself in a particular place. When a human sees the ghostly entity and tells somebody else about it, they start the legend.

A tragedy didn't have to occur to cause a haunting. Humans are the ones who get the haunting ball rolling by talking about it. Ghostly encounters make for good tales, and all humans like a little gossip. Consequently, the story of the haunted house is passed from generation to generation because someone years ago might have come in contact with a passing ghostly visitor.

Ghosts do not have to stay in one place. They do so because they choose too. Sometimes when they need a break, they may even have stand-ins, just as actors in plays do.

Usually, ghosts haunt a location for educational purposes and do not mean to upset or frighten people, unless it might somehow benefit them.

Other spirits want to tell a story, and if they realize you can see them they are able to do so, either by vocally or mentally — if you asked, that is. They may stay around a few years to lend authenticity to their tale.

Hauntings don't run on timetables, unless the apparition has decided on one. But the haunting can stop as quickly as it started. Keep in mind, though, that for ghosts, there is no such thing as time.

Anywhere a person who can see ghosts might be, there is a chance for a haunting.

Chapter Eleven

GHOSTS AND
THE LIGHT

Another area that needs to be discussed is the belief that ghosts need to "go to the light," as if they don't know where they are. Ghosts don't have to go to the light, as some say, because they are already a part of the light. Having free will, they can go anywhere they please.

The light these people speak of is the Light of God. Because of the ghostly people I have seen and interacted with, I know God is Light. When I had a near-death experience, I was in the Light of God. Knowing this, I can assure you that we are all in the Light of God's pure energy, whether we want to believe it or not.

As Human Genome experiments have established, we are all part of the same whole. All animals, they have found, have traces of the same genetic material. Chimpanzees and humans, according to scientists, have ninety-nine percent of the same DNA. As scientists look deeper, I think they will find that everything has God's lineage in it.

If we are connected to each other and to God in this way, then

GHOSTS TALK

it is surely feasible that man is always in God's Light.

When we make a conscious effort to establish that link to God by saying we want to be part of Him, then we can actually feel his presence. Most Pentecostal churches use this practice to bring souls to Jesus.

A person coming to the church with the willingness to give up the life he feels has been sinful asks Jesus to come into his heart. As he begs Jesus to forgive him, he works himself into an emotional plane that leads him to a euphoric place, and he can actually feel a physical change. Coming back to church is the only way these people can replenish that feeling because they feel they cannot get the sensation anywhere else. It is called converting to Christianity and gives them unadulterated proof that their lives have changed.

For many, this can be accomplished through meditation or prayer without the pleading to be changed. When a person decides to really feel how God manifests in him, all he has to do is make the decision.

To know this feeling, try this exercise: with your eyes closed, breathe smoothly in a meditative way. Ask that God or the Universal light enter the top of your head, flow through your body from your head to your toes and travel back up to become a cleansing exhaled breath. The tingling you feel at the top of your head will let you know that this is very real.

The energy is so effective that you can feel it course through your body before you are able to think where it should go next.

All it will take is the decision to consciously feel the God Light. Once this happens, you will have no doubt that God's presence is in your life.

The God Light is only giving you that little extra jolt so that you know for sure there is something to the energy stream. This does not mean we are held together with a silver cord, as some psychics say. I have never seen one.

Fear of this electrical contact worries many people because they begin to think that perhaps they are not grounded enough. After hearing so many psychics use the term "grounding," I have come to understand that they mean to ask for heavenly guidance to help them keep their feet on the ground. Some fear they will leave their bodies, never to return. They are afraid that if they allow themselves to experience too much of God's Light, they may float away and forget earthly life.

Ghosts and the Light

Without trying to insult anyone's beliefs or to make anyone angry, my thought is that when you are in the human body, you are more than grounded. The only way you will leave that body is for a vacation at night as in an out-of-body experience or when you decide to give up the ghost (which is another fallacy) to return to the Other Side. You are a ghost, either in a human body or without it, but you are a spirit nonetheless.

Don't ever be afraid to try anything that will bring you closer to God such as an out-of-body experience, which we will get into later. My thinking is that this body is mine for as long as I want it. In feeling this way, I know I am grounded. There is nothing like needing food or a bathroom that makes you know you are any more earthbound.

Even being grounded, you have that tie that God gives to all creatures by virtue of His essence. It is that energy that is everything. For me, it looks like a golden white light that is full of unconditional love. It doesn't matter who or what you are. As a part of God, you receive His full attention whether you know it or not.

People think they have done something marvelous by acknowledging that energy and finding it there. But that energy was always with them. All they had to do was focus on it rather than think God was out there somewhere doling out punishment for those who were disbelievers.

So many of us are not prepared to look because of fear. We think that we need to be free of sin in order to seek God. But as I have said, there is no sin, only choice. Man needs to believe in sin so that he can believe in good. We have the option of having only good, but we cannot fathom that.

Lots of people allow a minister or someone like me to dictate what God is to them because they feel they do not have the credentials to search for God themselves. God is always with them. He never leaves, but only waits to be acknowledged.

Most children know this. Even puppies and kittens know that they are in the full love of God, that they can do nothing wrong. With open abandon, they smell, touch, taste and experience in every way anything with which they come into contact. You can see God's wonder in any of them.

God is the string that makes the fabric of the universe. There is nothing this energy does not touch. In becoming more aware of this, then you become more aware of the spiritual implications this brings.

Since we are part of God, how can we ever be out of His Light? It makes no sense that we ever could be. We do not have to go searching for something that is always inside us. With this realization, most will approach life without fear.

When the spirit leaves the body, it becomes pure light again, like the God Light. Thus it never leaves the light and doesn't have to go looking for it. We on the earthly side need to believe that we stay in the same human-looking form on the Other Side, and we can if we wish. Each of us is an individual and recognized by spirits on the Other Side, but we are also part of the pure Light of God.

Many stories have been told of haunting ghosts who have been exorcised by a medium.

In their zest, the mediums tell the ghosts, "Go away, go into the light. Leave these people here alone because they are alive and you are dead."

The truth of the matter is that most ghosts know they are dead, although there are times when it takes certain spirits a while to learn it. Still, I've never seen one who had a hard time with knowing when to go to the light, because as I said, they possessed it all along.

Have you ever had to sleep in a strange place and then wondered where you were for a moment when you woke up? A ghost who did not expect to die is like someone who has awakened in a strange place. For a moment he is bewildered because he is not in familiar territory. But once he puts two and two together, he is able to focus on where he is. Other spirits are always there to help with the new arrival if needed.

Because of church rules, most suicide victims think before dying that they will cease to exist or go to hell. In watching them find the Other Side, I have been privy to some very different opinions of what they thought they would find. Even after they have been dead for a while, they will tell me, if asked, how it felt when they walked to the Other Side.

One such suicide, upon passing over, thought she would find a very different place from what she actually saw. Though she was a good Baptist before death, she did not really believe that she would go to hell, but she did not know what to look for.

This woman wanted to die so badly that not only did she use her car to poison herself by carbon monoxide, but she also used a pistol to finish the job. When she stepped through death's door, two females greeted her and guided her through what looked like a hospital corridor. Patients were asleep on both sides of the room, which stretched out a long way.

Two women guides, whom she recognized from their life with her on earth, walked and talked with her about the importance of life and the decision she had made. The look on the suicidal woman's face was something I will never forget. She had not decided where she would go before the death and was totally unprepared for the place she was in.

The ladies told her that she could sleep if she wanted but that there was no need since she had been quite psychic before her life ended. Though she didn't know where she would end up, she did believe that there was some place she should be.

Ever so gently, the ladies walked with her holding her on both elbows in case she thought she would fall, just as we would on this side for someone who had just been through a tragedy.

Whispering to her as they walked along the corridor — so as not to disturb the other souls' naps — they led her to a doorway at the end of the room.

I instantly knew that past that doorway was what one might consider heaven, but it is just a place for reviewing one's life and for higher learning. The walk would take as long as the lady needed to realize that she was still alive.

Some suicides sleep for longer periods on the other side before waking. If they think they are dead, then they stay that way for a while. When they awaken to find they are not alone, they appear confused.

Suicide is a choice that creates severe learning potential for all involved. When a person commits suicide, he will have to relive the circumstances of the life he left in some way in order to learn the lessons he wanted to experience. This does not mean that he has committed a mortal crime, but it is something he will have to revisit on the Other Side.

Everyone involved with the suicide is learning lessons. They are not the easiest in the world but they are lessons nonetheless. Each person who knows the victim has to deal with the effects of that death.

I believe that while on the Other Side, people involved in the sui-

GHOSTS TALK

cide drama may have planned together with the person to commit that horrible act so that everyone could use the death for an earthly instruction. Choice still had to be made by that person, while in human form, to commit the act.

This does not help the poor earthly humans who are actually in this kind of situation. The hurt and fear can be overwhelming. Handling this event is hard for the best of us, and we tend to forget that this is an earth school where we are learning by the consequences of actions we all take.

How can this be spiritual, we ask? Where is God in this kind of event? Why does this type thing have to happen to me? Caught up in the situation, we fail to see the whole implication of the learning process. All we can feel is the hurt. Why did they do it? Didn't I love them enough? What happened to make them feel they needed to die?

Anger, hurt, betrayal and love are all a part of this experience for the person left behind. Where is the spirituality in all this, we ask? Believe it or not, it is there just as living is.

Spirituality is not some transcendental illusion. It is living life fully with all the people, emotions, and choices we make. That is what true spirituality is. It isn't religion. Religion is bylaws of different churches.

Spirituality is the reason we are here on earth. It is the looking beyond what seems to be logical — keeping one's mind open to possibilities that defy logic.

People living their lives with optimistic values are among the most spiritual on earth. Spirituality is knowing that no matter what happens, it is all done for a reason. There are no accidents, only spiritual growth.

Living for happiness in everything you do takes you on a spiritual journey, while looking only for material gain can take a person further from what he seeks. Don't get me wrong — it is perfectly fine to be loaded with the material pleasures as long as there is happiness to go along with it. Happiness is one of the finest spiritual pleasures and is a sign of true spiritual growth.

Grief or unhappiness is a sign of spiritual struggle in which so many people find themselves entwined. There is no wrong way to become spiritual, but this is a hard way and comes with considerable spiritual growth attached. Each of us has to survive grief in some form,

Ghosts and the Light

but we can learn from it and grow spiritually.

Years ago, a psychiatrist sent a young lady of about sixteen to me. Her doctor had told her father that she would probably kill herself unless she was able to speak with a very good medium who could contact her dead mother.

The father, who had remarried, asked if he could bring his daughter to me. I told him that would be fine but that I did not want the stepmother to come.

A very good-looking dark haired man and his beautiful blonde daughter entered my home at the appointed time. We sat down in our breakfast area so that I could talk with the daughter. When a child is under-aged, I always want a parent there to hear what I say to the child.

The first thing that I saw was that the girl was being visited by her mother's ghost. Even the stepmother had seen the dead woman. Reading the child, I found that she believed her mother wanted her to come to the Other Side to be with her. This was far from true but was the whole reason the girl was repeatedly trying to kill herself.

Finally, I was able to convince the young girl that she was seeing her mother because she was a psychic and not because her mother wanted her dead. Of course, I had to relate to the child how the mother had died so that she would believe me.

While telling the father and daughter about the death, they were both dumbfounded that I knew so many details. Actually the father needed to hear this as much or more than the child.

Relating that the mother had left the house and asked the father if he wanted anything from the store, I told them how she was dressed and that she didn't look particularly unhappy. She acted as if it were any other day when she left the house.

Her death happened when she crossed a road and an eighteen-wheeler hit her car. She died instantly. The truck driver told the husband what I told them next, that the woman had looked straight at him before he hit her.

The lady did not seem alarmed or apprehensive but maneuvered right in front of the truck so that the wreck would happen. It was ruled an accident, but I knew better because the lady told me it was a suicide. In her last moments, she wanted the truck driver to know that he was not at fault. The driver knew she had seen him but did not try to get out of the way. It left an indelible impression on him.

There was no need for me to relate to the family that the lady had killed herself using the eighteen-wheeler as surely as one who takes a gun and puts it to her head. She was dead, and the family had suffered enough.

Anyway, the young girl was helped to overcome her death wish and realize that she was indeed psychic. Her mother's visits could now be looked at as something special rather than an invitation to death.

This did not suit the father, however. He started dropping by the house on the days he knew my housekeeper was there so that he could catch me without an appointment. I had seen his daughter and him without charging for my time because I really wanted to help her.

The first time the father dropped by, I was nice to him and took time away from what I was doing to talk with him again. He had brought his dead wife's wedding ring by to see if I could get any vibrations from it. After informing him that I didn't need the ring to feel his wife, I talked with him for a while and told him as nicely as I could that he needed to call before he came next time. "From now on," I told him, "you will need to make an appointment with me." But I knew that he was not going to quit coming by unexpectedly.

A week later on housecleaning day, the doorbell rang and there he was again. My husband had come home for lunch. Generally, I am a very nice person, I think, and so my husband tells me, but I guess this man needed to hear what I was about to do, so I was not so nice.

Answering the door, I stepped outside the door and spoke not so gently to him. "Why are you here?" I asked. Without waiting for an answer, I continued, "It is because I remind you of her, isn't it? Oh, it's not the looks, but it's something isn't it?"

He was actively nodding yes, and he agreed it was not my looks but that I really did remind him of her. Telling me that if I didn't help him, he was going out of the country and would kill himself, too, made me mad. He had no right to try to suck me into his guilty little drama.

Continuing my tirade I said, "You want to know if she killed herself because you were having an affair about six weeks before, don't you? You know she knew, don't you?"

He nodded his head.

"Yes, she did and, she didn't want to live any longer, but don't you tell me that you're going to jump off some cliff because I cannot give

Ghosts and the Light

you the answers you want. Do not try to involve me in that part of your life. If you are going to do it, then go but don't try to make me feel guilty for not talking with you about her. She killed herself. It was her choice. You have to make the same choice now. That is a purely selfish act, and I don't like talking with you about your possible suicide. Quit feeling guilty and get on with your life. You didn't kill her. She killed herself. Don't come back again without an appointment."

Stepping back into the house, I closed the door and left the poor man standing on the front step. My husband looked at me in astonishment. He told me that he had never heard me talk like that to anyone before. "Compared to the way he treated me, I was easy on him," I told Claude. Then I told him what the man had said to me. Claude still believed that I should have been a little gentler with the man, but I didn't. He needed a shock, and he got one from me.

In looking at the people involved in the woman's suicide, you can see how connected we all are — even the truck driver and me. The new wife was a part of the suicide, even though she was there long after it happened, because she had seen the ghost, too. We were all touched by that woman's death.

The lady knew she was going to die and even welcomed it. At the point of impact, her soul was standing on the corner watching the whole incident. There was no pain for her, and she was aware of all that happened. She knew that she was part of the whole of God and could watch the supposed accident as if it were a movie she was watching.

On the Other Side, she learned that it is not good to do what she had done, but there was no consequence for it other than that she would have to live another life in a capacity that would help her to learn to deal with her husband's infidelity. Jealousy is no reason to kill oneself.

As part of the Light of God, all people should live their lives in total respect for the fact that they are allowed the time and body with which to experience earth learning. Trying to make it a more positive adventure without jealousy, greed, and the other deadly sins the Bible speaks of makes life more constructive. Being human demands that we try to learn from all of our experiences.

In some accidental deaths, it takes dead people a moment to focus and realize what has happened to them.

If they expected to die, then they only worry about the pain cre-

GHOSTS TALK

ated for themselves and their loved ones and where their soul will wake up since they are not sure what the Other Side is like. Loved ones' pain at the death of the person they cared for can cause great concern for those who have died. Instinctively, they want to comfort those left on earth but are unable to touch them by earthly standards. Of course, they can touch those of us who have not passed to the Other Side, but it takes considerable effort.

Ghostly visitors can utilize touch even when a person is unaware that the spirit they seek is around. A lady friend asked that I try to speak with her husband's late uncle, a cancer victim, without her husband's knowledge. Before joining her husband on their patio, I told her that the uncle was a man with his own mind and may be anywhere in the universe but that if he wanted to talk, I would listen. The three of us sat in the moonlight talking for a good while before I noticed a tall man in a white shirt walk up behind her. Saying nothing, I waited and continued talking with the two of them.

The ghostly uncle was not content with waiting. As I watched him standing behind her, he stuck his left hand through her back. The moment he did, she looked at me in horror and screamed, "What was that? Someone stuck his hand through my back? I felt it." While screaming these words, she was leaving her seat. All the while, her husband's uncle remained silently behind her smiling at me. She instantly started to describe the sensation the hand had caused in her body, stating that it felt as if someone had put a hand through her back. Looking at me she asked, "Didn't you see him?"

Obviously, I was unable to keep silent myself any longer. The woman had panicked. Not only did she know that he had put his hand into her back as she said but she also knew it was a man. The lady is very psychic but still doesn't believe it. Trying to allay her fear, I described the tall man to the two of them, and they agreed that it was indeed her husband's favorite uncle.

He returned to reassure both of them that there was life on the Other Side, but he didn't want to have to stand around waiting. Ghostly visitors have their own minds and their own timetable just as we do. They do not have to wait on us to initiate what time they will appear to a loved one. When the lady voiced her desire to see her husband's favorite uncle because her husband had been missing him quite

146

Ghosts and the Light

badly, then he appeared and gave her a hands-on performance.

Not all spirits will do this, but he made my job much easier. In touching the person who had requested his visit, he gave proof that there is life after death.

Accidental death victims arrive at the Other Side in a confused state, as if they were asleep and have awakened in a room with which they are not familiar. Friendly guides help them to realize where they are and how to proceed. Those guides help them to focus their attention on where they are. They usually allow them as much time as they need to realize that they are indeed dead — or what we on earth consider dead.

When the dead person realizes that he is still alive, it sometimes takes an adjustment period. Preconceived notions can occasionally be hard to dismiss, but the heavenly guides help.

Most murderers go to the Other Side in a rage. Loss of control is hard for them to fathom. Their fury puts them into a dark place, from what I have seen. Though the Light of God is still a part of them, the anger keeps them in the dark. It is as if they have built a dark cocoon around them, which they carry from place to place. Like a badge of dishonor, any spirit can instantly recognize a person from the dark side and realize he still needs considerable spiritual development.

If the dead person believes he is going to hell, then he will for the amount of time he wishes to punish himself. Hell is anything a person needs it to be. Certain ghostly spirits feel a need for punishment. There is no one who sits on the Other Side waiting to send you to heaven or hell. Instead, each spirit deals out his own punishment according to what he feels is necessary. Those more enlightened spirits know that the time they waste with punishment takes away from their time learning from the experiences they had on earth.

Most believe that when they die, they will end up in heaven. Heaven is the light of which I was speaking. It is God's presence. Since we are all part of God, then we are constantly in His presence, no matter which side we are on.

There are ghosts who think that because they have committed terrible wrongs in life, they will never go to heaven.

If they believe in their hell strongly enough, they will go there on the Other Side. We spirits manifest what we need for our development.

GHOSTS TALK

In this case, the soul may feel it is far from the light when in truth all it has to do is change its beliefs. Then it is wherever it needs to be.

One thing I have learned from speaking with my ghostly friends is that a ghost is already in the light. We are the light, and we are conceived into the physical world already in the light as well. The light is God, and we are part of Him.

Chapter Twelve

NO GHOST FRIEND
OF MINE

A friend of mine has a young son who asked his mother to question me about evil spirits. He wanted to know if evil spirits would come to see him.

My answer came from the beliefs that spring from my experience in sessions with the spirit.

There are human beings we consider evil because they do not conform to what humanity subscribes to as law. They seem to be here only to further their worldly ambitions. These people do not care about anyone but themselves.

Greed, selfishness, hatred, and ignorance lead to the evil part of man on this side. He is trying to get something for himself and doesn't worry about whom he hurts in the process.

He uses murder and mayhem to attain what he wants in this life.

There are those on the other side who have lived this type of life. People who have died after a life of corruption on the physical side are not much different over there. Their personalities are much the same, even

GHOSTS TALK

though they can look over their life experiences with some hindsight.

Many have chosen not to change. Perhaps they don't know they can. At any rate, they like their circumstance because they feel that power is achievement.

These ghostly criminals need to feel the power they felt while physically alive, so they look for someone who behaves as they did while they were on the physical side. Rarely will they associate with a person who has only good thoughts and intentions. This kind of person is no fun for them.

When a murderer says that he heard someone tell him to commit murder, he probably did. He had one of those entities on the other side who didn't want to change but still got his kicks from helping a physical person in a life of crime.

The physical murderer had to have a killer's mind first. Then the ghost killer could find him. He had to ask for help either consciously or subconsciously. Then he would get the help he needed from his ghost killer friend who would hear him and say to himself, "This is someone I want to know."

The two of them have no regard for others. They only think of themselves and what they can gain. In believing in this manner, they are drawn together.

Ordinarily, responsible people will never hear from one who has learned to be evil. When a malevolent spirit visits a person who does not believe as he does, it is generally for a different reason.

There has only been one occasion that I had a ghostly visitor of this type in my home. Physical visitors who think like this are the frightening ones because they can do something about what they are thinking.

Going upstairs to my office, I encountered an odor just like rotten garbage. It wasn't very big, only about eighteen inches deep and long. It was on one stair, was standing still, and it felt very physical to me.

As I ascended the stairs my head went through it. Stopping when I smelled the offensive odor, I retraced my steps to see where it was coming from. Always the inquisitor, I tried to rule out the obvious.

It didn't take me long to figure out I didn't like the situation. Without thought, I demanded, "What are you doing here?" After all, he was in my home.

No Ghost Friend of Mine

In a flash, my head was filled with the question he wanted answered. In essence it was this: he wanted to know how he could change his spiritual existence because he wanted to be different from the way he had been on earth and on the Other Side.

Knowing I was not the one to be able to answer this question because I had never had to deal with something of this nature before, I asked my guides for help. They told me to tell him they were there. All he had to do was open his eyes and look their way. Then he would be able to see. He did.

The eyes they spoke of were of a spiritual nature. All he had to do was see that they were there to help him simply because he had asked. One soul loving another was the terms. That's all. When he allowed himself to ask and receive, then he was able to see.

There was no forgiveness asked. None was needed. All that was needed was that he see who he was and how he had affected others' lives. This he had started before ever visiting me. Otherwise, he would have never wanted to question me about progressing spiritually.

My guides were there for me to see. To my way of thinking, he could have seen them, too, without having to ask me, but he thought he needed my assistance. He was so focused on the worldly action that he was unable to look to a higher spiritual plane. My job, for him, was as a liaison.

The lesson was there for me as well as for him. He had that spirituality in him all along but was unable to find it. Thinking it would be hard to achieve, he had never looked. But all he had to do was to say he wanted to change. When he voiced his desire, it happened.

We don't understand that we are the breath of God. He never leaves us. We, in our ignorance, neglect to realize He is always with us. God is complete love and understanding. We are the ones who neglect to love and understand.

When this entity came to me, he used me as a medium or channel to another part of the Other Side. Both living and dead, we are all available to help one another — that is, if we are willing.

Most of us do not like thinking of or being around people who want to achieve power through murder or other criminal activity. Nearly everyone would rather believe that they have higher moral convictions than that.

GHOSTS TALK

Society dictates that we have to live together in a structured group with laws so that each of us can live with some semblance of peace.

Spiritual law dictates that we have the laws of society so that we can deal with them through compliance and non-compliance for the experience of life in a myriad of ways to ensure our divine growth.

This situation is terrifying if we are part of it. As a human being, this lesson can be the hardest one to learn. How could anything of this nature happen to my family or me? What did we do to deserve this horrible experience?

The answer is simple, although it is not a wonderful situation to be in. People who are most closely involved learn the lesson more quickly than those at the perimeters, but they are all associated in some manner.

Those who are more closely involved chose it on the Other Side in order to help everyone associated with the incident learn more quickly so that the divine spark of God could show more evidently in their souls' growth.

Both the murderer and the victim learn from these happenings. Some choose to be the murderer in full knowledge of what they will do while on earth, even though that is not how their soul feels. They do not have a murderer's mentality on the Other Side but are only killing while on earth to further spiritual development for those they love and themselves.

Again take a look at Hitler. He was not someone I would want to make a friend of, but he was good for the earth in the sense that we should have learned never to treat the family of man in that manner. Did we learn?

Most of us thought that was the most tragic lesson of the 20th century. Did that stop man from repeating the process? If it did, then Hitler taught an exceptional lesson along with all those poor people he killed. All of them came together in one massive play to ensure that humanity was never inhumane again. They did not die in vain but rather helped mankind to further both their physical and metaphysical soul development.

Some murderers are here for spiritual reasons, while others are here only to gain what they consider more power. In the heat of the moment, it is hard to decipher which is which. This is something none of us wants to be close to in any manner.

Try not to think of the Other Side as wildly manipulative. Rather, it is quite organized in its methods.

On earth our society is driven most often by consequences of actions, while on the Other Side they are driven by actions creating consequences. Most humans allow themselves to be participants rather than to realize that we are the creators of our circumstances. The Other Side realizes that each person creates their own actions even if they are only reacting to circumstances produced by others. In producing tests on the Other Side, ghostly acquaintances manufacture situations or consequences on the earthly side, and all spirits involved in the play wait and watch to see how the curtain falls.

If our world were ideal, we would never learn lessons of faith. As I have heard church people say before, we could all play our harps and not worry about tomorrow because there would never be a care. This would not promote spiritual growth but rather a depressed laziness. There are times when all of us would prefer not having a care, but that could become very boring.

Before you count yourself lucky that you have never been one of the figures in history that served to teach the masses lessons, be very careful. In your various lives, you may have had occasion to teach some critical lessons.

As related earlier in this section, my smugness turned on me one day when I in my holier-than-thou thoughts was discussing something of this magnitude with another. People usually see me as a pretty nice person, and I thought I was until this discussion. Feeling that in a prior life, I had been something of a Robin Hood, I had the smugness of my convictions while discussing murderers and people of that nature, but my sweet guides who never let my head get very big reminded me of a life that I could not fathom.

There is no smugness now. All of a sudden I found myself on a stage. That wasn't bad. I don't mind speaking in front of strangers, but the item I found in my hand wasn't what I would usually carry. I was a very strong man standing on this stage, but there was no pride in my heart. Looking down and to my left, I saw why.

A person I did not know was bound by the hands waiting with his head on a chopping block for me to use that axe I had in my hand. The one consolation I have now is that the executioner really did not want to do his job but felt he had a duty to do so. For me that is one of the hardest lives I can remember.

So again, before we go casting stones, we should look around our own lives to see if we have the right to pick them up.

That doesn't mean that we need to associate ourselves with people of that character on this side. On the contrary, we are to live human lives when we come here, and that does not dictate hanging out with killers, unless that is what we live for. Thank goodness most of society does not condone that sort of thing. Otherwise earthly life would be no fun at all.

After all, we pride ourselves on having higher consciousness than other animals on earth because we don't kill for the power but rather for food. To sustain life is instinct.

Reincarnation is also not a reason for doing anything because you think you'll get a clean slate on the Other Side. You will not, and you are your own worst judge. Don't think that someone who commits these crimes gets away free. It takes some time to redeem oneself from that type of incarnation.

One man who had killed a young girl, when confronted and finally realizing he was caught, killed himself and left a book on reincarnation at his feet.

Living for power is not what it is cracked up to be. Most people who live this way are frightened themselves or they would not have the wish to be more powerful. Insecurity guides spouse abusers, pedophiles, and killers. They are trying to live up to some conception of what they think they should be and find that their actions do not make them any closer to achieving their goal.

Power always leaves people wanting. They can never be satisfied. Seeking greater power does not allow any rest. Consequently, people who look for power are always looking.

In this world, there has to be good and evil in order to utilize the learning effort. Evil is not some imaginary being out there. People create evil by yearning for power.

When a person wants something he knows is not his and decides to take it by any means necessary, then he has broken the law. That is depravity in its fullest and is the birth of evil. There is no man with horns and a tail out there that is creating this, but it is one who is fully physical.

This comes back to responsibility. None of us wants to believe

No Ghost Friend of Mine

that we are responsible for the evil committed on earth, but we all contribute in one manner or another, although there are degrees.

Stealing is stealing whether it is a piece of penny candy or one million dollars. It took the same mentality to decide to commit the act even though, on earth, we punish the crime in different manners.

If you're not sure whether something is right or wrong, you might be best leaving it alone in order to further your spiritual growth. Either way you proceed will cause different conditions in which you will learn, but some are easier than others.

We on earth have a perfect right to feel threatened by powerful offenders. On earth, we are here to learn. Humans sometimes feel powerless, and that is part of the spiritual process, too.

Society's laws provide the boundaries that souls need for their evolution on earth. We all need to live with some guidelines for growth. If a killer kills, then he should meet whatever consequences earthly laws dictate.

As the soul grows, human laws change to represent the expansion.

Chapter Thirteen

IS POSSESSION REAL?

From what I have learned, possession is a real thing in the sense that a human has to invite the spirit into his body. There are those who have gone to the Other Side and want to guide or help people here.

Take the example of a little girl who is being sexually and physically abused by her father. While this abuse is happening, she retreats and calls out silently for someone to help her.

On the Other Side, someone hears this and says, "Maybe I can help her. Let me go try."

This person comes and tells her to be strong and that the ordeal will soon be over. In the spirit's opinion, it will be over soon because there is no sense of time on the Other Side.

This is not good enough for the little girl. Innocently she, subconsciously tells the spirit, "You feel good. I am glad you are here. Please stay, but I want someone who can help me get back at my father for hurting me."

Another spirit out there hears. He might have been Attila the

GHOSTS TALK

Hun in another life, and he knows how to get even. The little girl's expression of anger sent a hot signal to him because he has dealt in anger before.

He approaches the little girl with the same "I am here to help" attitude.

She has spiritually withdrawn to make room for the other spirit. Now she has two spirits with her who are willing to help her and work on her behalf.

One is a spirit who says if she can wait, this will stop. The other doesn't want to wait. He wants to take matters into his own hands now.

When he gets his chance, using her body with super-human strength because of the anger, he pushes her father down the stairs.

The girl granted permission for this by asking for someone to come and take revenge on her father. The little girl who was one has become three.

We have all heard of possession. The only way this can happen is if we have asked for it. Sometimes we are not consciously aware that we are inviting that kind of visit.

Acute anger and the desire for revenge promote this behavior. As long as people let their emotions and thoughts focus on vengeance, then people on the Other Side will continue to help those on the physical side through this type of behavior.

Any thought given great emotional weight will evoke help from the source needed, even if that source is not one you truly thought you wanted around you. Be careful what you ask for. Responsibility comes with the asking.

Section Three

KARMA AND REINCARNATION

Chapter Fourteen

KARMA AND REINCARNATION

Acording to Buddhist philoso-
phy, Karma means the sum total of one's actions, whether good or bad.

There are three kinds of human action related to Karma: mental, verbal and physical. Your future depends on how you concentrate
those actions now.

Each of these actions creates in life what you expect of yourself.
You are the sum total of those actions. As you think, speak and move,
you are.

With any spirituality there has to be a consequence of one's
actions. In my spiritual reality I believe in Karma.

The Bible says what you sow is what you reap. In essence, this is
true. The point that many people make—which I do not agree with--
is that you are going to be judged by a God who sits on a throne with
his pencil ready to mark you off and send you to hell. **You** are the judge
of **you!** As your worst critic, it is up to you to review your life and
decide what area of your life needs improvement. Then you will go

about making challenges to encourage the soul's evolution.

These actions do not dictate whether a person will face heaven or hell. They only serve to teach the individual who is living those actions. There is no sin, only education. Your reward is that you become more "God-like" in caring for yourself, and by doing so you can care more for others. In reaching towards God, one understands that we are all created in The Universal Source as one, but yet we are individuals of the whole.

My definition of Karma is preconditions made by a soul in past lives so that it can create situations in its present life that will extend to future lives. Our past lives have meaning in the present life based on the Karma we chose before. It is not a dirty word like sin, just the opposite. Like a savings account, it appreciates over time with our choices.

Karma is why we live our lives and is influenced by past and present lives. Between lives we create our Karma too. We decide what paths we will take on the physical side of life in order to work through our Karmic education. Setting up obstacles along the way, we can use freedom of choice in making our way to a better spiritual awareness.

As the only one in charge of our Karma, it is what we make it. Karma is eternal, as are we; we use it from one life to another.

Being the creators we are, our joys and sorrows of the future are chosen in the present. Then comes the experience. We set those times up for ourselves long before we touch them by the decisions we make.

Looking at your present will give you a snapshot of your future. Knowing what you want in your future can help you achieve it by working in the present. The very act of deciding what you want later starts the process. Your decisions along the way influence that future.

In Karma, a persons desire is their destiny and can be changed on a daily basis. Though it sometimes takes time to set it into motion, just the thought creates the motion.

Jesus said, "When you speak from the heart, it is so." I agree totally with this statement. Your desire, when expressed, creates your life or is in actuality reaping what you sow.

Plato thought that the soul is eternal, pre-existent and wholly spiritual. I agree with this.

He also thought that after entering the body, it tended to become impure through association with bodily passions. I do not agree with

Karma and Reincarnation

his implications of the word "impure." In some respects the impurities of his thoughts were correct. The body does alter the soul with thoughts on such topics as survival and procreation. Some people might consider those thoughts impure but they are not impurities. Instead, they are learning situations. The spirit always retains some knowledge of its former existences, even though consciously we may not remember those lives.

We come to earth as spiritual innocents who know their roots. As time goes by, the physical body, in its need to survive, asks for more. A baby's cry brings food and care. Learning the lesson that by voicing his opinion loudly, he can get the attention he craves too, this baby gets louder. As he grows older, he sees that others have material possessions. He thinks that there is no reason he shouldn't have those possessions, too. If he can't get them by asking or working for them, then maybe he can take them. In any event, they will still be his. He is no longer the spiritual innocent but is aware what he is doing is for his good now, not later.

I do not agree with Plato that the spirit became impure. It has only increased its knowledge via some of the imperfections on the physical side of life. Education is not impure. For me, the lack of it is.

Karma also dictates that reincarnation is a viable belief system because of the redundant lives we live in order to learn. From my conversations with the Other Side and my own experiences, I know that this is true.

Re-incarnation is something that most Christian beliefs have trouble with because they believe that incarnation is the assumption of an earthly form by God.

For instance, the Bible, John 1:14 says, "And the Word became flesh and dwelt among us."

I agree that the Word became flesh. As God, He can do anything. As a part of God, we can do anything too. Returning to bodily clothing at anytime, we can repeat the process of gaining knowledge.

With that knowledge, let us look to Jesus. He did not want us to worship him, as some believe, but only to believe the way he did. In the Bible under John 14:6, He said, "I am the way and the truth and the life. No one comes to the Father except through me."

For me, this means that we should follow his teachings. If we look at his teachings according to the Bible, he did not hate anyone. So

GHOSTS TALK

we should love everyone as ourselves. Do no harm to others. All are equal in God's sight because we all come from Him and are therefore part of Him. When we see that we are all one coming from the whole, then how can we wreak havoc on anything else God has made? Jesus was, according to the Bible, good to everyone he met and saw no one who was above love.

Karma means we need to forgive ourselves and go on living. Keeping our spirit clear for positive energy makes the soul grow. A strong active will and a desire for a pure heart are our best protections against negative energies that cause the soul to backslide. Sometimes we have to experience the unwanted energies of life in order to know the wanted ones. Without knowledge of what is bad for us, how can we acknowledge the good in our lives?

God did not make good and evil. Man did. We need to experience it in our lives in order to learn. Man gets bored so easily that he needs varied experiences to become more enlightened.

Even with believing in reincarnation, I do not believe in pre-destiny. Pre-destiny is putting a life challenge in place and having no choice but to live it. With Karma, there are always choices. Karma is cause and effect, which creates intelligence. Wisdom eases Karma.

Karma is with you always. It never leaves you. Whatever you do or wherever you are, it is there. Like a shadow, it follows us into the future making like situations so we can learn from what we consider our mistakes. In my philosophy, there are no mistakes, only learning experiences.

We are mirrors, waiting to reflect our image on others. We get what we give. Individually, we are all part of the whole. When a person, as an individual, starts to think that he can be dreadful to others without repercussions, then he is ignorant to the workings of Karma. How many times have you been driving and someone gave you that obnoxious finger? What is your immediate response?

Let's suppose someone did that to you. Without thinking, you threw your finger up to let him know how it felt. He didn't see you but the woman in the car next to him did. She thought you did it to her. Now, she does the same thing back to you. You don't see her doing it but the man in the car right behind you does. Not understanding what he has done to deserve such attention, especially from this woman, he wheels his

Karma and Reincarnation

car over in front of her causing her to hit the light pole. Then he gives her that same gesture and goes off before she can get his license number.

Who started it? How many others were brought into the process? All allowed themselves to be brought into the situation by the first person throwing up their hand with an obscene gesture. Any one of those people could have stopped that reaction by ignoring what they thought had been done to them and thus excluded themselves from this Karmic lesson. They were in complete control of their own situations at all times.

One individual started the process that caused the collision, and that person will have to account for that action somewhere down the line, even if he doesn't know what happened as a result of his action. The ones who participated are also at fault and will learn one day a valuable lesson from their actions.

Learning is like a chain reaction. It continues without end.

Energy begets energy.

Energy is usually associated with atoms, which are continuous. Atoms never die. They change and become something else after a short rest, but they never truly die.

History of Belief System

Ancient people believed in the life of the spirit. They thought that as long as food and drink were furnished to the physical body, the spirit could inhabit the body even though it was dead. Having no one to explain to them that the spirit continues to live on without the confinements of the body, they left nourishment for the corpse.

Because life was so hard for them, they thought only of their next food source, keeping themselves safe, having a group to live with and keeping the corpse supplied with food so that it's spirit would continue to live.

As civilization advanced, the belief in judgment after death was introduced. A standard of right and wrong was established according to tribal customs, and continues on today. Souls were made subject to the laws of retribution, because it was eternal.

They decided that man would have to live by the laws of the land or be punished in some way. What better way than death to the body?

GHOSTS TALK

Basic human nature dictates that we try to keep the body alive at all costs.

With failure to keep the body alive the next worst thing was for the soul to experience hardship. From customs, religion started to form and grow. Religion found ways to punish the soul in order to keep people in line: going to hell. Hell was a burning fire that was never quenched. Thus the soul would feel pain for eternity.

Christian doctrine includes the second advent of Christ, the resurrection of the dead, the last judgment, the immortality of the soul, concepts of heaven and hell and the consummation of the kingdom of God. The Roman Catholic Church additionally includes beatific vision, purgatory and limbo.

Religious beliefs have evolved from man's requiring a higher power to give life meaning. In looking at the different religions, we see that they are similar. All believe in retribution of some sort.

Religious leaders in the past have made a habit of destroying any literature in which they did not believe. The first Council of Nicaea in 325 A.D. is a prime example.

The leaders of that Council took reincarnation out of the Bible and substituted resurrection instead. If people could believe that there was life after death, and that they could be born physically again, then how could they be controlled? Religious leaders wanted control over their parishioners.

Society had to grow without chaos. Laws and justice had to prevail. The best way to control the masses was through the laws of God first. Then under those laws of God came the laws of the land. The thought that if one was not obedient to the laws of the land, then he would not be true to the laws of God. If this happened, he would die and his soul would go to a horrible place for eternity.

Constantine thought of this and brought to life a religion that has had a very large impact on the world.

In his early life, Constantine believed that the Roman sun god, Apollo, was the visible manifestation of the invisible Highest God. This Highest God was the principle behind the universe. He was also thought to be the companion of the Roman emperor.

Constantine was a warrior who was at war from 306 A.D. until 324 A.D.

In 312 A.D., while still at war, he had a dream that Christ

Karma and Reincarnation

appeared to him and told him to inscribe the first two letters of his name (XP in Greek) on the shields of his troops. The next day, it was said that he saw a cross superimposed on the sun and the words, in this sign, "You will be the victor." He went on to defeat Maxentius at the Battle of Milvian Bridge, near Rome.

My thoughts are perhaps that he could have been psychic with just a touch of ego.

Constantine went from being a pagan sun worshipper to believing that Jesus had helped him win a war.

As in any religious war people want to know whose side Jesus or God was on. Generally, that goes to the victor.

Well, we know Constantine thought he had Jesus' full authorization to go killing others. The good part of this war was that he stopped the persecution of the Christians.

In 313 A.D., he and Licinius (co-emperor) issued the Edict of Milan, which mandated toleration of Christians in the Roman Empire.

Licinius and Constantine, being human, both wanted to be the only emperor of the Roman Empire but Constantine emerged victorious in 324 A.D..

After such a long war and to unite his kingdom, he decided to intervene in ecclesiastical affairs and presided over the first Council of Nicaea.

He unified a teetering empire and reorganized the Roman state. Even though he brought Christianity to the forefront, he still tolerated paganism. Sometimes it's better to walk the fence than to let everyone know your beliefs. Walking the fence allows you to make everyone think you are on their side.

Now, I don't know about you, but if I wanted to make sure I had everyone's attention, being emperor and all, I would make church and state real close. That way, when people tithed, the state would be able to share in the church's wealth. Not only that but when you offended the state you would also offend God.

Constantine wanted to make sure that with God and state being unified that there was no way people could not understand that punishment for mistreating either would lead to dire circumstances. The bishops wanted to assist him at the time because it meant that their church would be recognized above all others. All but two bishops wanted to help him at that first Council. One recanted, out of fear for his

169

life, and gave into the others. The other was willing to speak his mind, though, and for that started a storm of his own.

The bishop, Arius, denied the full divinity of Jesus Christ.

Using the written Word, he felt that God was un-begotten, without beginning or end. Because Christ, as clearly stated in the Word, was the only begotten Son of God, He was unable to be the same as God who was not begotten. They were not made of the same stuff, God un-begotten, Jesus begotten. God, according to the Word, had never incarnated into man as Jesus had.

Arius believed that because Jesus had taken a physical body, which God never had, this made Jesus incarnate. If he could be made flesh once, what was to keep Him or any other of God's fleshly children from doing it again?

Thinking that Jesus had come down and taken a physical body in order to live as a human and teach others here about God got Arius in heaps of trouble with the leaders of the church at that time.

If we are to believe Jesus is the Son of God and man as the Bible describes, then he had to be incarnated into the physical as the ancient Greek and Roman religions thought. Again going back to the teachings of Jesus, He said that you could only come to the Father by going through Him, which meant, to my way of thinking, believing as He did.

Jesus was not afraid to see himself as the Son of God because He knew His origin. Others of the human persuasion are not so quick to take on the Divinity in themselves because they don't remember that the Spark of God is the spirit within. Without confidence that they are creators too, they shrink back from those beliefs, not remembering life on the Other Side and not having the realization of that memory that we are all individuals as part of the Whole called God.

Buddhism, Hinduism and other religions carry their thoughts a little further by believing that the spirit comes from God and is incarnated on the earth in everyone. As we are all are part of the Spirit, then we are part of God the whole in physical form.

Being part of the whole, which can take physical form means that we can return to the physical at any point in eternity. There are no limitations on what the spirit can do.

The Counsel of Nicaea along with Constantine had other thoughts though. Poor Arius, for his beliefs in reincarnation, was

Karma and Reincarnation

damned. Not only that, but anyone who believed as he did, was damned also. Then as it is today, we still have some who would persecute us for our beliefs.

Arius' papers were burned as heretic by the other two hundred forty nine bishops at the Counsel who had a problem with what he believed. There was only one other bishop who confessed he believed as Arius did, but he quickly changed his mind. He was prompted by fear of fire, no doubt, since fire was an accepted execution in those days.

Those bishops, led by Constantine in 325A.D., promoted religion of Christianity and effectively did away with the belief in reincarnation.

When the council came together, they had to decide which books would really be put in the Bible. How many men or women, for that matter, do you know, when alone much less together, have an easy time deciding on anything? If they were like our politicians today, they would never agree.

There is a story on how the council came to the understanding of which books would be in the Bible. It makes as much sense as any. Because they could not agree, the Bishops decided they would leave all chapters which they considered Biblical under a table. The parts of the books, which needed to be in the Bible, would magically jump onto the table over night.

With faith all things are possible. The next morning, miraculously, there were books on top of the table and thus the Bible was born.

Having reincarnation in the Bible created a small problem for those who wanted to control the masses. Church policy was built on fear. People need a certain amount of fear in their lives to appreciate living. If people didn't fear going to hell, then they would not adhere to church policy.

The policies back then were quite demanding. Tithing needed to be done to fund church and state. What better way to get to heaven than in the pursuit of giving up your worldly possessions to get there?

People who believed in reincarnation had no reason to tithe. They knew they would come back again. Making peace with their God, they lived their life without the need of church.

What did that mean to church as well as to state at the time? It was one less person to tithe to the church, which was part of state. That way of thinking might catch on and the Emperor just couldn't have that.

GHOSTS TALK

Besides that, a social question had to be answered. Lawlessness might come about. What is to keep people from trying to gain wealth without worrying about how they got it if they had no fear of retribution? There might be robberies and murder. After all, if one believed in reincarnation, there is really no hell-fire and damnation.

Knowing one might go to hell instead of coming back to earth again was a good way to keep parishioners in line. If a person thought they had to pay divine retribution, they would be better people on this side.

There are some good points to this way of thinking. Few people wouldn't behave if they sincerely believed they would go to hell for the sins they committed on earth. If the promise of a heavenly reward doesn't keep them straight, the thought of burning eternal retribution makes them a little more considerate.

Because Arius followers continued to believe as he did, in 525 A.D. they were considered damned again and the church put a little teeth into it.

Anyone who still professed to believe this way wasn't long for this world. The church was going to give them their chance, before they could contaminate others with their thoughts, to return to the earth again in another life.

Please don't think I am against organized religion: I am not. Preferring that you think for yourself, I ask that you study different religions and history to come up with your own answers. Thank God, I am still questioning.

I do agree with Saint Augustine's assertion that evil was not created by God, whose creation is entirely good. Evil was created by those who have choices to make. Thus evil is the absence of light in the Biblical sense, God being the truth, the light and the way.

Saint Augustine also believed that what first appears as evil may be inherently good.

For an extreme example of this, look at the Holocaust. We as nations allowed Hitler to kill the Jewish people for no reason other than they were God's chosen people, who according to the Bible killed Christ.

Jews were allowed to be killed by Hitler because most humans thought deep in their hearts that they deserved it. After all, Hitler was the one doing the murders, not them. They were a world away.

After witnessing the atrocities of the Holocaust, most of the

Karma and Reincarnation

world decided that this must never happen again. Something good came from what appeared to be a ghastly evil.

Another example of this is Native Americans who believe that everything is a part of God (whatever He is called) and that if you eliminate any one part, you have hurt the whole. For their beliefs, Native Americans have been hated, exiled, and called pagans.

Religious people originally wanted the Native American's land. It was, as it is today, easier to take possessions from those who do not have the same belief systems as the ruling majority. Greed becomes religiously justifiable. Religious wars are still being fought with the same fervor as they have been since the beginning of time.

I believe that each person is an individual consciousness within a collective consciousness. Even the trees, birds, etc. are a part of that awareness. There is nothing that is not a part of "It."

We are all able to make our own decisions separately but we influence the whole with each decision. That is why I say we must never hurt others.

On the subject of hurting others, I have heard many people say that they are vegetarians because they do not think it is right to kill and eat meat. Knowing what I do about animals, how they think, their feelings, their having souls too and how they enjoy life, it makes eating a steak a little less palatable.

Being a realist, I can't stand hurting anything but I also know that in order to survive and learn as human beings, we have to eat. Those vegetarians do not think for a second that vegetables have a consciousness too, but they do. So in killing them, you are taking lives.

We, as the American Indians say, should be grateful to the animal or vegetable spirit for letting us consume it, for giving its life so that we may have life. It is then a part of us and continues to live within us. Thus it continues to live as part of the "Whole."

Consider what happened when DDT was used to kill insects. Experts thought DDT would only kill bugs. But the animals that ate the contaminated insects were poisoned. Then the eagles and hawks that ate those animals were poisoned. It caused a huge domino effect that threw the environment off-kilter and took many years to repair.

If we are to survive on this planet God so lovingly gave us, we need to be aware of what we are doing and how it is going to influence others.

After all, it was His word that He knows every "fallen sparrow."

Human beings think that we are the only things that count in God's universe. Greed pushes us on. Worrying only about what is good for us, we don't take into consideration the consequences of our actions. Man touches everything and everything touches man. History has proven that we should check every available angle before irreparably changing our world, which would probably be better off left alone. This does not mean that we should stagnate before modernizing. It only means that we should make a thoughtful evaluation of the whole before we commit to change.

If we believe in reincarnation, then we will never get away from the problems we create. It would be better to keep the world unpolluted so that when we are born again we have a wonderful place to return.

Biblical comments regarding reincarnation

Several passages in the Bible relate to reincarnation. They cannot be discounted in one's quest for information on reincarnation. When read and dissected, they leave no doubt that reincarnation is in the Bible.

If the soul only had one chance at physical life, there would be no reason to continue striving to learn. "Get all you can while you are in a physical body because you can't take it with you," would be most people's motto. Then past lives would have nothing to do with the souls progression. There would be no reason to give them credence.

Christianity's central theme is that Jesus is the Son of God incarnate in a world of sin. He came here to teach us not to sin again.

Christianity also believes that after death there are only two choices for the soul, either heaven or hell. Christian leaders do not usually teach reincarnation.

As a child of God, we came to this earth to live life, learn lessons on this plane and evolve spiritually. God didn't make us do this. It was a conscious decision on our part. Being an individual who is part of the whole that is considered God, we must try to live our lives in the highest of spiritual – not religious – ways.

There is a difference in spirituality and religion. Religion is a belief system. Spirituality is living what you believe.

More people have been killed in the name of religion than in any

Karma and Reincarnation

war ever fought. Think of that. People, who make up religion, have killed more people in the name of God or whatever they called God than for any other cause. Who has the right to think that God wants them to kill another for not believing as they do?

Spirituality is not religion; it is a way of life. Loving others as you love yourself is what Jesus asked us to do. He was one of the most spiritual of men and one of the best teachers on reincarnation.

One of the more popular verses in our church was in Lamentations 5:7 which states, "Our fathers sinned and are no more and we bear their punishment."

Take a look at this verse with reincarnation in mind. Our father commits a wrong and then he dies. Now Karma takes over.

As an example, let us use a deformity in another life as payment for his crime. Even though that is quite simplistic, it might go something like this.

If that man returned to physical life by being born to his son as a deformed baby, making the dead man a grandfather, would it not look as if the grandchild was paying for the sins of the grandfather? In actuality it would be the very person who committed the crime who paid for it with the deformity. He just waited a family generation for justice to prevail.

What he sowed, he reaped.

Another instance of this is in John 9:1-3 in a passage concerning a conversation between Jesus and his disciples: "As he went along, he saw a man blind from birth. His disciples asked him, 'Rabbi, who sinned, this man or his parents, that he was born blind?' 'Neither this man nor his parents sinned,' said Jesus, 'but this happened so that the work of God might be displayed in his life.'"

Now to my way of thinking, how could this man who was blind since birth have sinned before birth? Either Jesus had a belief in reincarnation or reincarnation is truth.

Jesus even answered that neither the man nor his parents had sinned. He didn't say, "Are you stupid? This man wasn't even born yet. How could he sin before birth?"

Instead he answered the disciple's question. If he had not believed in reincarnation, then he would have gone into a dissertation about man only living one physical life. In other words, this was not a Karmic lesson but a lesson to be learned to glorify God and maybe Jesus even had the ulterior motive to make people aware of reincarnation.

In their innocence to learn from the Master, the disciples did not censor their words when asking Jesus about the blind man. To me this lends credence to the fact that the bishops took reincarnation out of the Bible at the First Council of Nicaea but they neglected to kill all verses associated with it.

There is another scripture quoting Jesus which states, "Except a man be born again, he cannot see the kingdom of God," John 3:3. According to some Bible scholars, the words "born again," as taken from the Greek manuscripts, literally meant physical rebirth. If physical rebirth is actually true, then are we seeing the manifestation of the kingdom of God, known as earth, upon birth as that verse implies?

My little dog, Muffin, demonstrated another version of being born again to me when, upon her death, her soul came back as the little black and brown puppy she had been when young. When asked why her spirit appeared in that form, she answered that she had been "born again." Her use of those two words, which were the last expressions that I would have expected at the time, made me take a look at the Biblical words, "born again," in a more educated way. Though she had just died, she returned in spirit in puppy form to let me know that she was indeed still alive.

Death is being born again and so is coming to the physical in the birth process.

In Mark 8:27-29, Jesus asked his disciples who they thought he was. They replied, "Some say John the Baptist; others say Elijah; and still others, one of the prophets."

With these words, the Disciples of Christ gave credence to reincarnation.

When asked by his disciples why the teachers of the law said that Elijah must come before Him, Jesus replied in Matthew 17:11-13, "To be sure, Elijah comes and will restore all things. But I tell you, Elijah has already come and they did not recognize him, but have done to him everything they wished. In the same way the Son of Man is going to suffer at their hands. 'Then the disciples understood that he was talking to them about John the Baptist.'"

What else can this mean but that reincarnation was a fact to

Karma and Reincarnation

Jesus? He didn't say that there is no such thing but readily admitted that Elijah had already come back and was treated miserably. As Jesus said the people had done to Elijah everything they wished. John the Baptist had his head removed for his beliefs.

For his beliefs, Jesus saw the death coming for him too.

Jesus realized that people don't always know the answer, even when it is placed in front of them. He even said that although people were waiting for Elijah to return, even though he had already done so, people didn't recognize him.

Jesus further admitted reincarnation and the fact that John the Baptist was indeed Elijah when he uttered these words in Matthew 11:13-15. "For all the Prophets and the Law prophesied until John. And if you are willing to accept it, he is the Elijah who was to come. He who has ears, let him hear."

He who has ears, let him hear is one of my favorite quotes from the Bible because it tells us to treat the information that we hear very carefully. Our minds only process part of what is being said. Jesus stated emphatically that Elijah had returned from the dead by being born again to physical life in the form of John the Baptist. He left no doubt as to what he was implying.

These Biblical notations for reincarnation are some that did not get left out in the first Council of Nicaea. They are in the Bible for anyone to read. When read in context those verses are proof positive that Jesus believed in reincarnation.

Many believe that taking the word reincarnation from the Bible and inserting the word resurrection was done to dispel the belief in reincarnation.

Reincarnations relationship to life

Karma is not an appalling event but rather the education of the soul. Enlightening the soul is what life is all about. The soul never dies as physical life does many times. It continues to live while only changing out the particular garment that it is wearing.

Reincarnation is like going to your closet to choose what you will wear today. Your feelings dictate your choice. The relationship between Karma and past lives is the choice of the life you want to live, just as if you were picking a garment to wear. When that garment is no longer functional for you, then it is tossed.

Reincarnation figures in much the same way. Once you have learned the lessons that you chose for yourself while on the Other Side in your current physical life, you toss your body away to look for another. Choice of that body will suit your needs for the next lesson. It is a never-ending circle producing the cycle of life.

The point one needs to learn is you are the one in charge of your own state of affairs, making you the creator of your fate.

Most people would rather believe that they are creatures moved by circumstances rather than believing that they are making their own situations in which to live. Responsibility is a hard teacher, with lessons that are not easily learned.

Reincarnation helps to reinforce the education of taking account-ability for one's own actions time and again. Lessons of the soul are hard to forget.

As creators, we challenge ourselves by setting up situations that call for experiences from which to learn until our soul is comfortable with our wisdom. At that point, without conscious thought, we are able to make the best choice for our souls' education.

Karma translated into reincarnation and education in the form of payment for our behavior in past lives does not necessarily mean that because you were cruel to someone in a wheelchair you will be strick-en to a wheelchair in your next life. There is more than one way that you can receive your karma. Taking care of the person in the wheelchair who may be your child, your best friend or the one you are in love with could be the way you pay your past life debt. An emotional invalid is another type Karmic lesson.

Karma has more situations for life's lessons than can be imagined.

The choice of Karma is yours, whatever it may be. God doesn't sit on a throne somewhere and say this is what you have to do. You as a creator with God make your own Karmic lessons.

There are no accidents of birth, only choices that are being and have been made by you. No one is immune to Karma. You might try to run from it for a while, but it will catch up to you in one life or anoth-er, just as your shadow follows you through life now. Making the best choices in your life is your way of staying ahead of your Karma.

Karma and Reincarnation

This does not mean that you have to go around with a perpetual smile on your face. Karma allows everyone the opportunity to live with every emotion, lifestyle, race, religion or culture. As physical beings we need to experience all the conditions Karma affords so that we can make the best choices for our soul's growth.

If we were only happy, only white or only rich, we would never learn the other conditions of life, which ensure the soul's growth, such as being poor, being another race or being sad. Our soul can best benefit by our visiting every life situation. That is why we come to physical bodies.

Living each day does not always mean that day should be a wonderful day— quite the contrary. Looking at it from the souls perspective, it will only make the soul grow stronger by experiencing the good and the bad. Past lives reflect present life for the soul just as a photograph of a child reflects upon that child's adulthood.

My only reason for looking to past lives is that you can learn from some to make your present and future lives better. Remembering the past allows one to learn from his choices and decide what best to do in the present. Thus one creates the best possible future in which the soul can continue learning.

Present life gives way to future lives, which can also be viewed in relation to what you are doing in your existing life.

One can review what has happened in the past, in their present physical life, to gain knowledge for their present and future circumstances. That same knowledge from past lives can be utilized to alter this life for the better.

Past lives are not events that stand alone in the soul's evolution. As a part of everyday life, they will affect your life in present-day circumstances. A past life is an event in your present life as part of the soul's growth just as birth, childhood, adolescence, young adult, middle-aged adult, mature adult and death are. Each cycle assists in creating the person you are today when taken in that context.

A past life may appear as something you loved such as food, actions, place of birth, home, likes, dislikes and a myriad of other things.

Certain cultures will be a part of what you love now. Foods from other countries might make you wonder why you crave them when you have never tried them. A certain part of the world might feel like home to you, even though you have never been there. Disliking a person the first time you meet them may relate to past lives. Fears of certain objects or ceremonies may cling to your life like a leech.

All these things cannot be explained by present-day life but are so simple if you only look to past lives.

One such past life, which affected the person living now in a most unusual manner, was something she would have never believed. With excitement in her voice, she told me that she was going to a wedding that was in a religion different from hers. The woman, a Baptist, was elated that she would get to see a Catholic church in all its ornate finery. What she did not count on, upon going into the church, however, was the fear she had for her life. She told me that she continuously looked over her shoulder to make sure no one was creeping up behind her to kill her, and she finally had to leave the church.

This lady didn't have a fear of church. Rationalizing didn't help her, she said. The panic was with her as long as she sat in that church. She couldn't focus on the wonderful wedding she was longing to attend; instead all she could think of was getting out of the church as quickly as humanly possible.

Telling me how beautiful the church was when she entered it; she described how she felt while sitting in this lovely church. Unaware that she was speaking of a past life, she was worried that there were people who would hurt her. In her mind's eye, she could see those people coming up from behind to kill her. As she described the situation to me, I saw that she was reliving her soul's history of the Inquisition even though she didn't believe in past lives.

It could have been something in the Church that made her remember that past life, or maybe it was just walking inside but something brought that life to the fore for her. An experience she was looking forward to suddenly became a miserable ordeal that made her feel as though she had to fight for her life.

Past lives will impact today's life in some manner. They may make you want to be a better person, or can even make you worse. Because you have free will, there are times when your present life is not much better than your past one. You have the freedom of choice to do whatever you want to do in each life. We sometimes commit to the same behavior as we have in a past life. After all, we have eternity to

Karma and Reincarnation

learn those same lessons.

Souls on the Other Side create, with the best of intentions, lives in which they know they can make up for what they consider past challenges. All those souls know that we are all in this thing called life together. What affects one affects all. Along with other souls, they all work to benefit each other and confront their destiny of becoming more God-like together.

After coming to physical form though, that soul knows that each of us has the freedom of choice, without the benefit of being able to see past lives as they did on the Other Side. Most usually cannot remember what they did in their past lives. Thus they may repeat, in the same manner, situations they were in before. Choices on the physical side are not easy because one doesn't have the benefit that one has on the Other Side to see the soul's life in its entirety.

Living does not come with a handbook. Going through life's ups and downs can be quite confusing, especially if you believe that any choice you make reflects directly on others. Most people do not want to hurt another person, even when that person has intentionally inflicted hurt upon them. It is not God's way.

We are what we make ourselves. The soul knows that it is up to us to decide how our life comes out. With each Karmic life, our existence may be different but the course of events, which were mapped out on the Other Side, isn't.

When you leave the physical side of life again, your soul might feel upon reflection, that it hasn't progressed at all. Thus it sets in motion a new set of situations in the physical arena in which it can hopefully learn the same lesson. The soul always allows itself another chance for education.

On the Other Side, your soul devises your karma so that you can enact it on the physical side. Thus what we consider life begins again.

Readings of past lives

Past life influences the way we perceive others as well as ourselves. Learning from our past lives and others' can lead to a better understanding of why we were born to the physical.

In the hope of helping others learn from past lives as I have,

GHOSTS TALK

included are some readings I have done for others and for myself. Each reading tells a story of how we can help ourselves, if only we try.

A young man in his thirties came to me for assistance. He told me he was unable to sleep at night and didn't understand why. I told him I knew this had just started and he said I was right. I referred to the fact that he had just bought a new bedroom suite. Puzzled that I knew this, he looked at me in wonder. How could I know this?

Then I told him that the furniture was a dark color, was immense and reminded me of the ship I saw him on in a past life.

I then told him that the man I saw in the past life was terrified of life in general. He had worked with numbers for a local import company. Anything that went against his routine created a real problem for him. As long as this shy man could go to work and go home alone at night, he was all right. Any kind of new event, or any relationship with others, evoked tremendous fear in this timid little man.

Being hijacked to a life on the sea was not a fear that his mind could comprehend or overcome. Life at sea was nothing that he would have ever chosen for himself, let alone the men around him. He was very frightened and in constant fear for his life.

Water invaded his every moment. Not only was it all around him leaving no room for escape, but it seeped through the very boards of the ship. Even the boards on which he slept were constantly damp, looking as if they had been rubbed down with walnut oil.

Fear kept him awake at night. The rolling of the ship and fright of the men around him made him feel he had to be vigilant. Finally, he had no choice. His body made him sleep for very small intervals. Lack of sleep made him more nervous and fidgety.

With his constant vigilance and lack of sleep, he began to give the other men the creeps. One of the more superstitious of the men decided he had enough and killed the poor, confused, little man. His fears of the men were confirmed when he was stabbed to death on the very boards on which he finally slept.

Upon finishing the pitiful story of the nervous little man, this young man looked at me and all he could say was, "You will not believe this. Not only is my new bedroom suite a dark walnut color and massive as you described but it is a water bed too." He also realized, after hearing the story, that he had become worried about dying only after

Karma and Reincarnation

buying the new bedroom suite. Plus, he was a single man who went home alone every night and didn't trust people.

Only after I told him the story of the poor hijacked man did these little tidbits make any sense to him. Later, he told me he was able to sleep again.

The new bedroom suite, its color and the rocking of the waterbed had subconsciously brought back all the fear and past-life memories from that horrible time. Getting in touch with his fear, exposing it, and dealing with it in this life allowed him to see the fear for what it was in both lives without the same outcome. Learning to trust was an issue that he had brought from that life to this. After learning how he had reacted in that lifetime, he could change his present life.

Fear generated by a past-life event usually surfaces when the person in present life is about two years younger than he was at that time in the previous life. Feelings of remorse and empathy can confuse a present day life in every decision that one makes.

The past life history of my chimney sweep is a good case in point. Being a good Baptist, he has a hard time with my gift, but his past life story, nonetheless, made sense to him.

The first time I saw him, he loved his occupation. Working on chimneys was what he had always wanted to do, he explained to me with a bubbling enthusiasm. His eagerness to do his job was a joy to behold.

Next time the chimney was to be cleaned again, he came. Although he was the same person, I met an entirely different man at the door. Without thinking or hesitating, I asked, " What is wrong with you?"

"Nothing," he answered, not wanting to tell a stranger his life story.

Using his name, I told him there was something about me he didn't know. Proceeding, without pausing, I told him I was a psychic.

Looking at me in disbelief, he told me he did not believe in that stuff.

I told him I understood, but I reiterated that if he would listen to me for a second I might be able to help him.

He stood there staring at me as if I was some kind of heinous thing, but I took that as an affirmation that I should continue and I did. Next, I told him about the heart condition he thought he had.

"How did you know that," he asked?

GHOSTS TALK

"Well sir, I just told you that I am a psychic."

He told me that he had a heart attack a few months earlier and that he wanted to sell his business. His profession now frightened him and he wanted out.

Being the helper that I am, I plowed right on with the conversation. I told him to get over the fact that he thought he had a heart attack. Saying, "Didn't your doctor tell you that you are okay? You didn't really have a heart attack at all?"

"Yes," he answered with a puzzled look on his face as if he were again wondering how I knew it.

"Then why are you holding on to that? If you continue to do that then your fear will be realized. As Job said, 'That which I fear most has come.' If you will listen to me for a minute, I might be able to help. I know that you don't believe in reincarnation but I do. Listen to the story I am about to tell you and see if it fits."

Although he wanted to continue his work and go on to his next customer, he listened while he worked. Since he believed in the axiom that "the customer is always right," he thought he owed it to me to listen. With his equipment in place, he worked fast so that he could get away from this weird customer as quickly as possible.

This man obviously needed help, and a psychic is a helper, to my way of thinking. Without another moment of hesitation, because I knew he was a captive audience, I jumped right into the conversation. "I see a house that looks to be about three stories tall. There is a light rainy mist falling. It looks almost like fog but is not as dense. You were in the same business in that life. That's unusual. Usually you change careers in other lives. In that life, you look to be about thirty-seven years old. I see you on top of the roof. The roof looks as if it is made of tile and very slick from the mist. You slip. Unable to pull yourself up from the lip of the roof after having slid down, I see you fall from the roof."

By now he has packed his equipment and started for the door. He puts it down in my foyer and with interest now he listens. I finish.

"The fall did not kill you. The fence upon which you impaled yourself did but it took a while. Alone, your last thought was that you did not want to leave your wife and three little children destitute."

Suddenly tears were streaming down his face. Without wiping the tears away, his full attention was now on my face.

Karma and Reincarnation

"Did you know that is my worst fear," he asked? "I am afraid that I will fall from a roof and leave my wife and two children without anything. That is why I want to sell my business now."

I told him that usually about two years before a person died in a past life, is about the time they subconsciously start to relive or remember the other life--especially if it is tied into the present life as much as his was.

There are even lifetimes you bring a war wound from another life so that you can remember that lifetime more clearly.

Further, I told him, while putting my hand on my own back to show him where it was, that he probably either had back trouble or a birthmark on the side of the back where the fence speared him.

When I did this, he said he had back trouble since birth, in that particular spot.

Next he explained that he was thirty-five years old, which fit what I had told him perfectly.

The next time he came to clean my chimney, he was in a much better mood. He loved his business again and had forgotten ever wanting to do away with his business.

His prior life had left him feeling as if he had not completed the task he wanted to perform in that life. Dying and leaving his wife and three children destitute, he felt as if he had failed. The chimney sweep came back into another life setting up the same situation so that he could live it again. In doing this, he thought he was giving himself a chance to get it right this time.

Bringing the injury with him since birth kept reminding him of that past life even if it was only in his subconscious. Becoming fearful that he might repeat the event and die again made him want to sell the company rather than deal with the situation. In his own way, he thought he was dealing with the problem by letting go the job he loved. What he considered a heart attack, even though the doctor said it wasn't, was an excuse for him to sell the business he loved before he could reach the age he had been in the past life when he died. That life was so entwined in his present life that his subconscious made him fear death at thirty-seven while leaving his family destitute again.

Instead he learned that he could leave the past life behind, keep his business and make the necessary arrangements for his wife and family just in case the worst happened. He visited his fear, made it useful in his present life and then dismissed it.

Sometimes a past life infirmity appears in the present life so that one can deal with the root cause of that medical condition. Since past lives affect future lives, at some point one has to come to terms with their fears and relationships from the past so that they do not have to continue revisiting the same issues. Bringing an infirmity into another lifetime makes some deal with the concern more quickly.

This was the case for a very nice lady who visited me at a psychic fair.

When working a fair, I am usually so busy that I do not look up to see who my next client is. She slipped into the chair in front of me and I started.

"I have to tell you about this past life or I will not be able to go on to other things," I told her.

She agreed without reluctance.

"I see a little girl around five or six years old carrying a big bucket from the barn. The bucket is almost as large as she is. This little girl has to lift her shoulder very high in order to carry this bucket full of milk. Because it is so cumbersome, she spills a little of it. A man, her father, I think comes running out of the barn and slaps her so hard that all the milk spills. The spilled milk starts a rage in him so much so that he beats her terribly. His beatings are why she died."

Without noticing the effect I had on this woman because my eyes are closed, I finished, then looked into her face.

With hidden emotion, she says, "You couldn't know this but I have to wear a brace. No one can tell as long as I have the brace on. One shoulder is much higher than the other. There is a problem with my spine."

Watching her then, I knew I had answered some questions she had regarding this deformity. She had bigger issues than the deformity on which to work. This lady, even though she was a child, had let another manipulate her life in her past life. As a child, she could do nothing about the father who ultimately beat her to death.

This was the problem she faced in her present life with all male relationships. After helping her to understand that she is master of her own fate, I suggested we look at her present life. In doing so, she allowed herself to acknowledge how she could stop the battering relationships.

Sometimes there is no way to correct the physical deformity a person might have brought from another life. Understanding the soul's emotional reasoning for including a tangible aberration in another life can help. Upon realizing what we need to learn and learning it, we can then prevent the same situation in another life.

Past lives also affect how others see themselves and the environment in which they live. Life for them seems out of place, as if they are not living in the right place or at the right time. One such past life caused even me to wonder at the ever-changing situations embodiment can bring.

Seeking a reading, a woman came to see me at my home. Seeing something that flabbergasted even me, I almost didn't tell her what I saw, but my ghost friends convinced me to continue.

What I was reading was a lady who looked amazingly like the lady in front of me except for the eyes and hands. Tentatively I started.

First I told her that she must have been born at the end of November or the first of December. When I finished that statement, she confirmed she was born December fourth. Her birthday with it's meaning was the whole crux of the reading.

The next issue I was about to relay to her needed veracity before I would admit that my guides were telling me she was from the star group Sagittarius.

Telling her how she looked in her past life, I started with her eyes in the other life. They were quite unusual, beautiful, but unusual. The pupil had an iris around it, as ours do, but then there was what looked like another pupil and another iris.

Long blond hair hung down her back. Except for the eyes and six fingers on each hand, she looked human. Her hands having six fingers each startled me a little more than her eyes. She was gorgeous but just a little different from what we consider normal.

After relating the specifics to this woman, she told me that ever since she was a little girl, she would go into the yard at night and tell anyone who would listen that she wanted to go home. Home was the star group Sagittarius, at which she was so used to pointing. When I explained that I was sorry this was the only information coming through, she told me that she had gotten what she came for, confirma-

GHOSTS TALK

tion of her roots. That was the only reading she wanted at the time.

Strange as it may seem, this really happened. Being as logical as I am, there are times I want to censor what I am being told or shown because I don't want to appear foolish. The fact is some already consider me to be out of mind for merely stating, "I am a psychic." I have come to terms with the idea that the thought of others that "psychics are foolish" is merely someone else's interpretation. As I see it, not acting on the ability I have would be foolish.

Each of us is always learning no matter what the subject matter, but sometimes the material from which we learn can be a little difficult to swallow. In this life, I have had my share of challenging items and have found that logic does not always matter.

As with the illogical reading about the lady from Sagittarius, because of the unusual circumstances, another past-life reading caught me totally off guard. Not only did I not understand it at first, but also it was one of my guides' best teaching lessons to me.

Although the man who was sitting in front of me told me his name, I did not know that he was Jewish. Most of the time, I am unaware what nationality a name stems from unless of course it starts with and "O," such as O'Malley.

It would not have mattered to me any way. Most of the time, I do not even listen to my client's names because I do not want my hearing their names to get in the way of my reading. Many times I will come up with their names in the reading if I do not know who they are. It is also better for me if I don't identify the person so that our subject matter can remain confidential and unprejudiced.

Generally when I remember the readings I am recalling now, it is because the person I am reading has stopped the reading in some way. When the reading is stopped, it encourages me to become the human, Da Juana Byrd, again and leaves the psychic for a moment. Without always remembering the person associated with the reading, I can remember those readings.

When I started this reading I did not know how truly surprised I would be. This is the day my ghost friends taught me more about the soul's evolution than I thought possible.

As I started the reading I was shaken physically by seeing a man in a concentration camp. Telling the man what I saw, I told him I did-

Karma and Reincarnation

n't understand what I was seeing because I knew the man I was looking at in the camp was him. To my logical mind, there was no way this
person could have been the man in front of me because he had to have
been alive and young during World War II. He validated that he was
indeed alive then and was about four to five years old.

This shook me even more because I knew the man in the concentration camp was a past life of the man sitting in front of me but I
wondered, how? Since both were alive at the same time, it was hard for
me to understand. Then my guide friends took over again. The shock
of what I was seeing psychically hit my logical self so hard that the
guides who were schooling me had my full attention and make this one
of the best lessons of my life.

In the concentration camp was the absolute twin in looks of the
man sitting in front of me. The only difference was how emaciated the
man in the concentration camp was. Bless his heart, the torture he had
been through and being starved on top of it was more than he could
bear in any form.

Relating the story to my client, I told him the man in the concentration camp was having medical experimentation performed on him.

As I proceeded to tell my client about the kind of experiments
being performed, my client gasped. Thinking that it was from the out-
rageousness of how one person could treat another, I went on to
describe how the German doctor drilled holes in this man's left chest
without anesthesia. While pointing to the spots on my own chest, I
heard my client swallow audibly. When he did this, I looked at him to
make sure he was okay. He caused me to temporarily come out of my
psychic place.

At that time, he told me that he was Jewish and reassured me that
he was fine. He also asked me to finish the story because he needed to
hear it.

My guides told me that the man in the concentration camp needed to believe that mankind was not totally without feelings. The mani-
acal part of the human race that was experimenting on him made him
reach out to look for a peaceful warm place with no Nazi experimentation. The need to feel human love was so great that he subconsciously sent part of his soul to the United States.

His soul would need a place of refuge in this agonizing time because it was more than he could understand. He chose to be born into a baby he knew would be safe from the type torture he had to endure. This was a premeditated psychic awareness deed; done before he could have encountered the torture he knew would ultimately kill him.

When the man died in the concentration camp, the part of his soul in that body left and joined the part that had been reborn a few years earlier and was living in the United States with loving parents.

After I had finished telling my client this, he told me why he had told me to finish the story for him. Although he hadn't been particularly intrigued with past lives, he knew I was supposed to be a good psychic and he would endure this part of my reading to get to the part about his future. The issue he had not counted on was that his past life story answered some very unsettling questions about his own childhood.

He recounted to me how holes had mysteriously appeared in his chest, during the war, in the same spots I had pointed at on my chest. Doctors in the United States did not understand it and could find no explanation for why it happened. One day they suddenly disappeared as mystifyingly as they had appeared. He had never found out the cause. Now he had his answer.

Past lives appear to me, as a medium, in a way in which the person who has had the past life can relate. In this way my clients can recognize themselves or some part of their lives for which their past life had meaning. This does not necessarily mean that you will feel about your past life as if you have a twin somewhere. It does, however, relate to your life in such a way where persistent questions of life can be answered. When related by a stranger, the impact of that past-life event on the present life is much more pronounced.

There have been times when, being human, I may have felt a little holier-than-thou because of my capability to use my psychic abilities the way I do. On one such occasion, I saw something in a client's past life of which he was not particularly proud.

Sitting there smugly satisfied that I had verified my clients past and feeling as if I were a wonderful human being for having never done something so terrible, my guides sliced away at that idea with a quick, efficient stroke. Thinking, because of my psychic ability, that I had always had the good of others at heart, my guides showed me that the only good I had in one life was what could be done for me.

Karma and Reincarnation

Believing that in several life times I had been on stage, my ghost friends showed me my stage. Most, as I did for a moment, would have enjoyed being on stage in front of a cheering crowd that included Royalty. The problem with this picture was my costume. Feeling the black leather mask on my face, I knew that I was the executioner. The rest of the story was not so good. In that past life I was executing some poor starving person who had wronged a nobleman. So that his family could eat, he killed a game animal on the Nobleman's land.

The lesson I learned from that past-life self-reading and keep still is not to become smug in thinking that I might be better than another in one respect or another. Very easily, there could be past-life skeletons hiding in all our closets as well.

In one of my past lives, I remember looking down at my beautiful shoes and seeing many precious stones on them. As soon as I focused on those shoes I immediately was filled in on the story for that lifetime.

The time was in about the fifteenth or sixteenth century with a grand royal ball in progress. People were dancing and having a wonderful time. The smell inside the room was a little overwhelming because of the warmth inside which permeated through the crowd of dancers. Outside the evening was cold and it made the gaiety of those in the room even more evident. Watching the party proceed, I noticed that the person of my past life stood at the fringes of the ball where different guests would come to speak to her. They greeted me with a mixture of curiosity and trepidation.

In this royal court, I was treated with the greatest of respect even though I had not been born in that country. My past life-skin was brown, almost black. Everyone in this royal court paid respect to me, even the Queen. Assessing my background with my knowledge of the time, the Queen should not have been nice to me because I was the mistress of her King.

Her Royal Highness would not sleep with the King. For that he came to my country and stole a person to make his royal whore. It wasn't bad enough that he took me from my country, but this man of royalty killed my past life by giving her a horrible venereal disease that ate away at her flesh.

Even though she died a horrible death, she did not hate the Queen. She felt sorry for her. The Queen's fear of sex with her King

GHOSTS TALK

kept her alive, but the decision she made to allow him a mistress killed my past-life body.

Past lives replay our weaknesses so that we have the choice to become stronger.

After the revelation in my middle years of that past-life incarnation, I made the connection between the past life and my present younger life. In my present lifetime as if I had no choice, I allowed a man to be my king and rule my younger life, too, just as my past life counterpart had. I allowed myself to be treated almost exactly the same way until I realized that, as master of my own fate, I did not have to give in to abuse. Finally, I learned that in this day and age, a woman no longer has to bow down before a king. She is able to stand up and take full responsibility for her life and actions.

Past lives will use all your senses to make you subconsciously remember the parts of them that you require. The memory of those lives helps you, in some particular manner, come to terms with your current needs.

Occasionally even your taste buds will help you remember a past life. As one of your more elaborate senses, taste can be psychically used quite efficiently. Thinking of Aunt Sara's apple pie can bring the warmth of the room in which you ate it, the loving concern of your aunt along with the cinnamon apple taste, texture and sweetness to your mind as if you are biting into its perfect crust. Reliving that whole sensation without the benefit of actually biting into the pie is quite psychic. Any memory that takes on that much importance is one that can bring profound insight at any time into your life. With the knowledge that the soul never dies but exists as one single life wearing much physical clothing, you can acknowledge how the memory would last more than a physical lifetime.

Without ever tasting it and for as long as I can remember, I hated Chinese food. Even the thought of it was revolting. It in no way occurred to me that since I had never tasted Chinese food I could not be a good judge of the subject.

Going through life without one taste of this food, I had no desire to change until I had what I considered, at the time, a dream one night. In it was a circle of Asian men chanting in some language I could not have known in my waking moments. The funny thing is, I somehow

Karma and Reincarnation

knew they were speaking Cantonese. How, I don't know. This was the first time I had heard that rather musical language.

Knowing they were discussing some sort of law, I listened intently. One man, who was not the leader, had my and everyone's rapt attention. They were all dressed in a taupe (brown-gray) looking color. As he spoke, I realized, he was me in that past life. Not a particularly handsome man, he was authoritative and carried himself with supreme confidence, which made him beautiful in my eyes.

His thoughts about law, human rights and justice have since made their way into my current lifetime.

Later, the dream over, I started craving Chinese food. Now, I love it. The dream brought out the memory of that past life, causing me to remember consciously that some cultural tastes are good.

As you can see by these past lives, not everybody is someone historically important. I do not remember a life that I was a figure who was well-known in history. But of course, we are all well-known in history by the mere fact that we are alive.

In living these lives, we must become different races and sexes as physical bodies in order to learn karmic lessons. Knowing this might help some be a little more tolerant of those not culturally, racially, or sexually like them.

Taking a physical incarnation on race, sexual preference or bodily appearance is a means to the ends in preparing the soul's evolution. Those persons having a problem with anyone not sharing what they believe to be the perfect race, sexual preference or bodily appearance will most likely have to deal with a situation involving that area of hatred in order to aid their souls. Unadulterated passion against another adds the impetus to make the soul learn more quickly the lessons of spirituality.

In one life a man may hate the very race he will become in his next life. With both lives he sees the implications of his thoughts and gestures. That is how Karma works. One never escapes their Karma.

Sometimes Karma has to make suggestions from past lives again and again until the person living those lives learn from them. Conscious choice is the proof that one has learned.

Following that extreme, either I am one of the most stubborn of souls or the most stupid. Several of my recalled past lives have had the same theme as my current existence.

GHOSTS TALK

Until I was in my late twenties, upon going to bed and closing my eyes in a vision, I would see a little girl looking at me. The scene was always the same.

She was a beautiful young child, eleven or twelve years old, wearing a blue gray dress with small flowers imprinted on it. Her soft, black and shiny hair was braided all over her head, as she stopped her work in the cotton fields to look at me. We instantly sensed that we knew each other personally, although no words are exchanged.

Fear gripped her and me when we see a man dressed in black on a black horse ride towards her. Totally unable to run from him, she waited motionless. Our extended knowledge in that he has a right to do anything he wished to her kept her frozen in place. Mr. Death is coming she thought, and I hear it. Both our hearts were racing so hard that they seemed to be trying to free themselves from our chests. She and I were held in this fearful grip as he approached. Though there were others in the field, we were alone.

I have other visions of her propped up against a plow in labor. She is always alone in a small wood plank barn in a barren field with no one to help in the delivery. Knowledge from my guides relays the rest of the story. We are one. Being impregnated by this man, she dies an agonizing death in childbirth.

Fear of death in childbirth followed me into this life. My labor with my daughter confirmed my fear. All the doctors present at the birth of my child, and even some who were not, confirmed that I had a very hard time giving birth. The feeling of being alone is in this life, too, as it is with most psychic people.

Mr. Death only appeared in vision form until I married my first husband. Then there were times I would wake at night with this man standing at the foot of my bed staring down at me. Glancing over to my right, I would see my ex asleep. One of the things my ex-husband did really well was sleep. At that moment horror would stop the ability to move or ask for help. The same uncontrollable fear I had felt while watching Mr. Death come for the young girl would hold me in it's grip, leaving me to silently pray that the man in black would leave me alone.

Now I know that my ex-husband was this man of which I was so frightened. While asleep, his spirit would leave his body and manifest itself in any life or any way it wanted. Assuming the life we once had together, his best shot at making me remember that life was through fear. As a spirit he could have won an Oscar for his thoroughly believable performance.

These fearful awakenings were done for my education. One part of my enlightenment was realizing what I was doing again in my life, and the other was to become a better teacher when I finally left the secure, hidden confines of my psychic closet. Memories of this young woman and her horrific life became more prominent throughout my marriage. When I divorced my ex-husband, Mr. Death left me too.

Another part to this story occurred when I was very small. My mother made me some flower-sack panties. Now, always loving anything my mother made, it was extremely out of character for me to turn down those panties. There was a problem with them though. They brought out an uncontrollable fear within me. Unable to stand even looking at them, I didn't want them anywhere near me.

Not wearing them was a waste and neither the Church nor my father could stand a wasteful child. My aversion to those panties was greater than the fear of my father's retribution. Mother, thankfully, gave them away because she realized that I would have taken a beating rather than wear them.

Now I know why I had such repugnance to those panties. My past life as that child wouldn't let me accept those panties. The material looked and felt as if it were the same material as that of which the little girl's dress was made. Past lives can touch some fear in the subconscious, and the memories are brought back by something so simple as a pair of homemade panties.

Past lives can also bring out social fears within human groups. When fear touches a nation, then inhabitants of that land can become ravenous with desire to purge their land of whatever they consider a threat to their welfare.

One of the subjects that people have many problems with is the sexual aspect of relationships. We hear so much about homosexuals and their being an abomination before God. In our society they have few rights.

When the world originated, it needed to become populated. With homosexuals there can be no population increase without the aid of heterosexuals. Thinking arose in Biblical times that homosexuals were bad primarily because of the need at that time to populate the

GHOSTS TALK

world. With the aging of our culture it would seem that we are more intelligent than the archaic notion that we need to populate more of an inhabited bulging planet.

As scientist have found, if you have a rat city, which becomes over-populated, rats will become homosexual in order that the city will survive. Nature takes care of itself. When the population decreases to a manageable size, then nature works again by creating fewer homosexual rats.

Just like wolves in the middle ages, anything that threatened mankind's food source or procreation had to be annihilated. Legends of werewolves were produced to stir up emotions in hungry people. Then man had a reason to kill out the wolf, which they considered wicked.

Legends like genes are bred throughout civilization. Gene memory and emotional legend memory stick with us like leeches. Emotional folklore strikes a cord of fear in the deepest regions of our psyche creating anxiety over achieving the basics of life such as eating, procreating and existing.

Being homosexual is not something most who are homosexual consider a blessing. Like being a psychic, it is sometimes a cross to bear.

Most children are taught to conform to societies wishes while young. Being homosexual, when young, does not allow you to conform. It only makes you alone in a world of heterosexual youngsters who can have no concept of how you feel. Society would not think of hurting a child, but a homosexual is something else all together. People who think in this manner have no concept that a child can be and is born homosexual.

Put yourself into another's shoes. Would you like to go against societies grain? Could you consciously choose a life where you felt ostracized and a need to hide your true feelings due to fear for your life? Most people would never consciously put themselves into this type situation. Karma, on the other hand, affords brave souls the opportunity to embark upon this path.

In this regard, my next reading involves a lesbian who really had a hard time coming to terms with who she was. She and her lover came to me at a psychic fair in another city. This lady wanted to be nowhere close to this fair but she came because her friend asked her. Not believing in anything psychic, she was there only to placate her girlfriend,

Karma and Reincarnation

who was interested in metaphysical topics.

Both appeared at my table at the same time. Because I do not censor my reading, I told them both that I might say something to the person I was reading that might offend the other. They agreed that it was all right and stated that they were best friends and would be fine with anything I said.

The girlfriend pushed her disbelieving lady friend into the chair and stood beside her as I began the reading. This lady was not comfortable and it showed.

As I started the reading all I could see was a past life coming through. My feeling was that this was not good. Not only did this woman not believe in the metaphysical, she sure didn't believe in past lives and quickly told me so. Her friend helped to calm her when I told her that I would have to relate the past life first. Otherwise I would get nothing. Reluctantly she listened.

My first impression was a woman walking along a boarded walk by the sea in what I presumed to be England. It was just past twilight when the dark was beginning to envelope everything completely. This young woman was happily swinging a small handbag as she walked away from the shop to go home. Passing an alley between two buildings, she was grabbed from behind by a man who clamped his hand over her mouth and dragged her into the alley.

There he and his three drunken sailor friends proceeded to rape her, tearing at her with hands and teeth until she was dead. I watched her soul leave her lifeless body and, as a spirit, hover above watching the crime below. Her thoughts mused that in the town in which she had always felt safe, four malevolent men had taken her life from her.

In her anger at the crime below, she vowed she would never be a weak woman who was unable to fight assailants off again. As a soul now on the Other Side she prepared a life that paralleled her past life promise. Now she was anything but weak but she was still a woman. Her being homosexual in this life effectively kept men away from her but gave her another whole set of lessons to learn.

Physically, she still could not defend herself against four men then or now. Not many men could. Her life went from being a carefree young lady who had no concern for life in that existence to becoming a lesbian who constantly looked over her shoulder in her present life.

GHOSTS TALK

As I finished the reading, I watched recognition come over the lady's face. She told me that she had the feeling all her life that she needed to be able to fight to take care of herself. Her partner said that I had given the reason for why her lover was so caustic to others.

This lady was not only angry with men but she was also angry about being a lesbian. With no patience for the treatment she received from society, she was a militant homosexual. Her past life gave her the knowledge of why she had become the individual she was. That reading was just what she needed in order to find why she had always felt that she had been maltreated by humanity.

Sometimes the subject of past lives can come from unexpected places, such as a child who is less than three-years old. This can be particularly disconcerting for a mother who doesn't believe in reincarnation and has never been around what she considers metaphysics. Children, being who they are, innocently go right to the crux of the matter.

Most times the parent wishes to believe that the child is making up a story with a make believe life. There are times, however, that the parent's soul gives them direct confirmation in truth of the child's tale.

A case in point is a woman, belonging to a Holiness Church, who was very upset when her daughter pointed to her mother's pregnant stomach and announced that the baby boy inside was the child's husband in a past life. Going even further, she told her stunned mom that they had lived in the desert together.

The declaration that she was carrying a son, which she was, surprised the mother. Also the fact that her two children had not only known each other before as her daughter stated but that they also had lived in the desert as husband and wife affected her most profoundly. The child and her mother live in a very humid southern state. Her child could have known nothing about the desert since she had not traveled there in her young three years.

The church that both attended does not teach nor do they believe in reincarnation. Church members would have had to pray very hard for the welfare of the "possessed" little girl if the mother had told other parishioners what had happened. Fear and innate knowledge kept her from telling her church. Instead she sought help from someone she knew would listen and not censor her.

Younger children have no problem espousing their thoughts

Karma and Reincarnation

because in their innocence they have not learned that they have to conceal their emotions or watch their words. Until they reach about age six, they are closer to the memories of their past lives than their current life. Though children usually are quiet about those lives because they sense fear from their parents, sometimes their mouth opens and words are said before they remember that they should hide those times. Their flabbergasted parents have a choice then. Either they can question the event or dismiss it as child's play. Most would rather dismiss the occurrence.

When the niggling words continue to haunt the parent, they have to investigate, as did a Baptist friend of mine. Without their knowledge that she was there, this mother of two young boys was watching her sons play wrestling on the floor. Listening she heard one of them say to the other, I took care of you before when we were brothers in that other life.

Because I finally told the mother that I was psychic, she decided not to continue our friendship and since had moved to another state. Knowing that she had eavesdropped on her sons' personal play, she felt in her heart that his statement was said in earnest. As soon as she entered the room, both boys hushed about the past life. The only person she could think of talking with about this incident was me. She called.

After listening to the story of her two boys, I told her that she could learn more about that past life of theirs together if she explored carefully with her two young sons. Most parents want to hear more about what their children are saying and in demanding to be told, shut the children up for good. If the conversation does not alarm the child, then they will usually expound more details of their past life.

Not wanting to upset a parent, children go silent when quizzed because they feel they might have said something wrong. Some will even tell their parents they were only playing. Parents know when a child is making up a story. If the parent is very gentle, they can generally learn more.

Children who have never been told that any thought they express about past lives and ghostly images is wrong do not have as hard a time telling their parents what they remember. Still, even the most enlightened mother may not be prepared for how close the past life relationship really was. Being open-minded is one aspect of spirituality, but seeing it in action is another. This could astound any of us, as it did with a mother

GHOSTS TALK

of a child who was just beginning to speak well.

Imagine this mother's face when her young child was asked, told everyone that his name was Barnes. That was actually his maternal grandmother's last name. In some cases that is all right but in this case he had never met his grandmother because she died years before he was born and his mother had never mentioned her name to him.

This lady and her mother had similar circumstances in life in that both were middle-aged mothers of first children. My friend, who thought she could not have children, found herself pregnant at forty just as her mother had.

Co-dependence was part of her mother's nature and she doted on my friend because her child was all that mattered in her life. My friend, after reaching adulthood and before having a baby herself, rebelled at the relationship. She vowed never to do that to her child if indeed she had one.

Since it was a co-dependent situation, both saw matters from their own eyes. Without benefit of walking in the other person's shoes, it is easy to speak against that person. With Karma, though, you get to test all the situations of which you speak. My friend is part of a very special Karmic lesson in this lifetime.

Before she became pregnant, her dead mother came to me one day as my husband and I were pulling into our garage. Thinking of my friend, I remember saying to her dead mother that she needed to help her daughter in working out the problems in their relationship that had existed before she died.

Spirits don't have to have a séance to manifest. They can come at the oddest times to get your attention, as she did with her response.

Instantly she answered that she and her daughter would be able to work it out soon. This lady let me know that she would be in her daughter's life shortly as her daughter's child. Like any mother who feels unappreciated, she added, "Then we shall see how she handles the situation."

About two years before this incident I had told her daughter that she would give birth to a son. Later she did. Her mother was reincarnated into my friend's son. One of the ways her mother substantiated the rebirth was to give people her last name when my friend's son was asked his name.

With my not wanting to influence this situation, I was quiet about my reincarnation theory. By not telling my friend that her son was actually her mother, I did not relate the message that her mother had given me. Instead, I was quiet until my friend brought up the possibility that her child was indeed her mother.

After letting her tell me why she thought so, I told her about the conversation with her mother. I also told her that although the child was her mother reincarnated, she was now another person with his own set of circumstances to learn from while on earth in his current life. Even though he would remember and sometimes verbalize his past life somewhat, he had his own goals for living this time.

Allowing him to reach some parts of that past life without feeling as if he is doing something wrong may help him in lessons learned in this life. Not only does it affirm for his mother that her mother is still alive, but she gets another chance to make their lives better for each of them while in her present life. Love can not only bring us back together quickly but it can also allow a mother to continue teaching her child even though she is supposedly dead.

This past-life story confirms that we do reincarnate in groups and that reincarnation is not done to solely relieve "Biblical" sin but rather to live and learn.

Reincarnation memories can move through out lifetimes. Personalities can remain almost the same in each life, but with enough challenges to make the lives different for learning purposes. Some lives can even be remembered because they ring some primitive soul bell for the person who wants to remember.

My husband, Claude, is always the one to test my psychic abilities. When I first came out of the psychic closet, he was not so sure that he believed in past lives but the metaphysical was beginning to make some sense to him. He decided to test me on past lives as well.

One day as I re-entered our living room, he surprised me with a question from out of the blue. "If I lived before, I want to know who I was from this time period to this time period, with a name and information I can find on that person."

Instantly I gave him the answer I heard, even spelling the name. Sure enough the person was in an encyclopedia and lived in the time period my sweet husband had demanded.

This was not enough for my husband and he decided to go to the library to research this person. When he returned from the library with his information, he was amazed. Based on the notes he took, he and the past-life person seemed to be very much alike. The one item that really got my husband's attention was that when this man had been buried, people from several different countries arrived for his funeral because he was so well-loved.

The secret my husband had always furtively carried was that he wanted people to attend his funeral. For him, people turning out to help bury him would mean that he was loved. In the past life, this very wealthy businessman, who helped anyone he could, was buried in a wooden box where thousands attended his funeral. This roused that memory in my husband and left him with the thought that he was indeed that person. His innermost fears, while in his present life, have been that perhaps no one will attend his funeral.

Past lives have to ring a bell in some manner with the life you are living now. Strong likes and dislikes, whether they are in body or mind, will surface again. Memories of places and tastes for foods, clothing and housing will sometimes awaken those lives and bring them to the fore.

Dislikes seem to come out more quickly though. One such dislike was brought to my attention when a woman told me that she had always made friends easily except for one time in this life. It had so upset her that she wondered about past lives because of the incident.

A friend asked her to attend her church, which she did. The pastor gave her dirty looks throughout his sermon but she tried to ignore him because her friend loved this church so much. After the service was over, her friend naturally wanted her to meet the minister. When her friend called the minister over to meet the lady, he said in a not too friendly voice that they had met, then turned and walked away.

The lady told me that she had never met the man before in this lifetime but that she had the same feeling about him that he had about her, only he verbalized it so she didn't have too. Her question to me was if it was possible that this had to do with a past life. My answer was that it most certainly was.

We don't necessarily have to spend time in our current lives with all the spirits we have had past lives with. Personalities may not mesh even between lives. It is just like picking friends while on earth: some are more drawn together than others. Between lives you tend to be drawn to those

Karma and Reincarnation

same friends and may at times allow other fellow spirits to become part of your spirit family in order to gain more experiences.

If a person, while on earth, stays at home always, then the only experience they are drawing while on earth is what being a recluse is like. As he allows more people to interact with him, then those others who are being received by the recluse are perpetuating more experiences with the loner. Now the hermit is no longer a loner, simply because he allowed others to become part of his life. In the same way, our spirits permit others to interact with us between physical lives.

As more people are introduced into the hermit's life, they bring added experience just as inviting other souls into your circle on the Other Side brings different comprehension to those souls willing to invite challenges for education.

Souls on the Other Side use their feelings just as they do on earth to make new friends, even though we all come from the same spirit.

One spirit occupies the Other Side, but that spirit has individual souls who make up the whole. As with any family, they may not all get along together all the time. Because they know what they do however, there is no real hatred there, only personalities who enjoy spending time together. Friends do not always offer differing points of view, and that's why continued interaction is needed among souls.

These spirits generally come back to earth together. Some may remain on the Other Side to be guardian angels to those who have come back. There is no waste for a soul, only recycling. Choosing differing personalities with conflicting viewpoints while in eternity is essential. Otherwise it might take one forever to learn all they need to know.

Some things only last a lifetime, but the spirit is permanent and replaces bodies with reincarnation just as one would old clothing. There is no sin involved, only learning. Karma is not limited to physical life. It extends to the soul's life, which is everlasting. Through Karma, a soul can experience all life has to offer.

DEVELOPING
PSYCHIC ABILITY

Chapter Fifteen

PSYCHIC ABILITY

A psychic, according to Webster's Dictionary, is a person apparently sensitive to non-physical forces.

"Psychic" also means of or relating to the psyche: lying outside the sphere of physical science or knowledge—immaterial, moral, or spiritual in origin or force. The psychic is also sensitive to nonphysical or supernatural forces and influences: marked by extraordinary or mysterious sensitivity, perception or understanding.

The meaning of the word "psychic" makes one think that this is a very hard inheritance to achieve. In fact, psychic ability is as simple as taking a breath. All you have to do is to use the talent that resides naturally inside you.

To use your psychic ability, becoming more aware of the six senses that you possess is imperative. The sense of smell, taste, touch, hearing, and seeing is all very important, but the most important of all is the sixth sense. Unlike the other five senses, it is considered intangible.

GHOSTS TALK

Like the wind, you can't see it but you most certainly can feel it. The sixth sense utilizes the other five senses to create feelings above what is considered normal or real. Knowledge that one has this sense and the decision to use it is a supreme sense. Because of that knowledge, reverence for the gift is undeniable.

Allowing yourself to use your sixth sense means letting go of what you have always felt was real. Such is the belief in God. We all know that there is a supreme energy, but few of us have seen it.

An atom is the perfect example of psychic ability. It is real, even though most have never seen one. They link together to form an object or person. Their decision to come together in a certain way determines what they are going to be perceived as for that object or animal's lifetime.

Perception is what we think. Awareness starts with the use of the five senses. As soon as we touch, feel, smell, taste, or hear, the brain is alerted. The brain is made up of two sections: the right and the left hemispheres. Integrating the two sides creates psychic ability.

According to science, the right brain is the intuitive side. This side is thinking of more than one thing at once. The right side is creative, visual, yielding, and subjective and wants an overview of things it's processing. The right side sees no restrictions.

The left brain is more logical. It has to process events in the brain in a step-by-step manner. This side detects features. Being aggressive and analytical, it is interested in minute details. This is the rational side of the brain.

Most animals employ one side of the brain according to what they are trying to achieve. Good psychics use both logic and creativity at the same time, thereby utilizing the whole brain.

Scientists know that the brain works subconsciously to keep the body functioning on all levels. People make conscious decisions as to what they will eat, where they will sleep and the type of life they want to live.

Even the conscious activity of eating is governed somewhat by the subconscious when it desires a specific food for the well-being of the body. Cravings are issued by the subconscious.

Becoming so tired that you must lie down and sleep is another method in which the subconscious enters the conscious state. Even the life one lives is part of the subconscious desire to create the best conditions for the body.

The subconscious is able to discern useful items for body and mind at such a basic level that most animals are not aware it is even happening. Awareness below the conscious level in hearing, seeing, or learning is called subliminal. Subliminal consciousness is such a strong learning tool for the brain that advertisers are taking advantage of it. All forms of consciousness affect brain function.

Psychic ability makes use of all forms of consciousness because it needs to experience completely.

In school, children are taught not to daydream. Instead they are told to follow a directed course of action. In telling children to stop the daydreaming and live in reality the teacher is actually saying that children should only use his their left-brain hemisphere. This severely cripples the children's education.

Had a bumblebee had that type of education, he would be unable to fly. Aerodynamically, a bumblebee can't fly, but no one bothered to enlighten the bumblebee to that fact. Subconscious knowledge in the bee allowed him to fly. The bee has a very good argument in his tail for discouraging anything or anyone trying to prevent his flying.

As with the child, all people should use the capacity to daydream and to follow a directed course of events equally. By creating a whole-brain attitude, we can employ both halves of our brain to their fullest extent.

When using both brain hemispheres and getting positive results, we begin to trust our abilities. Trust allows us to experiment more. Experimentation is testing limitations, and constant testing educates us wholly. This is not limited to day-to-day existence, but extends to psychic ability as well.

As we understand more of the psychic, we build our confidence and continue to research.

Psychics have to trust themselves because psychic ability is not clanging bells. It is like whispers spoken so softly that one has to strain to hear.

A quick experiment to see how much trust you have in yourself is very simple. In the comfort of your home, take a look around you and sit where you please. Close your eyes and take a few breaths. With eyes still closed, stand up and take three steps.

Those steps are probably very small. Because even though you know there is nothing in front of you, you can't really be sure if your eyes are closed. Losing one of the five senses causes you to feel very ill at ease. Even with the assurance that you can open your eyes at any time in the comfort of your own home, you are still pensive.

From birth, most people rely on the five senses. When using psychic ability, one has to call on hidden senses as well.

In the experiment with eyes closed, you had to bring in your psychic gift to help you move. Even though you crept along, you were able to make those three steps without hurting yourself. Memory is a part of the psychic sense by helping you place events, ideas and objects in their proper prospective. In your mind's eye, you could see where each object in your path was so that you could maneuver around it.

People who are blind use their psychic abilities without being aware of it. The existing senses amplify and compensate for the lack of sight, making the blind person more aware of odors, feelings, hearing, and taste. Projecting their aura on all sides, they are able to feel an object before bumping it. Smell and hearing help in this process, too.

Remember the feelings you had in the experiment as you stood there. Were you confident? Were you frightened, even though you were safely in your own home? Were you unsure of what you were doing? Did you trust yourself? Was this hard to do? Keep in mind the flood of memories you had as you started to take that first step with your eyes closed.

Try it again with your eyes open. Sit back down. Stand up. Take three steps forward.

The difference is amazing. Having more confidence, you walk as if you know what you are doing. Knowing you can succeed in this little experiment; you go at this task with ease because you can see.

Confidence plays a big part in your life. We are not all good at the same things, but that's what makes this world diverse. Otherwise, it would be a boring place.

Being confident makes us better at whatever we are doing. Feelings of inadequacy make us feel inferior. Like the little engine who could, we can. Acknowledge your confidence in the areas you excel in, and work on the areas in which you are not quite as confident. Pat yourself on the back each time you take a baby step toward your goal. In the psychic realm, we are all babies. Babies jubilantly learn from using all the senses. Enjoy the testing of your psychic ability as if you were a baby again using all senses to reach your goal.

Psychic talent requires confidence. Self-assurance creates progress in the psychic realm. With each new task satisfactorily completed, you can move on with delight to greater exercises.

Another psychic exercise is getting to know your bodies better just as a baby does. When you become aware of all the functions of your body, then you realize when anything out of the ordinary happens.

Start by finding and examining the third eye. Touch yourself between the eyebrows above the bridge of the nose. This is where most of you will get your first sensory manifestations.

After touching the third eye, close your eyes and look towards the third-eye spot between your brows. Notice the slight bit of pressure when doing this. While looking towards the third eye with your eyes closed, visualize a stoplight. Observe the red, yellow and green lights. If you cannot see the stoplight at first, do not become disappointed. It will happen. Give yourself a chance without putting too much pressure on yourself. As you become more secure, you will see the stoplight in your mind's eye.

Another experiment is to gaze toward an object. Stare at it for a moment without blinking your eyes. Now close your eyes. Notice that you can still see the object but now with your eyes closed the object consists of light.

Another part of the sixth sense is simply knowledge. That is getting an answer to a question or problem on a subject of which one has no prior information. When validation happens consistently with sixth-sense knowledge, you become more sure of yourself. Thus, trust in those answers leads to more knowledge.

Concentration and focus are also parts of the sixth sense. When you give an object or person your complete attention, you almost become a part of that object or person. This is feeling their vibrations.

The Sixth Sense, or psychic awareness, is processed in many ways and called by many names, often beginning with the prefix "clair," which means the ability to perceive something outside the normal range of perception. Some names used in psychic ability are clairvoyance (sense of seeing), clair-audience (sense of hearing), empathy (sense of feeling), channeling, auras, dreams, and psychometry. Clair-gustation (sense of taste) and clairolfaction (sense of smell) are two names

GHOSTS TALK

that I think might be added. Each and all of these psychic tools may be used in expressing your psychic gifts.

Purpose of Psychic Ability

Different people might have different ideas about the purpose behind psychic ability, but its only real relevance is centered on the person's becoming more spiritual.

All of us come to the earth for different reasons. Some come to help others and some to help themselves. Each of us is here to learn. Our own selfish motives in becoming more Godlike, whether we realize it or not, keep us returning to earth. Even the worst of humanity is striving to become better.

Spiritual growth is a matter of choice. Any choice you make is the correct one for the moment in which you are living. There are no wrong decisions. Choices you make enhance your spirituality in allowing you to look at yourself through the paths you choose.

Good experiences stay in our memories. Being rewarded with that extra special feeling— be it sex, winning a jackpot, being competitive and winning, or being Florence Nightingale — we all love that fuzzy feeling of having accomplished what we wanted. Good events happening in life, however, do not make us stretch the boundaries of our spirituality. That only happens when we feel we have made a wrong choice and take a hard look at it.

Even though an experience may have felt wrong at the time it was happening, it was a learning experience. There are no wrong decisions, only lessons learned. A good part of that learning encounter was that you did not want to repeat that event. The occurrence also taught something that might apply in another situation later. Sometimes we need to have difficult experiences, because they teach us more intensely and tend to create stored memories.

One such stored memory happened with our oldest child. At about three years old, my oldest stepson decided he wanted to see if the cigarette lighter in the boat was really hot. It didn't matter that his mother and father had told him it was.

Needing to learn for himself, he stuck the lighter to his cheek. The circular lines healed. This event was not one he would soon forget.

Psychic Ability

He learned two valuable lessons with one experience. First, he learned to be wary of anything hot and to be more careful with the lighter. He also learned that sometimes it's better to listen to those who have already stuck the lighter to their faces.

When you are in the middle of an experience, you feel it more deeply. Foresight might lead to dread of the situation coming, and hindsight allows you to feel better from having lived through it, but when you are in the midst of the situation you are living it completely.

Like my son, the human race as a whole sometimes needs to be terrified in order to recognize what is and is not good for them.

Race riots, as an example, bring out both the best and the worst in human behavior. People hurting others because they are not alike in skin color is a shame. Using the race card to commit crime is too. Racism is a fire that needs to be fed by all involved in order to survive.

Bigotry not only is an expensive lesson but is also a horrible human reaction usually based on a person's thinking he has the likeness of God. In being in His image, he has God's support, no matter how extreme his beliefs. And he is so dogmatic that he expects everyone on earth to believe as he does.

Hatred of others is often generated from a seemingly spiritual viewpoint. Using religion as a base of spirituality, people give themselves permission to loathe others they consider unlike them.

Again a good example is Hitler, who wanted to be a priest and was also interested in metaphysics. He had a strong belief in his ability to predict the future. Using his charisma, he united his countrymen by helping them identify and start hating the Jewish people.

The redeeming quality of that spiritual world's lesson, as expressed previously was that the human race said we would never allow such an atrocity to happen again.

Spirituality sometimes manifests itself in horrible events, but it most often comes on a daily basis in more subtle behavior with just the effort of existing.

Some learn from others' mistakes, while others are more determined to learn for themselves. They are unable to learn by watching someone else making hard choices or by hearing their experiences, and they have to learn on their own.

Teen-agers are a good example of this phenomenon. They continuously rebel against their parents because they know their parents are old-fashioned and truly ignorant. As a teen's experience grows, he or she begins to notice that those same parents are growing more intelligent with each passing year.

It's the same with psychic ability. As you grow in using your gift, you learn to become more Godlike. When you learn what God truly is, then you recognize that as a part of God, we are all individuals within a single creation.

Psychic abilities are only a road map to the inner self. When looking at the inner self, you come upon the face of God.

Psychic abilities are an instrument to help you find God. Our Creator, no matter how He is perceived, is the epitome of all things.

The gift of psychic abilities is given to all beings but is not used by everyone. Many people overlook it. Others use some, but not all, of their abilities.

People have different names for psychic ability. Some call it hunches, gut reaction, or female intuition. No matter the name for the psychic, it is a God-given birthright to each of us.

Police go on hunches to solve some of the worst crimes. Though they do not wish to call it psychic ability, they know it has credence when it continues to work for them. A hunch is only a tool of the inner self. It prompts them to look in the right direction.

Mother's intuition is widely recognized as viable. It is common knowledge that most mothers will protect her babies, no matter what their age, in any way they can. Psychic gifts are not frowned upon when called "mother's intuition."

Seeing ghosts is acceptable in most situations but can be very scary for the participants. People don't always consider seeing a ghost as being psychic, but it is. The very capacity for seeing a dead individual means the person seeing the ghosts has psychic gifts. The person looking at a dead person may not consider the sight a gift at the time, however. Being able to see ghosts make us realize there is more to life than the physical, and thus it is a divine experience.

The Bible is full of metaphysical experiences, with everything from miracles to ghosts, but most religions don't like to speak of the Bible and psychic ability being connected. Thinking of the psychic in a spiritual sense causes some religions to become nervous. It upsets

Psychic Ability

their religions foundation to think that one can find God without any ideology involved. Churches need participants to survive for capital reasons. Without souls in church, they can have no religion.

When a psychic espouses the belief that anyone can find God without pomp and ceremony but just by looking within, it can be very costly to religion. People who do that are feared by those of religious conviction and have to be dealt with in some manner. In the Middle Ages religious officials knew how to deal with people who did not believe as they did: such people were called heretics and were punished harshly.

Excellent values are found in some religions in that they help those who can't help themselves. Not to mention that attending church is a wonderful way to meet like-minded people. Socializing with compatible people in church lays a foundation of trust among the brethren.

Religions of the world help to keep those people in line who would otherwise wreak havoc on society, especially if they believed in past lives. Those individuals might use lives as their own selfish tools for greed, knowing that they will live again and again. Some people need fear in their lives. Otherwise, we would have more murderers, thieves, and hatred. Hatred and greed are the basis for most crime.

Churches teach people to be afraid. If you are not holy and don't go to church, then you will go to hell. This is like telling children that if they put their hand into the cookie jar, they will get a spanking.

Most churches, as well as psychic ability, are dedicated to teaching people to become more attuned to God while on earth.

God is the spirit that binds us all. His energy runs through everything and everybody. Knowing this truth, then, you also know that when you hurt any individual or the earth in general, you hurt God.

Psychic ability is spirituality and is lived every day as a source of information coming from God.

Psychic Awareness in Action

Psychic awareness encourages a person to investigate each portion of his soul's life. As a physical being there are a myriad of ways to explore this task. With psychic consciousness comes the knowledge that even the small things in life can be large in relation to all actions of life.

GHOSTS TALK

Becoming more aware means you realize that even words have life and should be used with great responsibility. Vocabulary is used for communication. Language can express feelings or emotions.

Be careful how you use words. Many of us choose our words with little thought. This can be hurtful to us as well as to others. We see in others what we like and dislike in ourselves. As individuals reflecting God as the Whole, it would be nice if we gave and received only the most positive words.

When we praise someone, his self-esteem rises. Criticism makes anyone close to the situation take a deep breath and draw inward. There is a sigh or huff as if the very air has been sucked from the room. The atmosphere becomes heavy, making it difficult to breathe. Realizing that criticism of any nature can cause this atmosphere, remember to speak nicely to yourself. In building your confidence by using high-quality words, you can accomplish any goal you wish.

Medical science is proving that words are effective when a person is in surgery. If, while his patient is under anesthetic, a surgeon tells his patient he is going to get better quicker and be healthier after the surgery, then it happens. The patient, listening to the doctor he respects, subconsciously believes what the physician is telling him. With that belief, the patient becomes stronger more quickly without side effects.

Prayer has also been found to help those convalescing even if they have no idea they are the subject of prayers.

Words are instruments of power. They can create. As such, people should be very careful in what they say.

Jesus put it very well in the Bible when he said if you speak from the heart it is so.

Putting emotion into your words creates whatever thought you may be expressing. **THOUGHT AND EMOTION MANIFEST!**

An example of thought and emotion manifesting is one all have heard. A co-worker might say something like this: "Everything bad is happening to me lately. Both kids had to go to the doctor. Johnny has to get braces. All I have done is spend, spend, spend! It's just been horrible. I guess the only thing that's working right now is the car, but it'll probably go out any second, just like everything else."

The next time you see that person, his car is in the shop. He created his own reality with his negative thoughts and the heartfelt way in which he said them.

As children of God, we are creators. As creators, we construct our own reality.

Words are psychic tools.

Part of psychic awareness is knowing that not all people agree with supernatural ability. Remember that when they use words of anger towards a psychic, it comes from ignorance brought on by fear. Until they learn that they have nothing to be afraid of, they may turn against you for your beliefs. Their words can sting, but understanding where they originated helps some.

Psychic awareness helps a spiritual person remember that he or she should never use words to manipulate others. Since words carry great power, both on paper and in the heart, when said, they create action. Psychics have to reach towards the highest spiritual goals with knowledge that in criticizing the fearfully ignorant, they could be hurting that person's soul. Allowing another to live on the level in which he feels comfortable is the best gift a psychic can give. Remembering your own fears can help.

When most people conclude that they are psychic they see the world in a whole new light. No longer is their day-to-day existence all about them as individuals, but it is about the good of humanity in general. Living with extra-sensory perception brings the good of the whole into focus and is just another tool of psychic awareness.

Life issues and the way you handle them bring spiritual awareness. Understanding others' motives increases, and judgment of others decreases. With spiritual enlightenment people understand that judging others is self-defeating. This doesn't mean that you have to tolerate injustice. Society has ways of dealing with injustice, but on a divine level we can look at the combination of events as a whole rather than separate. With that dimension of sight, understanding the soul's need for enlightenment allows us to be less critical.

Psychics take on a new political affinity of conservative liberalism. Seeing the world in a new light, they are aware that everything, be it animal or vegetable, wants to live a long and fruitful physical life. Acknowledging this behavior is part of realizing that God is everything. The cycle of life is brought to the fore and is now accepted with knowledge and gratitude.

GHOSTS TALK

As psychic awareness progresses, new recruits become more conscious that they always had the ability. Like a snail crawling to its favorite flower, memories etch into the mind recollections of past times when intuition raised its flowery head only to be trampled by logic. With the progression of acquiring our newfound knowledge, there is also the succession of past memories that return to remind us, even though we were not consciously aware at the time, that we always had our God-given birthright.

With recognition of our abilities we become more aware of life's intricacies. Colors become more acute. The senses are heightened, and bodily functions take on new meanings. Every item or idea with which one comes into contact heightens perceptions and creates the challenge of dissecting all its facets. Even sex can take on a new meaning. Enjoyment of life is at its maximum, even when life is not the easiest, because you know with confidence that you are building on your soul's progression toward becoming more like God.

Chapter Sixteen

MEDITATION

$\mathbf{M}$editation is a tool that is utilized to bring about psychic awareness more quickly. Using both hemispheres of the brain, it expands our minds and allows us to be more logical and creative simultaneously.

This powerful mind exercise can help reduce stress while helping us feel better physically. Its' breathing techniques supply large amounts of oxygen to the brain and can make you feel as if you have had a nap. A rested person is less likely to become ill. Meditation also rejuvenates the blood and lowers blood pressure.

Meditation use to control pain is called Biofeedback. Biofeedback is the use of meditation with technology to help people self-regulate physical functions. Because there is a connection between mind and body, Biofeedback has proven to help many emotional dysfunctions, disorders, and diseases.

Stress can produce many symptoms such as: increased heart rate, blood pressure, hyperventilation, excessive sweating, cold extremities, anxiety, headaches, and other symptoms. Some techniques used in Biofeedback are skin temperature training and muscle relaxation training.

The ability to alter skin temperature is directly related to relaxing and expanding the capillary walls, which increase blood flow and volume within the vessels. Increased blood flow warms tissue. Vascular relaxation stops blood vessel constriction that occurs with stress.

Tension is sometimes carried in the muscles. Most people have had their shoulders ache from tension, usually followed by a headache. When people contract muscles without being aware of it, they generally feel the ill effects shortly. With Biofeedback, people can become aware when they are placing undue tension on the muscles and can learn to stop it.

Biofeedback teaches a person to take more control of his bodily functions.

Being capable of increasing and decreasing brain-wave activity makes it possible to reduce the feelings of stress through Brain Wave Training.

Brain waves are measured by the electrical firing speed in cycles per second and amplitude in micro-volts. Without brain-wave firings, the body could not perform. Five types of brain waves have been measured, named and associated with particular processes. Knowing the technical functions of the brain can assist you in becoming more aware on a psychic level.

Beta waves fire at thirteen to thirty cycles per second with a very low amplitude and a high frequency. These brain waves are associated with sensory motor areas of the brain. This is the waking state, or what is considered normal consciousness.

Alpha waves vibrate at eight to thirteen cycles per second with low amplitude and are indicative of wakeful relaxation.

Theta waves span three to seven cycles per second with low to medium amplitude. A person emitting theta waves is sleepy, already sleeping, or in a state of sleep transition.

Delta waves fluctuate from two to three cycles per second with high amplitude and low frequency. When the brain emits these waves, it is generally in deep sleep.

Mu waves are associated with physical movements or the intention to move and diminish almost as quickly as they start.

Meditation

Brain-wave activities in meditation are best utilized between the Alpha and Theta firings. This is close to a wakeful sleep and allows our brains to roam.

The Mind

In medical science, the mind is an elusive item. Of course, scientists know we have a brain, which is in control of every function of the body, but they have been unable to find the area in which the mind resides. Mind, or consciousness, makes the physical body have a reason for being.

The physical body is the receptacle for the mind. The two become integrated when the spirit takes possession of the body. Then the body and mind are married until that body wears out. The mind or consciousness lives forever as the spirit that is part of God.

Descartes' quest for rationalism in the fifteenth and sixteenth centuries did not include the knowledge that the brain functions on different wavelengths, but he summed up the question of mind with amazing clarity: "I think, therefore I am."

In dealing with the brain, humans create physical limitations that can become mental limitations on themselves. The mind, being clad in a human body, knows that there are certain boundaries coming solely from being in a physical embodiment. One limitation put on oneself can cause a cascade to follow.

Take the example of the elephant brought into captivity as a baby. His handlers put a chain around his ankle and post him at a certain spot. Try as he might, he can't break the chain because he is too young. Continual testing of the chain as all youngsters do brings him to the realization that he can't get away from where his handlers put him unless they allow him freedom. As a baby the elephant mind comprehends that he is unable to break the chains. While growing older and still wearing the chain, he no longer tests the chain because he has learned that he is unable to break it. His handlers have won. As long as the chain is on his leg, the adult elephant believes he is still bound. Even though he could break the chain as easily as a hot knife slicing butter, he remains shackled. A powerful animal has succumbed to a much smaller one by being fettered in his mind.

GHOSTS TALK

Having psychic ability is like that baby elephant. As children we are fully aware of the ability God gave us. We use it. As we age and are taught that the psychic is illogical, the logical chain tethers us to the ground as surely as the elephant was. As adults, we abandon our gifts because we know the logical chain is still around our ankle, keeping us prisoner. With meditation, you can remove the chains. Opening vast universes of knowledge, you can access your higher goals.

Meditation as Prayer

Meditation is simply prayer. Prayers can be silent or forceful and do not necessarily mean you need to be on your knees to benefit. A thought to remember is that you need to be careful for what you ask because words spoken from the heart can manifest.

An example is a prayer I spoke many years ago before my first husband and I married which carried severe implications in my life. Before starting this life revelation, know that my ex-husband is not a bad person. We were young, and he was only mimicking what he had seen with his parents. He, as we all are, is living his life to learn to become more spiritual. Any routine experience carries us spiritually closer to God.

While waiting on him to visit one morning after telling me that he wanted to marry me, I said without thinking, "God, I want him at all costs."

After our marriage, the cost was extreme. My ex-husband ran around on me, beat me, and was constantly drinking and doing other recreational things. This was nothing compared to the cost I didn't think I could bear.

My fourteen-year-old daughter went to live with her father and stepmother after continued pressure and promises from them. This child, whom I thought I would be unable to carry to term, was every-thing I wanted in life. Oh, don't get me wrong — I did not want her to be the reason for my existence, nor did I want her to live for me. I did, however, as any loving mother would, want her to be close to me and to be a part of my life, as did her father.

My ex-husband and I lived in neighboring states. He reasoned that she had lived with me for the first fourteen, soon to be fifteen,

Meditation

years of her life. For the remainder of her life, her father wanted her close to him, which is perfectly understandable. The problem with that scenario for me is that I have missed a substantial part of her life.

This beautiful woman now lives far from me in that other state. The opportunity to be able to hear my door opening and hear her striking voice tell me she is visiting for a few minutes is missed.

The justification in life's dealings is that all life's tragic events only serve to make us grow. That is what we are here for. If everything were magical and beautiful all the time, we would take life for granted and spirituality would not be needed.

Living with this answered prayer, my best advice to another is, always be careful what you ask for. Your prayers will be answered, but you may not like the way in which they are.

Using Meditation with Open Eyes

Meditation can be employed to benefit the body, mind and spirit. Going within to comprehend who we are can be beneficial and medicinal.

There is no right or wrong way to meditate. Sometimes just the idea of meditation can summon the psychic sensation you're looking for. The purpose of meditation in a psychic sense is to receive knowledge above normal sensory expectations. Once you understand that you can produce this information by concentration through meditation, you might become more aware that you don't need to perform a task such as a long meditation to receive psychic data. Instead, processing psychic details is as easy as thinking once you become comfortable with the information you're receiving.

Comfort level and confidence go hand in hand to create the best psychic possible. Meditation can assist in raising a person's comfort and confidence threshold. This is one of the reasons that meditation is so important to the aspiring psychic.

Many people want to explore the psychic world through meditation but are afraid that they may encounter something ghastly. Some psychics encourage this belief because of their own fear. Either they have not asked or do not know to ask the "other side" about this irrational fear. So when teaching meditation they tell their students that they need to have the light of God around and through them for grounding and protection. As a child of God, you are protected from birth. Being human keeps one grounded and firmly on the earth.

When a spirit takes the body of a child at conception or after, that child is immediately grounded. God, being "All That Is," is part of that person and as such gives the highest form of security. The very event of becoming human lends divine protection.

Address fears, because they are hindrances to being the best psychic one can be. In acknowledging fears, you can put them to rest in an intelligent manner. If you have trouble believing you are grounded and that God is with you, then a simple ritual can ensure that you are protected.

With your eyes closed, ask for and see the white light of God surrounding your physical body. This should take care of any qualms about safety you have.

Setting the Mood for Meditation

Once you feel safe, you can move on to the next part of meditation. Soft music can be helpful, but only turn it up high enough that it is faintly heard. Get into a comfortable position lying or sitting. Rest with the palms of the hands faced upward rather than downward. This is another ritual but allows energy to travel into your hands or from them in a manner that can be felt.

Close your eyes and get comfortable. Once you're at ease, start to breathe in the following methodical fashion. Take a long breath through your nose to a slow count of three to five, whichever is more comfortable. Air should fill the lungs starting at the lowest point and working upwards. Make sure that your diaphragm or mid-riff is ballooned sufficiently with the breath. Breathing in this way will send more oxygen to the brain and help you feel rejuvenated. Hold that breath in the diaphragm for the same count of three to five. Now let it out through barely parted lips at the same slow count of three to five.

Concentrate only on your breathing. Make sure to continue to breathe. Enjoy the feeling, which should be a nice restful sensation crawling throughout your body. Just at the edge of sleep, you are nevertheless aware of everything occurring. Feel every part of your body while lavishing in this breathing technique. Continue without worry about time or sleep. If you fall off to sleep, have no fear. You will awak-

Meditation

en shortly after a very restful nap.

Practicing this method of breathing is important in learning to use your psychic gifts. Because of meditations use in one's psychic quests, one needs to relish all aspects of the relaxation technique.

Once comfortable with the breathing exercise, you can start another relaxation procedure that will carry you into a deep meditation. Deep meditation accomplishes many goals in the psychic world.

Some people feel more comfortable with structured taped instructions for meditation. If you are one of those people, make a tape giving instructions in a pleasant speaking voice with some of your favorite music in the background. Since your brain registers more quickly when hearing your own voice, this will help more. If there is no need for the tape, use the following instructions.

Remember to stay focused on your breathing and relax. Do not worry about trying to quiet your mind. Some meditation teachers advise students to clear their mind. If those students are like me, there is no way to accomplish this act. In my experience, the best way to meditate is allowing all images and activity in the mind without restrictions. Allow the mind the freedom to do anything it wants but use the structure of breathing to keep your meditation on the right track.

Slowly go through each exercise of relaxing while breathing. Take your time and enjoy all aspects of the meditation because that is part of the relaxation technique.

Start with your toes. Mentally invite them to relax. Travel up your legs to the knees continuing to breathe and instruct your legs from knees to toes to relax. Feel them as they become heavier with relaxation, sinking further into your chair or couch. Relax your thighs.

Using your mental voice to tell your subconscious that you will feel better while relaxing and when finished meditating than you have ever felt before.

Continue to breathe. Relax your hips and pelvic area and feel them sinking further into your sofa or chair.

Enjoy the expansion of your lungs as they expand with air. Relax your back and stomach. Sense that you are more relaxed than you have ever been. Your shoulders and arms are feeling very heavy and comfortable. Allow yourself the luxury of relaxation. As you feel more relaxed, feel the restful sensations spreading gently throughout your body.

GHOSTS TALK

Relax your face and the back of your head.

Continue to notice all sensations as you breath and become calmer. Mentally remember that all is right with you and God.

Tell yourself that your forehead and the top of your head are relaxing. Remember to continue to breathe. Enjoy the calming sensations drifting up your body as you quietly command your body to relax. Submit yourself to complete relaxation.

Focus now on the top of your head where your soft spot was when you were a baby. Feel the tingle of energy as you concentrate on it.

Tell yourself mentally that you are opening to the Universal Good that is God. Ask for the white light of God to enter through your baby soft spot opening and to permeate your body starting at your head, running down your left side to the left toes up the inner left thigh, around your pelvic area, down the right thigh, to the right toes, and up the right side of your body to your baby soft spot again and out. Make sure that the white light has left nothing out as it courses through your body. Feel its energy as the white light moves throughout your body with its revitalizing sensation.

Speak silently to your body and tell it that as you breathe out while focusing on the white light that any illness or uncleanliness which is in your body will be carried out with each breath thus clearing any disease.

The white light running through your body is a very real sensation that allows you to know that this energy can work and can be seen.

Find your third eye area right between your eyebrows. This psychic area can be utilized for seeing anything beyond the realm of items considered normal. If you look now towards the top of your head, you can see the white light entering your body. Connect with this energy and enjoy your new found ability.

Thinking of a place you dream of as being the most comfortable and safe for you, start painting a picture on the landscape of your third eye. Add items such as trees or water that increase your comfort level. When you are finished with this mind picture, it will be your secret escape when life gets to be too much or when you need to get away from anxiety.

The pictures painted on the mind's screen differ from person to person. What one may find comforting others may not. Immerse yourself in all your sensations. Allow the senses to sweep you along while

Meditation

painting. As creator of this palette, you may use any color, shape or item in your mind painting.

Some find a meadow full of wild flowers to be the best spot in the world. Feel the wind softly blowing across your body as the aroma of wild flowers is left dwelling in your nose. A mental creation is beyond description with anything being possible. Psychic ability uses all the senses to create its palette on the third eye area.

Others may find the ocean more soothing. Far enough away from the waves that they are not sprayed by the water, they listen to the sounds of the waves and the gulls as they dip down to the water and up into flight again. Sandpipers run along the beach using their long sensitive beaks to probe the sand looking for mollusks. Then raising their heads again they run to another hole while crabs sidle along trying to get back to tide pools. This could be a wonderful hidden place.

Still others might want to stay in their own back yard swing. The safety of home can be comforting and can make the best mind vacation.

Under huge old trees, by a creek, with the sunlight throwing little spears as it dances through the limbs onto the mossy landscape below is another inviting location. Hearing the wind lightly rustle through the leaves of trees while it caresses your body, as the water gurgles happily over rocks in the creek is a real stress reducer. The smell of the moss and the combination of shadows moving jauntily as the wind gently moves branches to let the sunlight touch virginal spots on the mossy land is very peaceful.

Any of these places and many others can become your secret hideaway. The place that makes you feel safe, well and peaceful is wonderful for your third eye mind painting vacation. It is your little piece of heaven. Make it your own creation without interference from anyone else.

Once you have done your mind painting enjoy the sensation for a while. Let yourself go. Don't try to think or reason. Just be.

Don't try to guide your mind. Let your right brain be creative. Allow anything that occurs to do so without fear. You are perfectly safe.

Once painted and finished, some may feel as if they are leaving their comfortable place. Know that your comforting safe place is with you at all times. At any time, you can go back to your safe place with a thought. Give yourself license to enjoy any and all sensations while meditating.

Don't try to guide yourself into any particular place— just enjoy. This allows expansion of the mind. It may even take you into situations you did not know existed.

An example of one of those situations struck me with the knowledge that my way of thinking was rather small, even though my meditation was taking me into a much larger universe.

I'm able to go into a meditation just by closing my eyes and thinking I can. You will easily accomplish this same feat once you realize the value of meditation. It will become quite easy once you have mastered your breathing techniques.

Upon going to bed one night I closed my eyes to go into a quick meditation before going to sleep and got a sudden surprise. As soon as I closed my eyes, I saw two eyes staring back at me. It was like watching a horror movie where the fiend is looking into the window at the same time his next victim looks out. It was so totally unexpected and shocked me so much that I jumped while rapidly opening my eyes.

At the same time, I said mentally to myself, "Boy he's ugly," and I realized I heard him say the same thing about me only he said, "She's ugly.". Before I could get upset with his analysis of me, my guides mentioned that not everyone looks the way we think they should. They added there is beauty in everyone just the same.

Upon hearing this message, I laughed. How many times had I tried to teach others not to judge a book by its cover and to try to look deeper? Here I was being completely human, which I find hard to take now and then, and I had just said someone else looked ugly to me without considering his feelings.

As soon as I closed my eyes again, there he was looking back at me. This time we continued to eye one another but stood back a little so that we could see our whole heads.

In looking more closely, I noticed that his skin was the most beautiful color of translucent blue over tan. His face was a little more wrinkled than what I am used to, but his yellow-blue eyes were full of compassion, even though a minute before he had said I was ugly, too. Undoubtedly his guides fussed at him, too.

We were seeing each other now through non-judgmental eyes, trying to look at the other individual not by our outer appearance but by what we had inside.

I could feel that he was unique and probably on the same spiritual journey I was on. When he turned to leave, I saw a female there with him. It was quite obvious she thought he was beautiful, too.

Clearly, these people were not from our world. They didn't even dress as we do. Though my guides told me that they were from another planet, I did not ask which planet nor have a need to know. Meeting them was enough.

Knowledge that there is more to life than earthly education denotes allows one to travel any universe unfettered by the usual restrictions. Please know that anything you see should not frighten but rather educate you. Fear stops exploration. While meditating, you can investigate without worry.

Life is not always what we expect it to be. It is possible while meditating that some may even see someone they know is dead or something that they think is not valuable or beautiful. Everything that is part of God's creation is beautiful and valuable. There is nothing so small that it should not be considered large in the relationship of the universe.

As an example, take the buzzard or vulture. Most people see the vulture as ugly, but let us consider its beauty. This large bird takes on the job of cleaning up the garbage in the world. Most of us don't want to touch carrion. The odor alone is enough to keep us away, but the vulture doesn't mind. He is doing the rest of us a very beneficial service while he works for his living.

When we look down our noses at him, we need to think what this earth would be like if he weren't in it. The vulture is beautiful. All God's creatures are.

While meditating, try to refrain from passing impulsive judgments on what you see. Wait and make observations based on all information received rather than one quick look. There are lessons in every happening. Allow meditation to enlarge your mind and potential fact-finding efforts by gleaning all information possible.

Creative Visualization

Creative Visualization is another way of using meditation to assist

people in their lives. This is done by the process of starting a meditation, getting comfortable within it, thinking about what you want to
happen, drawing it in your mind, and seeing it accomplished.
Afterwards and from then on, you need to believe what you imagined
is a completed act.

This form of meditation is the only one that I believe should not
involve other people. For instance, if you wanted to sell something to
someone, you could see a contract being written and signed with the
word "sold" on it without the insertion of a particular name. When you
put a name on the contract, you are being manipulative. Manipulation
brings strong Karma with it. As long as you see the product sold, you
are fine, but when you see it sold to a particular person, you have now
brought that person into your manifestation.

In using Creative Visualization, my prayer is always that all concerned with my meditation benefit from whatever my product is.

At one point I didn't pray that way and it cost me dearly.
Remember when I told God I wanted my ex-husband at all costs? I put
his name there and got him. That was a manipulation even though I
didn't believe it was at the time. Now in my case, my ex-husband wanted me too. His request was to make me the way he wanted me. Neither
he nor I won the manipulation we created for ourselves, but we did
agree to have this experiment together and both of us learned valuable
lessons. Always think before you act. Hasty actions are not always safe.

Meditation and Creative Visualization can be used to heal yourself and others with their permission. When endeavoring to read or
help anyone, a question I always ask subconsciously of them is, "May
I?" Generally the answer is yes even if it is without their conscious
knowledge. Invasion of one's spiritual privacy can be as upsetting as
physical invasion of one's space. Therefore always ask consciously or
subconsciously whether the person wants prayers or any kind of assistance. Some may not.

Once given permission, one can use meditation to find the place
that needs attention in a person's body and utilize Creative
Visualization to see it healthy and viable. Meditation allows a person to
see the body's parts and as a whole. With this capacity, one can hone in
on one portion and see them become well and vigorous. The amazing
part of meditation is that you might see the human body through med-

itation in ways that you did not learn while in biology class.

The potential for learning while in meditation is without end. If you set no boundaries, then the information to be discovered is endless.

Using Meditation to Meet Your Guides

Meditation can also help you get to know your guides or guardian angels. Starting with the usual meditation, and after painting your mental safe place, ask that one of your guardian angels or guides meet you there. Do not have a fixed appearance in your mind, because they can come in a myriad of ways. The spirit knows no boundaries. We in the physical need boundaries to feel safe. Spirit does not.

A case in point is when I first started meditation and learned a very important lesson. With eyes closed and deep into meditation, I saw a five-sided star turning end over end across my vision from left to right. As it got to about the mid-point of my sight a circle came rolling into my line of vision, too, and caught up with the star. They united. Now the star was within the circle. Without hesitation, I asked mentally of no one in particular, "What does that mean?"

Instantly I heard a voice state, "Man and God are one."

Next a purple pinpoint of light became barely visible straight in front of my eyes. As it moved towards me getting larger as it progressed, I got the impression that this was a person who came to help me learn. His personality was one that lacked social graces in that he seemed to have very little time when he spoke with me. Had this person not conveyed a hidden compassion— even though he seemed to want to make sure it stayed hidden — I probably would not have listened to his clipped sentences.

When I asked why he appeared in different hues of pulsating purple shapes, he answered, "Because I am a spiritual teacher."

In awe of this teacher and ever the student, but without wanting to appear stupid, I asked a sincere question and learned an even greater lesson. "What is your name?" Since then I have come to expect that a teacher not only teaches but also learns.

With an exasperated voice he acknowledged my question, but his answer was not expected. "Oh, that's right. You are human, and as a human you want to have a name for all with whom you speak." The words he sent to my mind were even more profound. "Do you have to know the name of every stranger with whom you come into contact? Some are here for knowledge or sight and no more. My name is Ramie, if you need a name."

Feeling as if I were in the first grade being chastised by my teacher, he led me to believe that he would not be around long. He implied that I needed to learn the lessons he had to teach swiftly. True to his word, he gave his message quickly and left just as quickly. Unlike John, he was not someone for whom I mourned, but he did give me very good advice.

Once out of the mediation, I called a psychic whose opinions I valued. Upon asking her about the circle and the star, I came to realize how people create and hold on to certain fears. Her first question to me was about the star and how the points were situated. I told her and she said, "Oh, that's easy. That means man and God are one." She gave me confirmation of the message I had heard.

This lady spoke from her fears when she told me about the points on the star. She explained that when they were pointed with two legs up and one leg down, it meant that it was satanic or evil. At that point I did not realize that a star could be used as an evil object when its points were set in a certain way. She thought it her duty to help me learn, but in teaching me that there was an evil symbol she allowed me to see through man's eyes. Man needs to see certain symbols as evil so that they can recognize that evil. In essence, man creates the symbol to acknowledge the sinister manifestation he invented. According to her, my star had its head up and therefore was a good star.

When asked about my purple gentleman caller, she replied, "Oh that is a spiritual teacher."

"That's what he said," I told her. Afterwards I didn't call her again for confirmation on other subjects. That would come to me in other ways.

The message for everyone in the lesson taught to me is that our guides are not always what we expect, and symbols were made by man as a forum by which to learn. Our guides use those symbols as part of their language because they know it is key to our understanding. Once they have given a message, guides generally send confirmation through some means, and it may be a very unexpected source. Be prepared for anything.

Meditation

One such confirmation came the day my little puppy, Muffin, died. In my grief I wanted proof that she was aware I was mourning and missed her. A friend had come over and we had gone to pick up a takeout order. Even though my friend was unable to comfort me I did not let her know it because that is not the Southern way. Instead I sat in the passenger seat allowing her to talk while I was in my own world. Her radio was turned down so low it could not be heard. Thinking only of Muffin, I could hear her words rambling on but was unaware what she was saying. At one point I realized I was hearing the song as stated in an earlier chapter that I so often sang to my baby, "You Are my Sunshine."

"You are my Sunshine" was playing for me as a message and gift from my little girl. Confirmation came from my guide, Muffin, as I had requested. She was indeed around and capable of letting me know it.

Sometimes confirmation of the meditation lesson comes in the form of someone you don't know using the exact words your guide used. This might happen over and over by several sources until you acknowledge the message received.

Each form of confirmation becomes a guide in itself. Our guides don't always have to be human or animate. They can come in many forms such as the words coming from a radio. Put no limitations on your ability to hear.

When using meditation to meet a guide, be prepared for anything. Some may take you completely off guard, but do not dismay. This is their way to let you know that you are not in control of them or how they appear to you. They are completely responsible for their own looks. In coming to you with an appearance you are not prepared for, they help you realize they are not of your making. They are their own souls and responsible for their actions.

After getting several people to acknowledge their initial meeting with their guides in a class I gave, I asked one woman to tell me who her guide was. Hesitantly she told me she didn't see one.

This was her first time to meditate and paint a mental retreat using the third eye area as well. Starting with the retreat, I asked what it was like.

"Like any other secret place you have heard today," she emphasized quietly, "except that it has a picnic table in it."

GHOSTS TALK

Trying to bring out the information, I explored further. "Did anything happen differently when you asked a guide to come?"

"No," she replied.

I kept on, "Any colors or anything different at all in your picture when asked about the guide?"

"No,' she answered again, "Except for when Jesus came."

The whole class burst into laughter.

"Jesus came after you asked for a guide," I repeated.

"Yes."

"And you say you don't have a guide." The class is still laughing as she looks about in apparent unawareness.

She went on to tell us that they were sitting down at the picnic table talking. Calling her name, I told her that she had a wonderful guide, which she did not even recognize as being an assistant to her.

A guide may show up as a plant, animal, color, symbol, person, or anything you may or may not expect. Keep an open mind.

Once you have met a guide or guides through meditation, you come to learn that you don't have to be in meditation to receive messages from them.

Using Meditation as a Psychic Tool

As a psychic tool, meditation is hard to beat. It allows a person full resources to any kind of information. Limitations are irrelevant.

Some people can call upon their spiritual selves to help them achieve greater accomplishments towards their psychic goals while others may use this tool to assist with physical health.

There are different levels of meditation that include everything from a five-minute breath renewal to a deep-level trance state. Any and all can help to achieve the desired response. With no right or wrong way of going into meditation, any exercise that one can use to achieve desired effects for themselves is perfectly satisfactory.

With many stages of meditation such as Simple Meditation, Creative Visualization, Self-Hypnosis, Extrasensory Meditation, and Trance Meditation to choose from, you can make meditation a useful part of your life. Understanding how meditation works and how each level can be achieved enhances its use.

Meditation

Once the meditative state is achieved, it is sometimes good when viewing scenes brought on by meditation to use the third-person presentation method. Allow viewing of the full image as if watching a movie without being part of the movie itself. As a spectator you can realize that except for the enjoyment or the learning experience coming from the production, you are not a part of it.

With Extrasensory Meditation, not all movies are love stories. Allowing yourself to be removed from the action but being able to see and comprehend the happenings will give you a greater advantage. Emotional viewing will not help you grasp all that is happening on the movie screen of your mind. When taking in the event as a spectator without emotion watching an incident occur, you can be more logical and understand all aspects of the situation.

Your logical mind will review the mind movie without prejudice and with logical deduction and thus be a better memory tool.

When you are in an emotional state of mind, you are unable to quantify all scenes you saw while using meditation. Being disconcerted keeps you from functioning in a thoughtful, logical manner. If you go beyond your secret mind place and feel hesitancy in any manner, it's good to observe your meditation mind movies in the third person rather than the first. In that way you can receive full recognition of given information without fear.

Meditation can make the transition from a light self-hypnosis with ongoing deeper levels until one reaches the deep trance state. This does not mean that you instantly go from one or another, although some can, but rather it's like walking down steps into a cellar. Light is behind you at the top step only until you turn on the light at the bottom of the cellar. Progressively you have less light with each step down into the cellar you take until you reach the light at the bottom and are able to flip the switch.

Using meditation, you can go as deep into the subconscious as you like. Some are not comfortable with anything but finding their own personal secret place, while others like to go down the steps of the mind completely into the trance state.

Seeing happenings at a different level from what most people in the alpha state realize, the person in the trance state may be quite proficient in recognizing that he or she is in the trance state as well as physical people who are in the room. People, while under the trance state, may be unable to communicate with others by usual means. Because of the second sight, they know who is around them and what is going on in the trance state as well.

Just because they are in the trance state does not mean that they are blind to the physical world. It only means that usually they cannot initiate conversation without another asking questions because they are too busy in the trance state world with its quickness of events to care about talking. They are too occupied recognizing what they see and making logical assessments of those sights. When asked a pertinent question, they can reply but may not have the Southern politeness most people try to exhibit when speaking with others.

In trance state, one is aware of every detail surrounding them simultaneously. While one can focus on one item with part of their being, other parts of their consciousness are fully aware of all that is happening, and thus the person who is in trance state may be a little less than friendly when answering questions. Any inquiry seems to limit the ability to sense every item at once because one has to focus on the question. Another part of that person's consciousness takes over, and the answer comes in an unemotional method, which can be alarming to the person who is initiating the inquiry if he knows the individual in the trance state.

Once people learn that the person in trance is not meaning to display obnoxious behavior but rather to learn more while in the meditative trance, they fully understand and generally appreciate given information.

Knowledge received from the trance source can be taken by a listening individual, processed, used or discarded in an unadulterated manner. The listener as well as the person in the trance state is fully aware that the schooling they are receiving is either earmarked for them or is not. Generally there are no mistakes when information comes from this source. It makes identification easily accessible.

In a few situations people who are in the meditative trance state are not consciously aware what has happened while in that level of meditation, but on a spiritual level they are subconsciously very much aware.

States of meditation are useful in achieving education on a personal level and as a teacher. There are no limitations when using med-

Meditation

itation except the confines we establish for ourselves. Allowing one-self to develop through meditation can bring huge rewards for our spiritual, emotional, and physical well-being as well as assisting on the psychic side.

Meditation is a formidable tool that can help us reach our full potential. Through Creative Visualization, Trance Meditation, Simple Meditation and Self-Hypnosis, people are granted higher spiritual access for assistance with their health and important spiritual growth potential. The importance of this marvelous self-improvement technique is beyond many people's belief.

Chapter Seventeen

AURAS

Webster's dictionary defines "aura" as "the atmosphere of a thing, a vague, luminous glow surrounding a figure or object. It may take the form of a sound, sight, smell or feeling not perceptible to others."

Although we are supposed to take the dictionary as infallible where definitions are concerned, my belief is that auras are perceptible to others, and I can prove it. Like a headache, although you can't prove it's there, you can feel it.

An aura is energy emitted by every living thing. It is the soul of the physical entity. When God said, "Let us make man in our own image," He was referring to spirit, not physical appearance.

This energy, or soul, can be measured. Auras emit light and heat. Body energy can be photographed using Kirlian photography, and heat can be electronically sensed. Thus, an Aura or the soul can be seen or felt. In Kirlian photography, and as seen by the human eye, auras assume many different colors. Color change depends upon the individual's mood and consciousness.

Auras are asymmetrical and constantly in motion. They do not have a set value as to how large or small they can be. Spirit may fill only the body it inhabits, or it can become the size of a room or larger.

Whatever the individual is contemplating will show up in the aura. A person's aura is a psychic tool that the physical person uses to retrieve subconscious, helpful information in the process of living. Using the aura as a tool, one can sense or see many of life's conditions such as health, spirituality, drug abuse, and much more. The aura can be examined to see when an individual is about to commit a dastardly deed or even die. An aura is a stockpile of information about the soul.

Every animal from the lowest, one-celled amoeba to man uses its aura to sense danger. For that reason when two people are meeting for the first time, each decides instantly whether he trusts the other. The two auras touched each other and subconsciously decided whether further conversation was due.

Auras from the two people either put them at ease or made the body kick into a protective overdrive of sorts. Like two dogs circling each other to get a feel as to who is the stronger, the aura allows two individuals to size each other up in a matter of micro-seconds. Sometimes a past life may help to form the opinion, but the touch of the two auras brought back the memory.

Auras do not stay within a certain range of the body but can travel great distances to sense what they need to investigate.

An example of this phenomenon is when at a hotel, a person has to sleep in a strange, dark room. Upon arising in the dark in the middle of the night to go to the bathroom, that person will generally feel an obstacle before running into it. The aura of the person is on full alert because it is in unfamiliar surroundings. Had the person been relaxed at home in his own bedroom, he may have smashed his toe because his aura was at ease.

Your aura is your best watchdog. While you sleep soundly in your bedroom, your aura is vigilantly watching over you like a guardian angel. Protecting your physical body is its object since that is its mode of transportation while on earth.

While sleeping, you feel someone enter your bedroom. Suddenly you jerk awake and sit up, as your heart pounds wildly, only to find

Auras

your husband finally coming to bed. Your aura did its job to alert your physical body to the entrance of another being. It has encircled you and filled the room so that anyone passing through your soul space will awaken you. Law-enforcement agents use this ability while awake or asleep to assess life-saving situations.

Auras are a natural in the field of love. Attraction comes from two auras touching before two people even notice each other. Auras seek out others who are most compatible with them. Once the auras touch and agree they feel good together, eyes of the two people meet. Now physical attraction catches up to the sense of spirit. Both start to display physical signs of interest. Floating across the room toward each other, they both feel the exhilaration of first attraction.

Although auras are perfectly capable of helping one find a lover, they are also just as capable of helping one to find an abuser. Auras accept the personality traits and challenges that the soul has deemed necessary for enlightenment. Thus, if a lady feels in her soul that she is not worth much, her aura will find a man determined to fulfill that prophesy, and vice versa.

Fill a room with one hundred people of the same sex who are looking for a mate. Make one of those people an abuser. Send in someone from the opposite sex who tends to attract abusers. She or he will find the one person in the room who is abusive instantly because both will feel the attraction. Like seeks like in auras until we learn valuable soul lessons. Then the aura, being educated, can move on to other life lessons.

Auras are utilized every day, all day long. They don't get to take a vacation. They work constantly in the background to maintain mental, physical, emotional and spiritual energy. As humans, we take the aura or soul for granted, but it never takes the physical body or any role created by the human condition for granted.

Empathy

When one aura meets another, they begin examining each other immediately. As they test the waters, they look like two lovers groping until they are satisfied as to the intent of the two physical beings. Once they have inspected each other sufficiently, they can make an intelligent decision as to whether to run from the other entity or make it a friend.

GHOSTS TALK

This examination is called "empathy." A person who knows that the soul is using this ability and utilizes this gift as a psychic tool is called an "empath."

Empathy is the soul's ability to feel another soul and understand the implications of that soul or aura. If the soul is sad, happy, dangerous, or even ill, auras will examine and show their physical counterpart what the other soul is feeling. Whether it is used for fight, flight, business, love, or otherwise, it is a healthy sense to have.

An easily recognized instance of aura use or empathy is when a person is walking down a sidewalk in an undesirable part of town. His aura is working overtime. This person has put his physical body at risk— and thus his soul's evolution while learning on earth. Now the aura has to really work to protect this person's physical body.

As he walks, this person sees someone come from around a corner a few feet from him. His aura has already started the body to work before sight of the person is even determined. Adrenaline is beginning to pump because the aura, after feeling the stranger's aura, is not sure that he should continue on to meet this unfamiliar person.

While feeling the stranger in an empathic frame of mind, the aura surmises that this new arrival is not there for his safety. Physical symptoms start to display such as the hair beginning to stand on the back of his neck. His eyes start to look the stranger over to see where his hands are. The aura is telling the body that it might have to run. Be ready, because this just doesn't feel right, the aura advises the brain.

In another case, a man could be walking down a street but this time in his own neighborhood where he ordinarily feels safe. Suddenly a large, strange dog emerges from a yard. His aura goes out to meet the dog's aura to see if the dog is well-intentioned. Upon feeling each other, the man feels that the dog is not one he wants to mess with and the dog feels a certain amount of fear from the man's aura. Now they have a decision to make. Is it worth a fight or should they allow each other to pass by?

Empathy will help both to make a good decision.

In everyday life, humans use empathy with friends and neighbors. When you see a friend who is emotionally down, you know it before that friend can even give every gory detail of their situation. That friend can look and act the same as always, but her aura gives the message that

Auras

all is not well. The first words between the two become a question, "What is wrong?" Rarely is the aura and empathy wrong.

When you cry over a movie or someone else's hurt, you are an empath because you have empathy for whatever another may feel even if it is only in the movies and not real.

A common example of empathy occurs when two people see each other on a daily basis. Take work, for instance. Each morning you see the same person when you arrive at work. You feel wonderful when you enter your workplace ready to face the day.

But the instant you walk through the door, greet the person whom you see every day with a smile and get a returned smile, you feel as if you need to crawl under a blanket and hide. Without quite understanding why, your whole attitude changed with your waltz through the door. You drag yourself to your desk to work out the day with one wish — that the day goes quickly.

If we analyze the situation, we can find the culprit. Look back with me now to see what went wrong or what is right. You felt on top of the world until you walked through the doors and smiled at your colleague. He even smiled back. Nothing was wrong, but you instantly felt as if your whole world had been turned upside down.

Go speak with the person who smiled back at you so nicely. Ask him how he is, and you will probably get another story. He is not so well. His face may have hidden that fact, but his aura or soul did not.

Another example of empathy can be seen in nursing mothers. When her child cries, the mother's milk begins to drop. The maternal condition prepares the mother to care for her child. The two auras are so intermingled that all the child has to do when hungry is cry and the mother instantly is ready to feed.

When a person allows his soul to exhibit physical or emotional symptoms from touching the aura of another, he or she is an empath of a very high degree.

Being an empath means feeling all the sensations others feel. You are no longer an island but a sensor of all energies around you. Even if someone is trying to keep emotional secrets, he is unable to do so. Without thinking, you feel everything he is feeling without being able to put a label on the situation. If he is down, you are. Conversely if he is up, you are, too. Because your aura is constantly seeking others' auras

GHOSTS TALK

requesting information about those people, you take on their feelings rather than imparting yours.

Using that important tool of feeling the aura, you can learn to interpret disease in another. Sometimes, you may even have symptoms of the disease, but you need only acknowledge the disease in the other person without actually allowing the symptoms to overcome you.

Being unaware the illness is not yours, you might think you are the one who is ill. As an empath, you must always ask yourself if this illness is yours. The answer will come instantly. Having gotten your answer, you can breathe a sigh of relief or go to the doctor.

Empathy is a valuable psychic tool. All plants and animals use it, as well as do certain inanimate objects. Because there is nothing that is not God, everything has an aura or soul.

Being able to empathize runs deep in a soul. There is nothing that does not touch an empath.

Psychometry

Everything emits certain vibrations, which is the aura. These energy units are electrical and create a little buzz that may be heard, felt or seen using the psychic senses. Just like those huge electric lines you sometimes go under, you can hear or feel that buzzing sensation even though you may not be consciously aware of it at the time.

As an empath, you can touch an object and pick up its vibrations even if it has not been touched for years. The object will retain any and all information it has ever been privy too. Touching objects to obtain information is called Psychometry.

This tool comes in handy when one wants to tune into information on something or someone who is not present. The person who touched the object leaves vibrations or aura imprints on it. A good psychic makes decisions while touching the object as to whether it is the object he is feeling or vibrations of the person who touched the object.

In murders or missing persons this tool is highly useful to the psychic. According to how open to empathy the psychic is, psychometry can have some very undesirable effects.

This has happened to me on more occasions than I want to admit when I touched another person's blood without knowledge it was there. In working murders, I have been privy to certain items that I would not otherwise come into contact with on a regular basis. Each time I have touched blood on an object, it has made me literally sick to my stomach, but it has also given me an edge to be able to see more clearly how the victim died.

There have even been times when the blood was many years old. One such incident was when a killer had not been found. A relative of the victim handed me a watch with dried blood on it. Without noticing the blood, I took the watch and became sick from the touch. Instantly I told the relative that there was blood on the watch because it made me ill. The family member explained that he was unaware that the blood would have such an effect on me, although it was the watch the victim was wearing when murdered.

In some instances, when touching the aura or psychic imprint left on an object by the person in question, a psychic is able to track that person much like a bloodhound. Once the psychic is able to find the aura of that person by picking up the vibrations, he is able to read what has happened and what is happening to the person in question. Because everyone is an individual within God, a psychic is capable of retrieving the aura of another and tracking it down to its source. If the soul has left the physical realm, in most times it becomes evident, too.

In this same way a psychic can interpret information given by inanimate objects as well. God is made up of every living thing, whether it is animate or inanimate. There is nothing He is not.

Using touch in psychometry is a wonderful psychic tool because it only expands on the human sense of touch and causes the psychic to utilize more fully the other senses.

Spirit or Aura

Each person carries a white light inside his body, which is his eternal spirit or soul. One's spirit, or "white light," is electrical and emits different light waves according to mood. The length of the wave determines what colors show in one's aura. As light shows through the spirit, one can see different colors. These colors change according to our mental, physical, and emotional health.

Everything, human or otherwise, has a spirit, or aura. As part of

GHOSTS TALK

God, we are different species, creations and individuals that are part of the "Whole." The "White Light of God" is part of everything. Inside and for a few inches outside the physical body, the "white light" is constant. When light goes through the reflected electrical wavelengths outside the body it provides color based on what is happening in our lives at the time.

White is the basis for all color and, as part of the "God Light" is a link between souls. That is why most people ask for the "White Light of Protection," although their spirits are already filled with that precious light of protection.

Spirit is the reason everything lives. Auras demonstrate what the spirit is feeling. Seeing another's aura is a true psychic revelation. Having the ability to decipher the colors of that aura takes some practice.

Even the earth as part of God displays its aura easily at sunup and sundown. The mood of the earth is evident when you look toward the horizon to see the color of the earth's aura. People have been using those colors for years to interpret nature's climatic events. "Red sky in morning, sailor take warning," and "Red sky at night, sailor's delight" are two sayings used by seamen to interpret weather patterns.

Nature in all her splendor is allowing you to see the color of her being when she displays magnificent colors at sunrise and sunset. Sometimes it is a wonderful orange or pink, but in tumultuous times it is the color of slate.

Our soul or spirit influences our physical lives so that we reflect our auras in daily life. Colors we choose in our aura offer the opportunity for all to see what life means to us at the time of choice. Like the chameleon, colors alter to suit our spiritual needs.

Human beings wear colors in their auras that express needs of the spirit. Like shoppers in a supermarket seeking to improve their health by choosing vegetables of different colors, humans use more than one color in their aura for their mental, physical, spiritual, and emotional health.

Going further with this premise, people like to wear colors that are generated in their aura also. For instance, a single woman who wants to be noticed will generally wear red because she is looking for passion and excitement.

In the animal kingdom, red is a significant color that signifies willingness to mate. Certain flowers have red petals to entice a bee. Monkeys

246

in estrus have red bottoms. Red is the color of blood when it hits the air. This all has to do with the sexual. The old "Red Light Districts" were purely sexual. If you want to be noticed, then red is the color.

Disease of the physical body can be detected in the aura first. If it is not dealt with in the spiritual body, then it grows in the physical until it is either healed or the physical body is stopped.

Black is generally the color of disease and is the void of color; its wavelengths absorb light rather than reflect it. The person carrying black in his aura may have something either mentally or physically wrong with him.

Sometimes the black is indicative of a person who is involved in some very detailed project. He needs all his energy and prefers to become reclusive with that energy.

Auras are one of our most important psychic tools, because is it is the first to greet others. Consequently, we all should pay more attention to that first impression. Reading auras can give you the inside track on everyone.

Mothers realize that their children are ill by instinctively feeling their baby's aura. Businessmen have gut feelings as to what their customers want by touching their clients' auras. Using this tool, people recognize whom they can trust, although many tend to ignore the feeling.

Auras are not just a tool for psychics but a means for everyone to become more perceptive. Everyone uses this sense on a subconscious level without being aware of it. It is always in the foreground, helping you to make intelligent decisions.

Your aura can become your guardian angel at times. Feeling leery of a person or situation makes one tend to be a little more watchful. The aura presents physical manifestations such as the hair rising on the back of the neck. This causes one to take notice of that particular situation more carefully.

Clichés have been made with auras in mind. Using color to describe feelings of the spirit manifesting in the physical has made the country-music industry more than a little money. Such phrases as: "I'm so blue today," "Look how red she turned," "She's green with envy," and "Don't it make her brown eyes blue?" are part of everyday conversation.

Moods of auras influence colors and textures.

Favorite colors dictate personality traits and change with time.

GHOSTS TALK

While getting dressed each morning, a person looks for a certain suit or dress. If he is unable to wear that piece of clothing, then the whole day seems to be ruined. The person who was unable to dress as he pleased because of an unforeseen event feels out of sorts, as if he just doesn't look quite right. His confidence is lowered because he couldn't dress as he wanted.

The aura affects the color and thus the attitude of the day.

Housing decor directly influences life with the colors chosen. As we change the way we think and the direction in which our life is going, we grow out of colors.

Spiritual growth commits us to learning the significance of each color. There is nothing in life that is not important.

Out-of-Body Experiences

Spirit or aura is not confined to the human body. It does not have to use the physical body for movement, but it does need the physical body for spiritual motivation. The spirit accomplishes education in physical form.

As a result, the aura or spirit can leave the body at any time it wishes without death occurring. Bodily functions are not hampered when the spirit takes a small vacation or checks on other souls. Physical life continues as if nothing has happened.

Sometimes this occurrence is described as "daydreaming" or being "off in your own world." It is not something to be dreaded but rather an exciting change. People use psychic ability every day without being the wiser for it. Choosing to call it something innocuous such as gut, intuition, or déjà vu takes some of the superstition out of it, but it is still psychic ability.

An "out of body experience" is not a terrifying event but a wonderful change from the humdrum physical world. The soul's escape from the physical body allows it the ability to go into the past or the future.

Any event is left open to scrutiny by the soul. It can converse with other souls to set up new tasks for the good of spiritual advancement for all souls involved. The soul is capable of doing anything its heart desires. There are no boundaries for the spirit.

Soul travel is one of the easiest feats the soul can carry out. It is an experience that is taken for granted by the spirit. Often, the physical body is never aware the spirit even leaves the body. Occasionally, the feeling of déjà vu makes one question the events the spirit has previously witnessed in its out-of-body traveling.

Once you realize that your spirit can leave your body upon command, you will no longer live life in the same way. Memories of the spiritual side of life begin to reappear to the conscious part of the mind rather than being buried in the subconscious.

The subconscious, both in and after out-of-body travel, hints at psychic ability seemingly forgotten while living in the conscious world of physical form. Memories brought to the surface of consciousness cause the spirit to start to remember its birthright.

When a soul consciously realizes that it is capable of astral travel, it starts to seek information on how to accomplish the act while conscious. One such person came to visit me for help on astral travel. After taking this person into a deep meditation and making him comfortable, I told him that the soul could leave the body without fear through the area right under the heart, whenever he was ready.

His soul left his body with some hesitation after I let him know that his astral self could re-enter his body anytime he wanted. At the moment of his soul's departure from his body, my home became filled with other spirits to cheer him on. They sat around looking like a church revival waiting on him to become aware.

Once he had a chance to play outside his physical world for a while, I called him to come back home. While he was still in astral form I asked him to ascend a stairway in my home, but I also asked him to stop on the top step of the stairs. He had not seen anything at the top of this stairwell when he came to my home because the stairs made a turn with a high wall concealing anything above. My request was that after doing this he return to his body, which he did.

Once inside his body and out of meditation, he was fully animated in appearance and speech. His first words were, "Are there ghosts in here now? I saw them come in as I left my body."

"Yes," I answered. "You are right. They did come in when you left. Now what did you see at the top of my stairs?"

"I saw the head and shoulders of someone." With those words I sent him to the top of my stairs. At that point, I heard the exclamation,

GHOSTS TALK

"That is what I saw."

At the top of my stairs was a mirror placed so that when someone reached the top of the stairs, all that could be seen were the head and shoulders. This was proof positive he had left his physical body upon conscious request to explore the astral world. Seeing other astral visitors there was added confirmation.

Any soul can go out of body without fear of losing the physical container in which it resides. All you have to do is ask your soul to allow this to happen while you are awake. Many souls find themselves traveling out of body when at the point of sleep and wakefulness. As they are waking they become aware that they are drifting back to the other dimension.

When a person is sleeping soundly but awakens suddenly with his heart pounding, it is generally because his soul was traveling and decided to re-enter his body quickly. The surge of activity causes the physical body to react. Later the person having the out-of-body experience may have a touch of déjà vu. This is only a conscious reminder of a subconscious event.

No fear should be associated with out-of-body travel because as part of God, all souls are safe in the astral dimension.

All individuals' souls are connected with the God source, but they do not appear tethered to that source with a line. Instead there is a divine connection within each of us as individuals of the Whole. Upon that realization, one can see the blanket of souls who are separate yet united. The aura is only a soul or spirit wearing the clothing of the physical.

Detecting Auras

Different techniques can be used to detect auras. Some require feel, and others use sight. All necessitate focus and concentration until one becomes aware how easy it is to perceive another's spirit or aura. Once you consciously achieve sensing auras, you will become aware how this was always a part of your life.

There is no right nor wrong way to access auras. Whatever works for you is the right way, just as it is with any metaphysical lesson. Confidence grows stronger, and psychic ability comes more readily, if we compliment ourselves upon each achievement. Never belittle yourself if you do not achieve what you wish on the first try. Keep trying and keep patting yourself on the back. Knowledge will come.

For more ease in sensing auras it is always good to have at least two or more people together. Heightened senses develop more easily when you have people who think alike. The old adage that says, "Three gathered together in one mind with faith can move a mountain" is quite true.

Make sure that you are with people with whom you have extreme trust when trying to view auras the first time. Otherwise, learning how to sense auras might be a little more difficult. When we trust our friends, we allow our auras wider capacity to give and receive information. People have told me that once I had told them about auras, they had seen auras on their friends while sitting with them. Souls as auras are touchy-feely by nature and decide instantly whether a newcomer is acceptable in their presence.

Once you are comfortable with your environment and the people you are with, you need to give yourself permission to see what you may consider extraordinary. Consciously and aloud, each person should speak the words, "I give myself permission to learn." These words can be used for any opportunity in life and are some of the strongest metaphysical words that can be spoken.

You should also say aloud that you wish your aura to expand both in and away from your body so that it is more easily sensed or seen. Because one's aura can fill a room, this is not a difficult task. It does this on a regular basis for the protection of the physical form.

To become familiar with feeling auras, place your two hands in front of you with palms facing about three inches apart. Without touching, slowly move your hands toward one another in a pumping motion as if you are pushing on a ball. When you feel a little resistance between the two hands, you are feeling your spirit or aura. The sensation of feeling can be spongy, hot, cold, or tingling but it is a tangible sensation.

Close your eyes and feel the sensation grow stronger. Become aware how you sense the sensations. Realizing how you react to each new metaphysical act can help you in recalling other psychic knowledge. Allow yourself time to enjoy this conscious newfound knowledge.

While continuing to feel the aura in the pumping motion, move your hands apart slowly. Focus and concentrate as you feel the aura growing to the width of your two hands. It will continue to grow with you as far as you can hold your hands apart.

After feeling the sensation of your aura between your two hands about a foot apart, invite another metaphysical student to join you. With your eyes closed so that you cannot see movement, still using the pumping motion you used before and your heightened senses, ask your partner to move her hand between yours. Tell your partner when you feel her hand between your two outstretched hands. Both you and she will be amazed that you have felt her aura block yours.

Now you are aware how your aura works when you are asleep. It is constantly on guard protecting you from any other aura influence. That psychic sense is why you awaken so easily when another person enters the room in which you are napping.

Return the favor for your partner by letting her feel you interfere with her aura.

To try another method, have your partner face you. Extend your palms face-up at arms' length. Close your eyes. Your partner then needs to place her palms face-down over your hands about a foot or two above your hands. With your partner using the same pumping motion over your hands and moving slowly down, tell her when you can feel the aura. Open your eyes and see how high her hands are over yours.

Again, the same sensations apply. They may be spongy, hot, cold, tingling, pushing, pulling or as if small breaths of air are brushing your hands apart. Some even feel the sensation as energy that pushes itself into a point and touches the other's hands. Some feel what seems to be magnetic repelling of the other. As long as you realize that this is the sensation you will feel when touching someone else without the use of physical limbs, any feeling you get will do.

With your eyes now open and feeling the sensation as your partner pushes her hands palms downward in a pumping motion over yours, have your partner lift her hands higher and away, in the same jerky motions from yours, until you can no longer feel the aura. If your partner is unable to move her hands any higher, turn your hands toward each other as if you were two children playing "pat-a-cake" and move away from each other. See your aura growing to meet the other.

Generally the aura is about half-way between the two students unless one or the other has retracted her aura.

Again, return the lesson for the gracious partner so that she can become aware as you did how the aura feels when being manipulated by another.

Once you have accomplished this feat, you are ready to see auras on other humans, animals, plants and rocks. Everything has a spirit and is tied to God in the same way you are. The quicker you become aware of this truth, the quicker you are able to use all your psychic abilities.

Another method for sensing auras in a group situation, after you have learned how they feel, is to form an energy ball. With your group forming a circle, each person needs to point his hands palm in "pat-a-cake" fashion towards the center of the circle. The intention is to try to create an energy ball in the center of the circle. With thought coming from each person, this is easily manifested.

Feel the weight and width of this ball and make it increase in size until it is about the size of a large beach ball.. Have fun with it as if you are a first-grade student. Eagerness and open-mindedness are part of this creation. Once you have the ball created, an appointed person needs to take it from others' hands and hold it in his own.

The object of this exercise is to be able to toss this beach ball to each person in the circle just as you did when you were younger with a physical ball. Each individual in the circle should be able to feel the ball when it is tossed his way and feel the weight of the ball leaving his hands.

This energy ball is created when everyone in the circle shares an individual manifestation and each person gives permission for it to be built. Thus, it takes on a life of its own while the circle is involved with tossing it around. Once they quit, the energy ball dissipates back into the universe.

To learn to see auras more easily, ask one person from your group to sit in front of a lightly colored wall. The reason for this is so that the wall will not absorb light flowing through the aura, thus allowing the other people in the room to see the aura more clearly.

Although it is generally impolite to stare at a person, that is exactly what you need to do. Look at the person whose aura is being read without blinking. Defocus on the person and see the outline of his head and hair. Notice the bright white color protruding out from his head about an inch or so. Continue to look out as the light passes through that aura and other colors start to emerge.

While still staring at the person, close your eyes. Become aware of the light that stays in your eyes outlining your friend and filling his body. With third-eye sight you are witnessing spirit energy. Some, when dead, are called "Light Beings." That is where the term originated.

Open your eyes and enjoy the light show.

Look the whole body over to see where the aura is consistent and where it is not. If there are spots that look different or have a different color to them, there are special reasons.

While the group is looking at the one person's aura, encourage everyone to talk about the colors they see and how the aura is shaped. This confirms that they are not only seeing auras but are also seeing the same colors.

Each person in the group needs to sit in front of the wall to be scrutinized by the others.

Once you've grown comfortable maintaining the sight of auras in humans, take a look at your dog or cat. Or look at a favorite plant. Since everything has an aura that reflects its physical condition, you can monitor anything you care about.

Another method of sensing auras is to learn how each color feels. To do this, pull different colors of cloth from around the house. Lay out the cloth so that it does not touch another piece of cloth.

Raise your hand about two inches above one piece of cloth and feel the color. Close your eyes and sense it more strongly with focus and concentration. Understand how that particular color feels to your senses. Once you feel you have the color sensed, move on to another color until you realize how each color vibrates, and you recognize the particular feeling that comes from that color.

To further your education in color, put several strips of colored fabric into a paper bag. Decide the color you want to pick before placing your hand into the bag. Put your hand into the bag without looking and choose the color by feel.

An additional way to sense color is by using an ordinary deck of playing cards. Shuffle the cards and put the deck face down. Take the first card and lay it face down without looking at it. Hold your hand about two inches over the back of the card. Decide whether the card is red or black. Although every card has a color on the back, you will be able to feel the vibrations from the face of the card and decipher whether it is red or black.

Continue to work with the playing cards until you feel comfortable with your ability.

The ability to see auras allows you to read any individual. The colors you see will give you an accurate picture of what is going on in that person's life.

Colors

Colors are not only beautiful to the eye but considerably influence a person's actions. They evoke physical emotions and are even part of the ritual in our lives, even though we're often not conscious of it.

Color is so taken for granted that even though people revel in its beauty they tend to overlook it just as they do when hearing a bird singing outdoors. It is a wonderful part of life that people have come to expect should always remain.

Funeral dress is traditionally black. A chaste new bride wears white in her wedding. Some years ago, brides that were not quite as chaste wore beige. Newborn boys have blue as their color and girls are pretty in pink. A person who has a green thumb is generally envisioned as one who can grow anything.

Color influences our lives in many ways.

Sight, of course, is enhanced by color and would be much less enjoyable without it.

Some colors have been found to help in certain areas of physical life. For example, pink helps soothe anger. Some prisons use a pink room for calming down prisoners. After about 20 minutes in such a room, inmates who were angry are more docile.

Doctors' offices generally use mauve and aqua colors. (And since they always seem to be running late, they usually don't put a clock on the wall.)

In older hospitals, green was considered the color of healing and is still found in some hospitals today. When you think of green you think of trees or, in a broader sense, of nature. Nature is healing.

Color is alive and has spirit, just as everything in the universe does. As a tangible entity, it can be seen and felt. Each color has meaning attached to it and determined by the person observing the color.

People's preferences in colors give us information about their personalities. Changes in their lives find them preferring different colors at different stages of their lives. Because color vibrates at different frequencies, it can aid our self-esteem or it can cause us to feel worse.

Mood is influenced by color.

Wrapping up in a snuggly old pair of pajamas or sweats is reassuring when we have had a bad day. Why do we pick a particular piece of clothing to be our comforter? It is because of the color. That color either lets us wallow in our emotions or brings us out of despair.

All color must have light in order to be seen. Light waves and their lengths determine the color. Intensity is another attribute of color. When you take the color black and add light, the light darkens as it approaches the black because it is being adsorbed.

The combination of hue, saturation, and luminance dictates the impact of color. Hue is the actual color, saturation is the purity, and luminance is the degree of darkness of that color.

If an object is black, then it absorbed all the light in order to retain the color. No light is reflected.

Light waves can only be reflected, absorbed or transmitted. When light waves hit an object, all waves — not the color of the object — are absorbed. The actual color of the object is reflected. A yellow flower absorbs every color but the yellow and reflects that color so that someone looking at that flower perceives it to be yellow. In the same way, our spirit reflects the color of our aura from the boundaries of the physical human form, absorbing light it does not want to reflect.

Light traveling away from our body in waves is part of the "white light" or our spiritual being. White light is composed of colors recognized by their own wavelengths and actually comes from the sun. The tendency for some psychics to ask for the "white light" to surround and protect them may have originated with old religions that worshipped the sun, and from the sight of "God."

Light from the sun is white and contains all the wavelengths of color. Visible colors radiating from the sun make up the colors of the rainbow: red, orange, yellow, green, blue, indigo, and violet.

As the waves travel away from our body, they appear in our aura so that we reflect whatever is happening with our spiritual selves.

Auras

Spirit and physical bodies are intertwined for learning purposes. Our spiritual selves give off a second-by-second display of our everyday lives in the form of "auras." In either conscious or subconscious ways, others pick up on colors of auras and use them as a tool.

When looking at an aura, the definition one gives to each color is very important. It can help you make wise decisions when it comes to meeting other humans, animals, plants, or minerals. Everything, including Mother earth, has a viable aura. Everything is alive with spirit.

Shades of color give us a true interpretation of the spiritual and physical body. As a color moves from light to dark, the meaning of that color changes; the deeper the depth of color, the more intense. All this needs to be considered when reading an aura.

Be careful to examine auras thoroughly when reading them. Look for any variations of color that might give insight into the soul or personality of the person being read. When two colors join to make a new color, you must consider the meaning of both colors that are joined. If the combined color is darker, it lends itself more to the darker of the two colors' description. For instance, red blended with white may make pink. Both the red and white color description combines to give the explanation for the pink color in the aura. If the red is more prominent, it is vying in interpretation for its position in the combined color aura.

Muted shades of color in an aura usually indicate problems with the individual such as temper, drug or alcohol abuse, or something equally undesirable.

Looking at an animal, plant, or mineral's aura, you generally see the white light from within first, but there may be times you don't. That may take an entirely different interpretation. For instance, a man with black coming from within may be a child molester, or he might not have long to live. Remember, the aura is reflective of the soul within. Your reading of the aura is based on your perception. Listen to your inner self. It will guide you.

Auras, like humans, are complicated. Therefore, no aura is the same, and usually they have more than one color in them. As with all living things, they have a lot going on at any given time. It takes time to interpret all the colors, even if they are represented only by a thin line or spot within the aura.

GHOSTS TALK

Knowing what color means to you will help you in reading auras. Take the following psychic interpretations of color based upon the personalities of the aura you are reading. Use them as a guide and expand upon them. The descriptions include negative and positive traits for each color. Remember, even positive traits can become negative if abused. Decide for yourself what characteristics each color should have. Allow your own psychic senses to assist in your description of each color. When viewing an aura, ask for help from your inner spirit and listen to the answer. It can come in a myriad of ways.

Black

Black is one of the most beautiful of colors and yet is the void of color, too because it absorbs all light producing color.

In an aura, it is the color of detail. People who have this color in their aura are eager to work in detail-oriented careers. They don't get bored with statistical projects.

If a job needs finishing, these are the people to finish it. When put in a place to find the mistakes of others, they are right at home. Working on puzzles and finding others' mistakes bring out their tenacious spirits. Black personalities will sometimes intentionally find mistakes just so that they can repair them.

These personalities need leaders, though, to tell them what needs to be done. Under guidance, they are able to get to the crux of the matter and solve very large problems. Although they are not what one would consider outgoing, creative personalities, they are creative in finding and solving problems.

This color also indicates that the person is holding things inside. Feelings of vulnerability plague people who have black in their auras, and they are very unsure of themselves.

When it comes to clothing, black indicates that one does not want to be touched. Black puts a barrier between the wearer and others. Holding their energy in is something that is needed at the time. Building a reservoir of energy for these people is of extreme importance. This color is also effective in helping them keep their strength inside so that they can better protect their emotions. Although they want to be part of the world around them, they want no one to tug at

Auras

their sensitivity to that world.

Black is a relief color for most people, like "Mom's apple pie". It makes them feel comfortable and even, in some cases, makes them feel smaller, allowing them to hide from the sometimes cruel world.

Black or brown, when viewed in an aura, can also indicate illness. Its location and hue can be an indicator as to where the illness is and how severe it is. For instance, if the person who is being read shows black around the right knee, it could be an indicator that the person has knee problems or will have shortly.

Some child molesters, rapists, and killers have black in their aura. Since black in the aura harbors physical illness, it can also appear in people with spiritual or mental illness. A person who wants to take the life of another, rape someone, or control a small child, has an illness all his own.

It takes a lot of planning to put such manipulation into practice. This type of person shows the conception for this behavior in their aura when they are deciding to complete the deed, as did a person who came to me for a reading. My first sight told me that he had the thought of molesting his four year-old daughter. Upon telling him what I thought, he confirmed that I was right. Admitting it, he said he really didn't want to do this terrible thing but was constantly thinking of it. When we discussed the matter, I was able to send him to a psychiatrist for help.

When an aura has black throughout, then death can also be close.

Learning to read these very real indicators of a person's health is a daunting task but can be accomplished. Listening to yourself and those from the "other side" can guide you. Consistent surveillance of others' auras is the best teacher.

Black in an aura can be a cloak of sorts. Since auras are constantly testing and touching one another to learn what is going on in others' lives, it allows the wearer of black to mingle yet resist others' approaches to touch his aura. Like a shield, it keeps him safe from the continuous bombardment of fellow auras.

A shiny new black car is a sign of mystery and intrigue, an item to be valued. Some black in the home is tasteful, understated and cozy. This color is neutral and goes with anything unless there is too much of it. An overabundance strikes visitors with a feeling of sorrow, and with good reason. It is the color associated with funerals.

GHOSTS TALK

A person with black in his aura can be in any kind of profession that requires attention to detail such as accounting, engineering, programming, or navigating. Anything requiring him to be precise is right up his alley.

But black personalities have negative features: they may become too reclusive and deny anything or anyone access to their worlds. Being alone is not good for the soul's education in life, unless that is the lesson the soul wants to learn while in physical form.

Giving up on life is another negative quality associated with a black aura personality. Over-emphasizing detail and forgetting to look at all other aspects of life is a negative characteristic. As with anything, too much of something is not always good for the soul.

White

White in an aura is the color of purity, the "Godlike" or sun color. It generally stays right below the skin and shows outside the physical body for approximately two to three inches. This color usually shows up on everything that has an aura, which, as we have learned, includes everything.

Because everything is attached to God through our spiritual beings, everything has this color seeping from the physical body or held captive within. Therefore, everything has some of the traits realized from the "White" personality no matter what shape or color it may take in its corporal physique. No one is immune to this color.

Ghostly presences sometimes use this color to express themselves because most people expect to see spiritual entities in either angelic white robes or misty white smoke. This is supposedly the signature of a ghost.

The color of new snow or light from above makes one see the beauty and none of the frailties. What we fail to see is that snow and light both have impurities but look as though they are purest of sights. Though our originating aura looks pure, it carries with it all the imperfections of past lives. There is no true perfection in life; only the yearning for it.

Although this color is a "Godlike" color, it bears a heavy burden with it when people choose it for their aura. Being spiritual in nature dictates that as a part of God, we all have this part of Him within. The

Auras

colors we mix in our aura along with this color illustrate the personality of each individual. When people decide they need more white in their auras, they are asking for more spiritual lessons.

The white of the beginning aura brings ego that is sorely needed if a soul is to live a physical life. Ego is there to keep us going and to remember our primordial instinct for survival. This need for survival is not a bad character trait as long as we don't allow it to become an obsession. Anything carried to extremes can cause the soul problems.

A white personality sees itself as very special because of this color, sort of above it all. Watching others with interest, it blends in with its surroundings. Like a hawk sitting in a tree waiting for its next meal to scamper by, it waits for someone to need its opinions so that it can express them appropriately.

Shyness comes with this color, but it is not a true shyness. Waiting patiently for others to notice them before they make their thoughts known, people with white dominating their auras tend to appear shy, but in truth they are very outspoken.

Virginal attitudes abound with these people. They feel pure no matter what they do. Others attribute the virtue of purity to them as well, whether they deserve this characteristic or not.

With sober sight, they tend to look others over with a very critical eye. Even while this is happening the people they are appraising do not feel they are being criticized but analyzed instead for their own good. If they win the approval of the white personality, these people act as if they have just won the lottery.

White personalities feel they are right in their belief structures although they are not sure they want to discuss those beliefs with others. The fact that they know they are right is enough for them. When asked their opinions, they give them. It is not uncommon to notice a slight smile cross a white personality's face when another acknowledges truth in the white personality's' beliefs.

When a person wears white, it can be for a different reason than "It looks good on her." She could be seeking a more "Godlike" attitude in life, or she could be showing that she feels she is better than others. For some it implies the feelings of sackcloth and ashes from Biblical lore, which is putting others before themselves or believing they need to be more humble.

White in an aura outside the body more than a few inches can indicate that the person being read has a need for God to guide her life more. Where the white appears indicates what lessons the reading should take. Sometimes the white can appear in such a way as to show the negative personality traits of the person being read.

Perhaps the white being read demonstrates the need for more ego in the person. Maybe she is critiquing her own soul and looking for answers.

As with black, white in certain areas of the body can mean some type of disease. Epilepsy, nerves misfiring, and other brain malfunctions carry white in the aura. If it looks like snow after the shows have gone off on a television around the person's head, that can indicate a brain ailment.

In home décor and automobiles, white is used extensively. It is bright, easy on the eyes and reminds those living with it that their roots begin with God. Adding other colors to it only make the color white more vibrant and does not detract from it. White is very popular, with other colors added to the furnishings. On the other hand, white is hard to keep clean, but its impact with other colors is worth dealing with that one negative aspect..

People with white in their auras often work in the service sector. They might work in medicine, psychiatry, the ministry, or social work. Any field where they can feel self-important and guide people is a good choice for them.

Self-importance is a part of their personality but does not interfere with their higher motives, unless they are a negative white personality. Becoming too critical or judgmental is one undesired trait of the negative white personality, even if it is a part of the soul's learning process.

Negative white personalities deal from a feeling of piety, believing that since they know God's way so well, they are better than others. These people don't mind being a little smug in that knowledge and lay in wait for others to make a mistake so that they can "Lord" it over them.

Negative white personalities have hard lessons to learn, but those lessons eventually make their souls richer.

Red

Red is the first primary color to appear in a rainbow. As such, it

Auras

calls attention to all who see it. This color makes the eye wander across the rest of the rainbow looking for the other delightful colors in such a spectacular event.

Red is the color of passion, energy, and moneymaking. People who keep red in their auras run the gamut of personality traits. Their auras shine as an invitation challenging all to help these people achieve what they want most. It has powerful significance. This color is not for the wallflower.

Stop signs are red. Red gets your attention. These energetic personalities crave attention, and what's more, they get it.

Being quick with their emotions, they may erupt like a temperamental volcano, then simmer down just as quickly.

Quick to give others responses to any question, they feel they know all the answers. If their reply is wrong and it is proven, you will find them trying to learn why. They are not frightened of not knowing the answer but only of appearing stupid.

It is all or nothing for red personalities, but they always expect to win it all. If they don't get what they want, after a good rest and time to re-group, they are quick to bounce back.

Because they are quick-moving people, they want everything done in a hurry. When tired, they have to lie down to rest right then because they feel as if all their energy has escaped them. Once they have taken a quick nap, they are up and ready for almost anything life has to offer them. Red personalities feel invincible, and others tend to think they are.

Even though red personalities have all these personality traits, that does not make them good leaders. Red personalities are movers and shakers but need someone to point them in the right direction. They are loyal as followers once they decide they are being led wisely. They do not hesitate to do whatever it takes to get the job done.

Red personalities have a tendency to go off on tangents. Their attention spans are not all that they should be. When focused, they are very determined. The trouble is getting them to stay focused on the task at hand. As daydreamers of the color world, they are always ready for the grand adventure.

Reds are quick-minded, brilliant people who may not be well-educated but are quick with answers because they have lived the circumstances.

GHOSTS TALK

It is the color for someone who wants to be powerful and in control. Business people who want to win wear the power color red to meetings in which they want to stand out. The red personality makes one feel more energetic or motivated.

In nature, red is a color that involves procreation. Monkeys in estrus have red bottoms. Women who are fertile menstruate. This is the color that puts people in mind of sexual behavior. For this reason, in a group of women if one woman is wearing red, though she may not be the most beautiful woman, men will look at her more quickly than all other women.

The term "red light district" refers to prostitution.

Red personalities, when in their true red mode, are sexy and seductive. They walk with the atmosphere of one who wants to be noticed, basking in being watched intently. .

People with red auras are looking for the next quest. They are never satisfied with the ho-hum life of nine-to-five. Even if a red personality has a regular job, he is waiting to leave work to become his alter-ego, always looking for the next grand adventure to take him away from anything boring.

This color needs to be mixed with other aura colors for balance. Otherwise the person wearing the red aura cannot withstand its continued pressure to perform.

The color red in an aura can signify a need for sex, money, or power, and even the need for a thrill. This color, according to where it is located, can also indicate injured feelings.

Different shades of red have different meanings. If an aura is a more brick (reddish brown) red color, there can be addictions to drugs or alcohol. It can also be interpreted as an eating disorder or emotional instability. Anytime a muted shade is noticed in the aura, it implies that all is not right with that entity.

Red-orange auras are not only dynamos but love the outdoors and anything to do with people. Red with blue overtones in the aura can be energetic people with high emotions.

Red in home décor or automobiles implies that one is adventurous and passionate. Red cars are considered quite dynamic. The color red demands that one keep moving. It needs other colors to dilute its impact and make people feel more restful.

Auras

People with red in their auras can choose a career in anything from a soldier to a train engineer. Their choices vary widely. There is always room in any business for people who prefer red in their aura.

As with other auras, a red aura can have a negative side to it. Negative red personalities are never satisfied. They may be people who want attention no matter what the circumstances, and they will do whatever it takes to be in the spotlight.

Some may be control freaks. They need to handle everything because they think no one else can do anything as well as they can. Some negative red controlling personalities are abusive, especially to those they love. Love gives them the opportunity and motive for controlling lives.

Other negative red personalities are unable to concentrate on a given assignment for any length of time. Daydreaming tends to vie for their time.

Negative red personalities can also come across as threatening by exhibiting a bad temper over a minor infraction.

Orange

Although orange is not the color you would usually associate with nature, you might want to re-think that. When most people think of nature, they think of green. But if you look at the earth's aura at sunrise or sunset, you will see the unmistakable orange glow surrounding the fringes of the earth above the interior "white light."

Since the earth manifests nature by being the harbinger of everything living on its body, we can conclude that nature has an orange aura. Following that train of thought, then, people with orange in their auras are nature lovers. Being sports-minded, they love to do anything having to do with the outdoors. Taking long walks in the woods revives them. When forced to stay indoors for long periods of time, they might become ill.

Trees and animals mean a lot to them. They want to be a part of nature, and they are, just by the very fact that they are alive.

People with orange in their auras rarely meet a stranger. Their outgoing attitudes make them good friends. Because of their personalities, others speak highly of these down-to-earth people. Although they may sometimes invoke anger from others, it usually doesn't last very long. No one can remain mad at someone so helpful.

Persons with orange in their auras are good lovers and can be kinky where sex is concerned. But they don't consider themselves kinky — just willing to try what their partners like.

A person with a predominantly orange aura tends to take up for the underdog and will enter any situation in which he feels someone is being battered.

Orange personalities are loud. They talk a lot and know enough to be dangerous about most subjects.

In most cases they are the nicest people one could ever meet, but don't dare try to push one. If you do, you'll be sorry. You'll feel as if you have a tiger by the tail, and you won't know whether to drop the tail or continue running in circles trying to stay away from its teeth.

Orange personalities are always aware of their surroundings, but they appear to be more adventurous than most because they take premeditative chances. Even though they seem impulsive, they generally are very much aware of what they are doing and even have a plan, as haphazard as it may appear.

They learn and remember through experience. People with orange in auras are on a quest to learn, testing the boundaries of each challenge they come into contact with.

Orange personalities believe God meant for them to have any good thing in life they want.

When orange occurs in a person's aura, it can mean that the person wearing the color wants a vacation or needs more laughter in his life. Perhaps boredom has set in, and he needs some adventure. The amount of orange in the aura indicates the person's attitude.

Possibly this person needs to be able to speak up and is drawing the color to him so that he can talk without fear. The color of the orange in the aura is a good indication of what the person being read requires to help him deal more effectively with his life.

It takes a very strong-willed person to live with orange in the home or within his car. Taken in small doses, orange can set the mood and be quite charming, but when in large amounts this color can get on one's nerves quickly.

A person with predominant orange in his aura can choose any

career that has to do with the outdoors: river guide, construction, farming, ranching, sports. Even clothes designing or stand-up comedy can capture this creative person's attention.

Negative aspects of the person with orange in his aura is that he might want to spend too much time outside and might be considered flighty. He might not want to devote much time to anything that keeps him away from his ultimate high, nature. Easily bored, he continually seeks distraction. Fun is the center of his life, and he doesn't want anything to divert him from that.

He likes people, he might give too much of himself and his time. This can create negative effects upon the person whose aura is orange. Because he always sees other people's problems as his own, it can get to the point of being harmful to his own life.

Yellow

People with yellow personalities are a business-minded lot. These people want others to know they are well-educated, whether self-taught or otherwise, and that they strive to succeed with mental prowess.

They make good leaders, and they generally make up their minds in a methodical manner. Every detail needs to be analyzed before they make a move. Any strategic game such as chess peaks their interest. The true yellow personality makes wise decisions based on consideration of all points of view.

This personality can be a little stubborn, especially when they believe they are right. Although they are willing to listen to others' comments, they still analyze each part of the problem to come up with what they consider to be the best solution.

Yellow women personalities would rather be in business than be mothers, but they can excel at both jobs. Adaptable under any circumstances, they are able to meet challenges. They truly believe that they can adapt to any situation, and do this quickly and without showing emotion.

They can sometimes appear cold and disarming. When these people are under stress, they feel they need to keep their emotions hidden. They believe that if they show stress, it is a sign of weakness. They try not to let you see them sweat.

Yellow personalities keep to themselves and generally only have one or two good friends. These friends are usually people who are business-minded, too. The true yellow personality depends on no one but himself.

Both sexes generally appreciate tailored clothing and prefer to dress quite professionally. Although women might add accessories to their attire, they dress with the thought of keeping it simple.

When yellow appears in the aura around the head, it can mean that the person wearing the color needs assistance with important questions in his life on anything from finances to health. There is a need to make intelligent decisions without emotion. Perhaps he needs to become more adaptable to a current situation. Another possibility is that he needs to put distance between himself and others. Check the location of the color in the aura for that indication.

The color yellow is too bright for people to be around for long periods of time. They need a break from this beautiful color because it can be too demanding. In home décor, people generally tend to mute yellow colors with other colors that tone down the radiance of the yellow. Otherwise, the color needs to be very pale. No one can look directly into the sun without pain. As with looking into the sun, yellow can cause pain by demanding too much attention to the fine details of one's life.

Good careers for the yellow personality can include anything from politics to the clergy, and include any vocation involved with making decisions for others.

On the negative side, people with a yellow personality tend to appear as know-it alls. They think they are the only ones who can make an intelligent decision on any subject. When the color goes more toward a mustard shade, these personalities know that they are the only people making the right decisions. It distorts their mental aptitude. Other people become suspicious of the mustard-colored personalities' motives.

Businesswomen who have negative yellow personalities look down on their counterparts working from home, rearing children. They consider this beneath a real woman's intelligence. Their state of mind suggests they believe that the stay-at-home mom is lazy.

Extreme stubbornness in the negative yellow personality can cause them to miss part of life's bounty. Steadfastly continuing in one direction can cause one to lose sight of the important things in life.

Green

Green is the color of healing in an aura and is seen in nature, as well. People rejoice in seeing trees giving birth to the first leaves of spring. Getting outside to smell fresh air in spring is a restorative experience.

Green personalities take the word "care" to the extreme. As natural mothers, they want to help everyone. In order for green personalities to feel good about themselves, they have to be helping someone or something. Nurturers by choice, they are the ones who take care of animals, humans and plants.

Preferring to watch rather than to become involved in another person's private matters, they usually keep their thoughts secret. Because the green personality would rather listen than speak their opinions and possibly hurt another, most people see them as good listeners. Others take for granted that the green personality can see more than one side to a situation. Therefore, they hold the green personality's comments in high regard.

Green personalities make people feel at home by putting them at ease immediately. They try to take care of others with all the care their mothers gave them, even if they never had a mother to give that care. A person with a green personality instinctively knows what other people need to feel comfortable, and they excel at providing it.

People with green personalities also have a lot of pride. They walk alone into the face of any challenge but do not expect others to do so. Ego dictates that they face their demons alone. They consider doing otherwise to be a weakness.

They consider it their sworn duty to be peacemakers. They want harmony in everyone's life. A green personality may even stop an argument between others by starting one himself.

These wonderful personalities do not take the earth for granted; rather, they find amusement in all its details, challenging or otherwise. Their sense of humor relays how they feel about life. They are loyal to a fault, because they know a friend would never hurt them on purpose, and they will fight for that friend to the death. Most believe that green personalities make the best of friends because they are jovial, caring and can keep a secret.

When green is present in an aura, it can mean that the person who shows this aura color needs healing on some level. Noticing where the green is located can be an indication as to where the healing needs to be directed. The amount of color can be a gauge. Green in the aura can also be an indication that one wants the qualities that the green personality presents.

In home décor, green usually is seen in its darker forms because people need the healing touch of the forest. When it is combined with yellow color to make chartreuse, it can be a harder color to take in great quantities. As a clear shade, it is one of the easiest colors to enjoy and has a formidable vitality.

Green personalities usually excel in the medical profession or some occupation that aids people. This characteristic makes them wonderful counselors.

Green personalities need to be careful not to make martyrs of themselves. This negative trait is easily accepted by green personalities because they give too much of themselves. Sometimes they care for others to the point of self-harm.

Taking the underdog's side, rather than listening to all sides of an argument, is another negative trait. Learning that the person they are trying to save might be as bad as others claim can lead to great depression.

Making people feel too comfortable around them can create problems when the green personality needs time alone. People take for granted that they love having them around because they are made to feel too welcome. The negative green personality would rather have company than ask for some time alone.

Negative greens cannot speak up and ask for anything. Pride makes them think they should accomplish the act by themselves. It is too much trouble to ask others for help.

Blue

One of the most beautiful colors in an aura is blue. Both the sky and the oceans can attest to the heights and depths this color can reach.

Auras

Blue is the color of emotions. The hue and its depth of color are indicators of emotion and how it is affecting the person being read.

People with blue personalities tend to think with their emotions. Either they are way up or way down; sensing all the emotions they can experience on their way to either point.

As feelers, some may cry when happy or sad. Having a need to feel every thing, they leave themselves open to others. They take the mood of any person they are around, whether that person is upset or elated. Feelers don't even know why they run the emotional gambit. They allow their environment to guide their emotions.

Feelings can be overwhelming when one is in a "blue mood." Mood is the state of mind in which a person functions. People can never be in one state too long. Thus the blue personality does not stay in one frame of mind for long periods of time. It needs to create diversity to keep from feeling stuck.

Some personalities of blue stay within themselves and do not trust people very much because when wearing a blue aura they are easily mentally and emotionally injured. Afraid of trusting and being hurt, they feel the need to keep their distance from others.

The paler shades of a blue personality indicate people who want everything in order. Their closet is immaculate. They know where any piece of clothing is and most likely how long it will take them to get it out of the closet. Although they appear to be perfectionists, they are not. Instead they enjoy the ability to be able to itemize everything.

As the blue moves to the deeper hues, it becomes more moody, and that becomes apparent to anyone paying attention. With royal blue, one can be on a high or in the deepest of wells. A person making a decision to parachute for the first time might wear this color in his aura because it means he needs to make a quick emotional decision. Whether this escapade is to be an enjoyable opportunity or the last of his life takes considerable fervor in making the decision.

Navy colors in an aura personality occur in people who are highly emotional but want to hide that fact. They tend to try to ascertain their feelings and put them into an itemized report to be read only by themselves. The darker color is a comforting shield that allows them adequate room to justify their mental and spiritual behavior. Most aura personalities this color are closet perfectionists.

Reading blue in an aura indicates as many diverse meanings as there are moods. If you see a pale shade of blue around the head, for instance, you can conclude that the person you are reading wants to organize her mental house. Life might be frustrating at the time, and she needs to compartmentalize some behaviors.

Seeing clearer shades of blue might mean that the person being read is aspiring to become better in mental aptitude. She might be excited about an upcoming adventure.

When reading the deeper shades of blue in the aura, a reader might find that the person being read is in emotional turmoil and is trying to find clarity.

In home décor, blue is used extensively because of its emotional qualities. People enjoy seeing the same mental qualities they possess in their homes. It comforts us to realize that not everything is perfect.

Too much of a good thing can be depressing, though. An example is putting a baby boy into an entirely blue room. Once I got an emotional call from a new mother. She told me her baby boy was crying all the time, and it was literally driving her crazy. After listening to her exasperation, I told her that the baby did not cry all the time. He quit when brought out of his room. She acknowledged that I was right. Then I explained that the baby's room was painted blue although I had never seen it. Again she said I was right. At that point I told her to paint the baby's room another color or balance the shade with other colors. I told her that most babies put in a totally blue room cry from depression.

Careers for blue personalities include anything dealing with the arts or anything creative. An artist, chef, or a designer has the emotional aptitude to perform tasks effectively.

Negative blue personalities expect others to be down when they are. If they are not, these negative blues will do their best to infect others with their own depression. They can be perfectionists who are never satisfied with anything done by anyone, including themselves.

Co-dependency is a negative side to the blue personality. They need approval for all their endeavors. Afraid to take risks, they curl up into emotional fetal shapes waiting for hurts to befall them. Imaginary hurts inflicted by others become all too real with the negative blue personality.

Fearful of venturing into unknown emotional territory, some

negative blue personalities will not even give others a chance to become friendly. Their motto is, "Be safe rather than sorry."

Purple

Purple is one of the most beautiful colors and is the color of spirituality. It is a shade not easily obtained in life and is sought after as a prize. Purple is the color of aspirations of a higher sense.

People with purple personalities are always striving to be better than they consider themselves to be, both on a spiritual, emotional, and a mental plane.

Needing more knowledge, they become avid readers, only to discover that they truly know nothing. They never give up the acquisition of learning. Trying to become what they think they should be, they search their own lives and the lives of others to find the answers.

The studies of all religions make them feel as if they are accomplishing something bigger than themselves in life. If they find a point that they don't understand they will continue their quest for answers until the question is resolved. Reading other people's opinions about religion is good enough for them. Thinking their search for God by reading others' material will help them find answers, they forget to look to their own souls. Searching for answers is a good spiritual quality, but knowing your own soul is better.

A good theological discussion is right up their alley. Wanting to help as many souls as they can, they are more than willing to give anyone the benefit of their education.

They try to achieve perfection, and they seem to struggle with themselves more than most because they are so critical of themselves. These personalities do not think they are being critical, but analytical. Analysis of every aspect of their physical lives ultimately gives them an answer to their life's purpose.

The deeper shades of purple show someone working hard to find inner peace and love, not only of their fellow man and themselves but also of a higher power that many consider God. Spiritual fact-finding is their ultimate desire.

Purple personalities make good friends because they always give of themselves, though they might want to know why. Generally they do not ask much for themselves in return.

These personalities think that because we are supposed to be "God-like," people should be able to understand each other's needs. Acting upon that understanding, one should give without hesitancy for the asking. In that manner, they are uncommunicative in asking for help. This causes problems in communication when their needs are not met in what they consider a proper manner.

When purple shades of color are seen in the aura, it generally means that the person being read is aspiring to become a better person. The place the color appears gives even more details as to what the person being read is feeling. For instance, if the purple color is around the genital area, it may mean that the person being read is having a spiritual problem in the sexual area of his life; the head might mean that he is on a spiritual learning expedition. The color gives many more clues. If the color is completely around the body, it may mean that he is trying to reconcile his spiritual feelings with those of living physical life.

When reading a muted shade of purple in the aura, the reader may see the person being read as a religious zealot who thinks he should enforce religion in the way he believes. A pink-purple or violet shade of the aura might indicate someone looking for spiritual peace.

Home décor is enhanced with purple, but it is too hard a color for most to take in large doses for any period of time. When purple is mixed with other colors, it can become very striking.

Careers for purple personalities might include religious studies, writing, or social work.

Negative purple personalities could become self-martyred by believing that the world is against them for their beliefs. They might become overly demanding that others believe as they do. These purple personalities might even decide to die for their religion and take others with them. This goes against the ultimate goal of God. A spirit takes a physical body to learn, not to force religion onto other people.

Some purple personalities think they give to relationships without reciprocation. When they do not receive what they think they should, they turn silent and think of themselves as the only ones who work in the relationship. This type of behavior is resistant to hearing

Auras

that there may be two sides to a story.

Pink

The color pink is subtle and undemanding yet cannot be passed without appraisal. Coming from the combination of red and white, pink is the color of peace. When we mix red with large quantities of white it combines the best of both to make a wonderful blend. It is so pleasant that not only can it be seen and felt, it can be inhaled.

People who love the color pink usually are either in a blissful state or looking for one. They are the smiley faces of the world.

Truly loving everyone, they try to see the best in others. If he doesn't find the best in a person, there has to be a very good explanation in a pink personalities' mind as to why not.

Those who have this personality quietly study the best approach to problems and then act on their thoughts. Because they tend to research ideas this way, they may be seen as slow, although they are anything but.

Pink personalities see the world through rose-colored glasses. They desire a pleasant place to live, and they manufacture that place in their minds if they can't find it realistically.

These personalities are shy, very intelligent, hard-working people who wish they were more a part of the mainstream but are frightened of moving too quickly. Stepping lightly, they fear hurting others. They are full of good intentions. Pink personalities watch what they do or say because they are afraid that others might see them as harsh. They try to make everyone happy.

Others notice their wonderful senses of humor, though the pink personality might not laugh aloud. Some might even say they have a dry sense of humor.

Pink in a person's aura indicates to the reader of that aura that the person is looking for peace and tranquility. The person might want to become more conscious of others and try to learn to stop and smell the roses. The place pink appears in the aura dictates the meaning. If pink is right above the shoulders, maybe the person being read needs some relief of stress or grief. When the aura is pink around the middle part of the back, it could indicate that the person wants peace with someone he wants off his back. In the small or lower part of the back, pink might indicate that the person being read wants peace in financial aspects of his life.

Home décor is influenced subtly by those brave enough to use this color in their environment. Outside, pink is enjoyed immensely on favorite plants such as sweetheart roses.

Careers for the pink personality might include gardening or library work.

Negative pink personalities can overdo the niceties of life. The perpetual smile on pink personalities' faces can grow thin when you are not in the same blissful state they are.

They can be hurt too easily and give up trying because of this. Because they truly love others, they might feel they have hurt someone and then socially retreat.

Another way they might become negative personalities is by trying to push their ideas of moving slowly onto others. They might become too preoccupied with thinking their own moves over so that they stagnate mentally.

Gold

Gold represents wisdom of the highest kind. Angels or light beings have appeared in this color. This magnificent color typically covers unification of religions back to divine spirituality. An open-minded gold personality generally realizes that all religions have something to offer people, but spirituality is inherited from God.

Gold is the color of souls having acquired wisdom from previous lives. That knowledge is used in present lives to assist the soul in acquiring more divine education.

People who have gold personalities have a mixture of white, brown, green and yellow. This mixture has the perfect balance of qualities of all those colors. White inserts purity. Brown adds detail and concentration. Green imparts healing. Yellow includes inquisitiveness.

When white is added to this mix, it helps people carrying the gold color realize that they are not better than others. Their lessons have taught them they should be more accepting of others. Ego takes a back seat with these people, who have learned that everyone has to progress at his or her own level.

The abundance of yellow in this color creates the desire to gain more intelligence through life's events. The driving force of the yellow effect in the person with gold in their aura makes them continually seek out information on a physical, spiritual, and mental plane.

Green color in the gold aura allows the personality to realize that healing is always there to be called upon when needed.

Brown color in the gold aura entices the individual to be meticulous in searching for information from life. That search means giving careful attention to the details of ordinary life while not being caught up in ego or feeling as if you are better than others. Brown is the grounding color. It makes one focus more intensely on the reason one is in physical life when applied in the golden color.

This prized color reflects what our civilization holds dear. Having this in one's aura could be seen as the highest spiritual value. People who carry this color in their auras have overcome many obstacles to obtain knowledge they hold dear. They have no need for others to acknowledge their progress.

Gold is a forgiving color that aids people wearing it in their auras to understand that others need to learn through spiritual lessons while on the physical plane. That is the only way these others can gain the wisdom to fulfill their mission of becoming more God-like.

Brown

The color brown is a mixture of the colors red, black and yellow. As with all combined color, brown takes personality characteristics from all the colors that combine to create it. The quest for detail comes from the color black, passion for the quest comes from red, and inquisitiveness comes from yellow.

In an aura, brown like black can be seen as disease when being read. In most cases the illness might not be as progressed when this color appears in the aura. Because brown is taken for granted, it can sometimes be overlooked.

Look at the mixture of colors that create the brown color in the aura. If there is more red in the brown, then the person being read is leaning more towards characteristics of the red color.

Gray

Gray is the color of judgment. Black with its love of detail is mixed with white and its purity of consciousness to create gray, from which decisions are formed.

Judges, because they make decisions that affect others' lives, have this color in their auras when working. Other people choose this color for their auras when making decisions. This is the color of hard-working men and women who have to think clearly while working such jobs as an air traffic controller, pilot, or bus driver. Others' lives are in their hands, and they have huge responsibilities toward their fellow man. Because of this, the gray shows brightly around the heads of such individuals.

Chapter Eighteen

CHANNELING OR MEDIUMSHIP

Webster's defines channeling as "the course or agency through which something passes." Channels are sometimes called mediums. The definition in Webster's of a medium is "a person thought to have the power to communicate with the spirits of the dead or with agents of another world or dimension; also called psychic."

Speech is not the only form of communication. Touch, smell, taste, hearing, and sight are other ways to share. When these senses become heightened in using one's psychic ability, a person is able to reach a different vibratory rate and thus come into contact with entities that have a different electrical makeup. Since everything is made up of energy or electrical units that vibrate at one rate or another, we are all part of the divine energy source called God.

As a part of the whole that is God, psychics' souls can enter other dimensions. There they are able to spiritually raise their vibratory rate in order to communicate with whomever they seek.

GHOSTS TALK

All knowledge comes from God. The data may be perceived in different ways. A medium or channel is not obligated to speak only with what physically live persons consider "dead people." Channeling live people, animals and other life is possible when giving a reading. Being able to describe for the person being read other live persons' thoughts, demeanors and physical attributes is all part of a mediums abilities.

This is not only because the soul never dies but also because there are, as with everything, different methods for communication. Different languages spoken and signed among humans attest to that fact. Feelings of a higher magnitude using empathy, a mode for becoming one with another entity, are another manner in which communication takes place.

Some of the entities a medium might communicate with are our highest spiritual selves, other people, both alive and dead, plants, animals and inanimate objects.

When channeling our higher selves, we are actually requesting our highest spirituality and knowledge for service to the body, mind, and spirit. This is the part of the soul, which is generally deep in the subconscious. It has not forgotten that we are one with God. As a part of God, we are responsible for all others as well as ourselves. As the old cliché says, "No man is an island."

In working with people and animals, a medium may be trying to learn about or communicate with the person, either dead or alive. Then she or he can give precious information to loved ones waiting to hear from their departed friends or family.

Inanimate objects usually give channels a history or a story of some sort. Sometimes what people consider inanimate is truly animate when giving details about its' lives. They have spirit just as everyone does and as a part of God deserve the same respect we humans want.

Plants are fully capable of being channeled, too. A green thumb will say that she just knows what the plants need. Some don't even know how they keep their plants alive, but they have what it takes.

Energy can be channeled just as you experienced when working in the Aura chapter as you tossed the energy ball from person to person. This consists of using your psychic senses to send and receive messages to and from others. Channeled energy can also be used as a method to promote healing of yourself and others.

Channeling or Mediumship

Methods of channeling vary. Though you are reading this book in search of knowledge to help you in channeling, it might only provide a portion of methods one may use to channel. Learn from reading, but consider your own methods as well.

Channeling sometimes happens involuntarily. When you are driving and pass the street you want because you are daydreaming, that in a sense is channeling. Listening to birds sing and losing yourself in the melody is channeling. These events are escapes from hum-drum life but can also, if used properly, become a source of enlightenment.

People expect channeling to be direct and possibly even painful. If that is what you expect, then more than likely you will receive painful information until you become educated and realize there is an easier way.

Although I have been a medium all my life, when I came out of the psychic closet I thought I needed more concrete evidence that I was channeling than what I had received all my life. When someone asked me a psychic question, I knew I was getting the correct answer when I felt a very sharp pain in my stomach. But it was fear of being wrong that caused that pain. I continued in this manner until the "other side" called a halt to this hurtful method. They told me that if I would listen, I could hear the answers. Psychic ability does not always come in the form of a clanging bell, but a whisper.

There are times when you may hear a voice scream at you out of nowhere, but this is generally only used for warnings when the spirits want to get your attention quickly.

Most of the time communication comes in softer forms. It may be accomplished with a soft voice murmuring in your head or ears. You also might see pictures in the third-eye area, or you might experience dreams, feelings, scents or tastes.

Prayer is one of the simplest forms of channeling. Some have even prayed and heard God answer them audibly.

Belief in channeling is sometimes hard on us. We have to use all our senses in order to give credence to something that appears to have no way of being proven.

Take the case of Michael Servetus, a Calvinist in Geneva, who accurately described blood circulation in 1553. His contribution to science and religion caused him to be burned at the stake. As is so often the case, if it can't be proven tangibly, people don't believe.

GHOSTS TALK

The more you come to believe in your channeling abilities, the more answers you will get. People on the "other side" are more than willing to speak with people on the physical side.

Many people believe that if a person is talking to someone who can't be seen by everyone, that person must be nuts. But the same people who don't believe in channeling will go to church and talk to God with the expectation that He is hearing and answering their prayers. For them, talking with God, whose existence cannot be proven, is all right because everyone knows without a doubt there is a God.

Saying things such as, "I can feel God in my life," or "He has spoken with me," is acceptable when used in religious context. Others will say they have seen God with a little less enthusiasm because that might be broaching insanity if the other church members have not. All of these people have been channeling information under the context of religion.

Religion does not have to be a part of channeling, but spirituality does. People channel through their birthright, which is a gift from God. As with all psychic ability, every entity has this birthright when born. Not all decide to use the gift, but all have it.

Channeling is a skill that can be utilized easily, just by the asking. When we give ourselves permission, we can revive the talent. Then all that remains is the method in which we receive the information.

Sight is another form of channeling. When a person sees a ghostly entity, he has increased his vibratory rate along with the entity having lowered his so that the entity can be seen by physical eyes. The person seeing the ghostly entity has certain physical symptoms that accompany the sight. Although these symptoms occur with sight, they can also occur with other channeling methods. They may include a dry mouth, a tingling or itching sensation in certain areas of the body, chills— either localized or all over the body— and feelings of heat or cold.

There are times an entity will appear as you normally go about your day-to-day business. Sometimes, you don't even know you have met a person who is actually dead to the physical world because he might appear to be flesh-and-blood. At other times it might be someone you know is dead, but you see him as clearly as if he were alive. There are times ghosts appear as mist, mini-lights dashing across a room, smoke, or a light being.

A light being is someone who looks like a human form made of light. They might also be called angels. To recognize the sight of a light being, one can get in a very well lighted area with a friend. Have the friend stand across from you in the light. If possible, have him or her stand with the light flooding his or her back, head and shoulders. Stare at your friend without blinking for a moment. Then close your eyes. You should be able to see the person's form filled in with light even though your eyes are closed. From now on you will recognize light forms when you see them with your eyes open.

Seeing other forms of ghostly energy such as a mist, smoke, shadow, or haze where they should not be — and ruling out logical reasons for their appearance — is a good indication you are seeing a ghostly presence. You can either watch until it disappears or close your eyes and ask that it leave.

You can ask either mentally or orally, "Who is this?" The answer will be immediate, either mentally or audibly.

Dogs often sense or see ghostly entities. Our dogs have separate methods for dealing with ghostly sightings. Mysti, our oldest, ignores them unless they do something totally foreign for their particular species. Madeline, our youngest, does not like any strangers in the house. Giving them her complete attention, she growls as she watches them move. When she sees shadows, Madeline gives them the same attention because she has seen ghostly entities appearing in this manner. Animals do not know that they should not see this type personality so they express in their unique way their thoughts on the subject.

Spirit can find more ways to appear to humans than we can ever realize. After ruling out all logical phenomenon, ghostly specters are the only logical reason left. Each ghostly sighting is, in effect, a channeling event.

Ghostly entities can be seen as an invisible movement like that of heat waves coming off the pavement on a hot, humid day.

You might have another type of ghostly encounter. From the corner of your eye, you catch movement. You know you saw something, you turn quickly to catch it, but it is not there. Even though what you saw is gone, you know exactly what the apparition looked like.

On occasion sight is achieved with the physical eyes closed. For instance, if you look at an object, then close your eyes and continue to see that object, you are seeing by using another psychic sense. Similarly, when you close your eyes and see colors manifest in front of your eyelids, you are also channeling. This also occurs when you close your eyes and see a face or another person standing there. The spirit person being seen behind closed eyes has three-dimensional properties, just as anyone in the physical world.

When viewing ghostly entities, try not to be shocked or show that you are fearful, because you may alarm your visitor. Remember that they are cognizant of your presence and feelings. If they think they have upset you, then it may make them retreat back into their invisible world. Try to be calm and ask who this person is if you don't know them, or just allow the entity to be there without speaking as you enjoy each other's presence.

Meditation is another form of mediumship and is popular with first-time mediums. Using the techniques in the Meditation chapter, ask to see anyone who would like to speak with you. Lie back and be prepared for anything. Symbols, colors, persons, animals, plants, and just about anything you can or cannot perceive will come to you. Enjoy the performance and learn.

Symbols and their interpretation represent another channeling method. These may come to you more easily when meditating but can be seen at any time. For instance, repeatedly seeing the same symbol can be a message. Within a few hours or days a friend or family member might bring it to your attention as well. At this point, a good medium will probably ask what message this symbol is trying to impart.

Some symbols relate to specific events going on in your life. A stairway going up means those affairs are taking a turn for the better. Just about any symbol that reaches upward can have that meaning. A circle is infinity, just as the parallel eight figure is. Any sign that appears to be leading downward indicates a period of challenge in life. Spirals can mean that you are working very hard to get where you are going. How you feel your life is moving depends upon the direction of those spirals and whether they have an upward or downward motion.

A box, for instance, can mean that one feels they are being boxed in or caged by their actions and circumstances. A star can be man or can have other grim meanings such as the ones placed there by Satanists in the form of a pentagram. Knowing the difference between the two is important.

Animals can become symbols as well. Take the snake for instance.

Channeling or Mediumship

It was used in the Bible to describe the ultimate evil and everlasting life as infinity when it had its tail in its mouth. In the medical profession, the Caduceus is an insignia showing two snakes intertwining around a staff to signify something good and welcoming if you happen to be ill.

Symbols can take any form, from nursery rhymes to rocks, in order to give people images they recognize so that they may derive the underlying meaning the spirit wants to impart.

Another tool for channeling is touch or psychometry, such as was described in the Meditation chapter. When you touch an object, you are giving permission for your channel to be activated. Information can flow into the consciousness of the reader.

Dreams are one of the simplest forms of channeling. Either when asleep or awake, you can make use of these very insightful events.

When asleep, you might dream of the past, present, or future. Precognitive dreaming is more easily interpreted because it generally appears just as the event is going to occur. Symbols in dreams may be a little harder to decipher, but they may contain information pertinent to your life. Dreams that appear in the past typically include vintage dress, the speech patterns, or even languages from other countries. Usually the dreamer is able to understand the language even though he can't when awake.

Daydreaming affects everyone and is a more subtle form of channeling. It has a calming effect and allows us a vacation of sorts, just as meditation does. The problem with daydreaming is that others can become a little agitated at the daydreamer's lack of attention. When asked what he was doing, the daydreamer usually answers, "I don't know." This usually isn't something you consciously decide to do but just washes over you before you know what's happening. It provides a needed break, although the rest of the body is still functioning as if one is fully awake.

Drivers experience channeling by daydreaming when they miss a street they use everyday. Doing a job that is not challenging such as driving home each day allows the spirit to excuse itself while the rest of the body is driving the automobile. After passing the street, you realize that you should have turned onto your street. Berating yourself, you turn on another street to work yourself back around to your own street without any idea that you were channeling.

GHOSTS TALK

These are just a few methods we use in our continuing evolution towards the "true source." Opening channels with love and care allows us to use this information to make our lives and others' more profitable. Remembering that everything has a spirit will permit people to get acquainted with items they never believed had a soul. The same spirit exhibited individually connects everything.

Sensations of Channeling

Channeling or mediumship can cause many sensations as you open your mind to it.

This book discusses some of those sensations. There are many more that may happen to mediums that are not covered in this book.

The most widely felt sensation is just the same as breathing. It is a bodily function just as taking a breath is. Channeling is so simple that it goes hardly noticed, such as in daydreaming or dreams at night. A medium's body might not change in any manner other than the fact that he or she is channeling. This generally occurs to people who are unaware that they are mediums. Using their resources as an everyday occurrence they have no idea they should feel any differently.

Upon discovering that mediumship is a viable event— and an important one at that — people tend to believe that channeling should create some extraordinary change in their bodies. As you go further into the study of channeling, it might.

Some sensations you might experience during channeling are dry mouth, tingling in localized areas, localized pain, extreme heat or cold body temperatures, uncontrollable shaking, body color change, itching, ringing or buzzing in the ears, hearing someone speak who is dead, smelling odors foreign to the area, chills and chill bumps in localized areas, tasting a foreign taste, and crying. None or all of these symptoms can apply and might be totally unexpected.

For the trance medium, other spirits may be invited into the body for a limited amount of time in order to supply their message. The medium may allow partial or total body control with which the spirits may work.

You don't have to worry about a spirit keeping possession of your body. It cannot without permission. Channels, or mediums, have complete control and authority over their bodies.

It is not uncommon for a medium to feel different vibrations when channeling. This assists the medium in understanding that the information is coming from an outside source. Without this feeling they could not be sure. Family or friends of the dead give confirmation of data received, but mediums need to feel their own sensation of channeling so that they can acknowledge and develop their ability.

Channeling is taken for granted by those who have a natural ability to do so. After coming out of the psychic closet, I listened to some mediums say that channeling is hard to do and should have some visible sign. Even I became confused about channeling for a while and thought that there should be something spectacular to this event although I had been using and taking this talent for granted since birth. Speaking with the "other side" is as easy as speaking to a friend or family member. Sometimes you might both speak at once, and at other times each of you might listen to the other. You might even argue. Emotions run high in either situation.

When I finally came out of the psychic closet, I thought that it had to be harder because mediums kept telling me so. My guides and spirit friends gave me what I asked for until my lesson was learned. The key for mediums is to find their comfort level with their body and the information received.

Spirit guides or guardian angels gave me what I needed to ensure that I was on the right track. They told me I was open to channeling. When my body went pale white, as if all my blood had been drained, I knew they were giving me evidence.

This not only affected me but my husband, Claude, as well. On a particularly good day of working with my spirit guides, I noticed that it looked as though all the blood had left my body. After pinching my cheeks, I could not even get a pink blush. While the paleness raged, a tingling sensation like pins and needles swept my entire body, with particular emphasis on the crown of my head. I enjoyed the sensation as proof of my ability, although it did cause me some concern.

Upon walking into my office and seeing me, Claude became very upset. Excitedly, he said, "You are as pale as a ghost! Let's go to the hospital!" After I told him what was happening, he still didn't seem convinced. He let me and my guides know he didn't appreciate what had happened to me — as any good husband would have.

All the while, I was content with the knowledge that I was opening to channel. I worked intently to better myself for the job of allowing information to travel through me. Helping others, as well as myself, was and is my goal.

Graduating from that form of enlightenment, I went on to less painful methods for retrieving data from the "other side." Sometimes I still feel as though I'm sitting in a freezer when I'm channeling. The violent shaking is not as bad because I realize it doesn't have to be, but it still has a manner of manifesting that catches me off-guard.

Sometimes when an entity speaks to me, I experience itching. Chill bumps in localized areas are not uncommon and give comfort and confirmation — confirmation that you are undergoing channeling at its finest.

All the senses are heightened when one is channeling. Taste, smell, hearing, sight, and touch are on the metaphysical level. This enhanced feeling is wonderful in itself, but when you get extraordinary information also, then it is a real bonus.

Remember, too, that you are always in control of your body, mind, and spirit. This will enable you to enjoy the channeling experience much more. It's up to the channel, or medium, to manage his or her abilities.

Trance mediumship initiates sensations that involve more control. If you are a person who cannot stand giving up control, then this kind of channeling is not for you. Allowing others to inhabit your body for even a few minutes can be a challenge. To start, you must decide how far you are willing to go with the trance state. Will you allow full or partial use of your body while in this state? You also have to decide how you want your own consciousness to react. Should you have your spirit conscious of the events taking place, or would you rather be unaware of the experience? Once these questions are answered, then all you have to do is ask that trance mediumship begin.

Get comfortable and allow the entity access to speak through you, using the voice it prefers. It looks theatrical but can give the listener valuable information. It's an amazing experience when someone who has asked for a reading hears from a dead loved one in that loved one's own voice.

Channeling or Mediumship

I prefer to know what is happening at all times. It can be disquieting when you allow someone else to enter your body and give him or her permission to use your voice for a while. These entities do not always have the same likes and dislikes as you. For instance, a person speaking through me in this manner loved talking with Claude but did not care for my dog. She totally ignored my beloved little dog, Muffin. Muffin was uncomfortable and growling at her because she had a definite problem with another person speaking through my lips with a British accent.

Within my body, I was waiting and listening to this other woman speak to my husband without ever acknowledging my dog. The experience wasn't bad but was not my cup of tea. I would rather sit and talk with these people than to allow them to take control of my body in such a way.

When working murders, the channeling can be almost the same, with only minor differences. Generally, I take on the role of the victim, which is not always easy because I feel the effects of whatever death role they played.

This is another sensation that needs to be clarified when channeling. When you decide to start the channeling process for the first time, you need to make the rules.

Because a medium needs to know and be able to describe the manner in which a person died, one of those rules is, "How will I let the manner in which a person died affect me?" For instance, a medium would not want to feel the full force of a strangling if that is how the person being read died. The medium would like to feel only the most minute of details related to that strangling while still being able to describe the death.

In channeling for murder victims, I generally feel the death as a thud wherever the victim was shot or stabbed and as a slight choking if there was strangulation. Water deaths feel different from strangulation deaths. Pneumonia might show up as a water death, as would tuberculosis. Learning to use your own interpretation is part of the channeling experience.

When working murders from the murderer's point of view, I am able to watch and sometimes become a part of the murder. This is not my favorite viewpoint for obvious reasons, but neither is being a victim. From the victim's standpoint, I feel and see. In either case, I am part of the situation.

Murder investigations are not for all mediums, but some are very good at identifying both the murderer and the victim. Giving pertinent information and being able to identify the killer is compensation for the work they do.

Mediumship does not have to be hard on the body of the medium. It can be as easy as one wants or as hard. Learning to read the feelings is the most important tool for a good channel.

Getting Ready to Channel

Giving the invitation to your ghostly friends initiates communication. The medium has to learn how to recognize the gateways for learning to channel. Previously we have looked at how to recognize spirit, past lives and auras along with other psychic phenomena.

Another good idea for the novice medium is to surround himself with like-minded individuals who either want to learn psychic work for themselves or are excited about being part of the medium's education.

Remember too, that the spirits who come to you will not hurt you. They are there for a purpose, too. Either they want to be heard by you and a loved one, or they are there to assist in your education. In my classes, it is not unusual for several spirits to come and observe or assist.

Spirits on the "other side" keep the same personality they had when on earth. They might change some, but not much. On the "other side" though, they can see the reason behind all events of life, according to their spiritual education.

The exceptions are those people who are on the lower levels of learning. A murderer, for instance, keeps the same personality but fails to see the larger picture. Still involved with the desire to control everything that comes into contact with him or her, the murderer creates a very miniscule place in which to reside. Because he wants to control, he doesn't look to see if there could be a larger picture. He cares only about the world he is creating where he is king. This personality is truly nearsighted until he begins to wake up and realize that we are all connected to the Supreme Being. What affects one affects all. Waking up can happen at any time a spirit decides. All it has to do is make the deci-

Channeling or Mediumship

sion to look beyond its own personality and become aware of the higher meanings of life.

All spirits have their own personalities, even though they are part of the whole. Uncle Joe or Aunt Ruth will return as spirit keeping the same personality they had while alive physically. For this reason, there will be times that you channel an entity for which you don't particularly care. It is the same as with physical life and meeting people every day. If this spirit is someone you don't like, you can be sure he probably feels the same about you. With this in mind, he won't enjoy spending time with you anymore than you will with him.

People tend to look at spirits as if they are far removed from us when in actuality, we on earth are only spirits in physical clothing. A good medium needs to take that into consideration when conversing with other worldly entities. Do not try to endow these spirits with the greater attributes humans sometimes think they should have. Though they are without physical bodies, they still carry the personalities they had while physically alive. This will make the medium's job much easier. The only exception is those spirits who have never had an earthly incarnation.

Techniques for Channeling

Everyone who channels has a different method. There is no right or wrong way. As has been stated throughout this book, you are the only one who knows what is right and wrong for you.

There are many different levels and procedures you can start with. Some may be easier for you than others, but all have their merits. These procedures are a basis for learning. The best way to learn to use these tools is to take them, change them to suit yourself, and make them your own.

Becoming a channel is easier when you first realize you are seeking an education yourself. Asking questions is the quickest way to learn. In the same fashion, making detailed inquiries of the spirit being read is the quickest and easiest method for retrieving information. Don't be shy. Ask all the questions you want, as if you were meeting someone for the first time and would like to strike up a friendship. You may even ask some questions that you wouldn't ask a potential friend.

As a channel, one needs to be open to all possibilities. Nothing is impossible. With that in mind, look at rocks or crystals. Everything in the universe is made of the same energy units but is compiled in different forms such as human, mineral, or plant. For ease in beginning to learn to channel, the crystal emits more easily readable information.

Gather a group of like-minded individuals. Get several crystals together. Each person in the group needs paper and pens. Take a crystal, hold it, close it in your hand and with eyes closed request information from this stone. If you need to, then you may do a mini-meditation while holding the beautiful rock.

The easiest manner in which to receive information from the crystal is to ask questions of it. For instance, what is its color? Instantly, you will hear or mentally see a color. Ask if it the crystal has a male or female energy. The answer will come just as quickly. Ask if there is any other information it would like to impart. Again it will happen.

Any information you get from the crystal needs to be written down without letting the others in the group see your answers. Pass the crystal to your partner and receive their crystal without talking.

After both of you have had a chance to read each crystal, compare notes aloud. Start by reading what this inanimate entity told you about itself. Do not be surprised when both you and your partner see much of the same material about the particular crystal you are reading. Others find it astonishing that these rocks can actually impart information.

The next step up from inanimate objects is something that stays relatively rooted, too — plants. Plants are easily channeled and are quite ready to tell you what they need in order to survive.

Have your group of beginning mediums circle one of your favorite plants. This channeling session will begin with finding the aura of the plant as you learned in the Aura chapter. Seeing auras is a form of channeling because you are looking at the spirit. Stare at the plant without blinking if you can. See the outline of the plant and watch the white light coming from the plant branching out into other colors. If there is a need, look at the plant with closed eyes with the "third eye" so that pertinent information about that plant will come into focus more readily.

Ask the plant questions just as you did when channeling the crystal. When asking direct questions, you are more apt to get quick, intelli-

Channeling or Mediumship

gent answers. Write your answers on paper. Discuss your findings with the other mediums as you did after the crystal channeling session.

Each person in your group needs to have brought a picture of someone he or she knows but others in your group do not. This can be a person long dead or someone who is alive. According to the size of your group, each person in the group can hold each picture and use psychometry as explained in the meditation chapter to receive channeled information about the person in the photo.

Questions to ask yourself about the person in the photo are as easy as the questions you asked the rock and plant. Obviously the one difference is that you will know whether the person in the photo is male or female. Asking for clarification on characteristics of this person help you to be better able to read the person in the photo. Of course, you may also ask if the person is physically alive or dead. Request information from the person in the photo as if the two of you are speaking in person. Glean any facts that might help the person who brought the photo to know clearly that you have honed in upon the vibrations of the person in the photo. As you hear that you are getting correct data from the person in the photo, you become more confident. When you become more confident in the method in which you receive your facts, the better you become at mediumship.

Remember that you will receive details about the life of the person you are reading not only through speech but also through sight, other sounds, odors, tastes, thoughts and feelings. There might even be a motion-picture effect. These are all techniques in which a medium receives pertinent statistics about the life of the person being read.

Learn to believe and speak all information you receive, because it might be pertinent. If you see a goat push a boy into a pond, as I did once, say it. Otherwise the man being read might not believe that you really saw the goat push him into the pond when he was a boy. Although you might give him information about the event right down to every animal there, if you don't say you saw the goat push him in, then he has a problem believing you are really psychic.

There is the possibility that you might hear another language and have to repeat it to the person being read. Taking it on faith that this is part of the reading is the medium's choice, but if you don't say the word then you will never know if it was pertinent.

GHOSTS TALK

Once while giving a reading, I told a man that I saw his uncle come into the room. Then I proceeded to describe the uncle to the man for whom I was reading. Each time I mentioned his uncle, he would use the term "relative" instead. Finally the uncle spoke in what I now know is a Yiddish word. With my southern accent, I was having trouble speaking the word that I kept hearing, but I was able to say it well enough that the person for whom I was reading was astonished. Upon hearing the word, he said, "That is my uncle," which I had been trying to explain to him since the uncle had come into the room. With that I asked him what the word was and he replied that it meant "relative." My use of that word had made the man for whom I was reading a believer.

Dive into mediumship with your mind, body, and soul once you decide to become a channel. Trying to censor the information can be a disaster. When you decided to become a medium, you opened yourself to criticism from others. Once the decision has been made, don't worry about the possibility of being humiliated. Allow the information to flow through you. There are no right or wrong answers, only information being interpreted by you and the person for whom you are reading. If you are going to do this, do it with your whole heart. In this manner, you can give the best information possible.

Remember, too, that channeling, as with any psychic ability, has a very heavy responsibility associated with it. When you give out of compassion, then you have everyone's best interest at heart.

Another method for channeling on a psychometric level is to have someone cut magazine pictures or draw simple pictures and put them into manila envelopes. Number the envelopes and make sure each person in the group has the chance to touch each packet and write down their impressions. Invite the people in your group to look for color, shapes and sizes. A picture might be one of water and people in your group might see a certain blue shade that may later turn out to be the color of the water in the picture.

Once all the people in the group have had a chance to write their impressions of each packet, hold up the numbered envelope so that everyone can see. Now ask your friends to read their impressions of the packet before opening it. After each impression for that number has been read, open the package and show the picture. The group will be able to give and receive instant confirmation.

Channeling or Mediumship

Psychometry can be used on handwriting too. Each person in the psychic group can bring a note written by someone they know, or something he or she has written. Let each person in the group touch the handwriting; each individual can then write on paper his or her impressions of the person who wrote the note. Once all notes have been examined and your friends have written their thoughts, then start with the first note and allow your friends to reveal their channeled thoughts on that subject before revealing the author of the note. While holding the note, you might ask the sex of the person, what color hair the person has, is this person single or married, or what does his or her mate look like? These are not the only inquiries to be made but will give you a jumping-off point.

When I read handwriting, I don't examine the actual verbiage of the phrases. Holding the paper, I feel the writing and get impressions from it. They might be in the form of pictures, words that I hear, or feelings that come upon me. Actually reading the note interferes with process for me.

Another form of psychometry channeling is having individuals in the group bring a piece of clothing or an item that belongs to an acquaintance. Using what you learned previously in the Aura chapter, hold each item in your hand and write down impressions you receive from the item. Again, for efficiency, ask questions of the item. Answers will come.

Have fun while channeling! It makes the experience so much easier. All you have to do is focus, concentrate, and enjoy. The next scenario for channeling will increase enjoyment even more.

This channeling experiment deals with methods for observing past lives. You will need a piece of cloth and a flashlight. Place the cloth over the flashlight so that light can come through the cloth. Hold it in place with a rubber band wrapped around the flashlight.

Have one person sit in front of the group, holding the flashlight under his chin and turned up toward his face so that the light hits under the person's chin and reflects on the face. Turn off all other lights. Watch as past lives appear on the person's face, hair and clothing. When the group starts to talk about what they are seeing, all will realize that they are seeing the same change.

For the next exercise, one needs to stand in front of the mirror in a darkened room. This is not necessarily easy because people do not generally like looking at themselves in this way. As with looking for auras, you need to stare into your eyes while seeing the outline of your hair. Notice the change as your mirror begins to become cloudy and then blacken. At that point, your whole face turns into someone you do not know. Try not to become uneasy because when you do, you will lose the past life image. Do not be concerned if, while you are observing the image, you see another entity appear beside you. This is quite common.

Dreams offer an easy avenue for channeling. As with an out-of-body experience, an old friend or family member might come to you in a dream. In the dream state, you might even announce that you are dreaming and that the person you are witnessing is actually dead. That is when he will pronounce that he is indeed alive and well. This is one of the most effective and easiest forms of channeling and has happened to many people, some of whom do not believe in psychic ability.

Dreaming can also carry one to a future or past life, giving you the whole scenario and the reason for having the dream. Some say the eyes are the windows to the soul, and I agree, but dreams can provide the history of the soul for anyone capable of watching, remembering, and interpreting.

Precognitive dreams are a channeling tool because they show an individual events that will happen in the future. But you have to learn to decipher which dreams are precognitive.

My precognitive dreams usually begin at my father's house or look coppery like the old tintype photos. Once I understand that this is a precognitive dream, the dream takes on everyday colors and situations to make sure that I understand the nature of the event.

A form of channeling using meditation occurs when you want to meet your guides or someone who passed on to the "other side." Before going into the meditation, you need to be specific in your desires. Once in meditation, be prepared for answers.

Meditative quiet is another way to channel. Talking mentally to spirits will allow them the opportunity to approach and speak back to you in the same mental manner. In this way, you can get answers without anyone being the wiser other than the nice spirit entities that want to assist you.

Using this same method, you can get a live person's attention by

Channeling or Mediumship

simply saying "hello" mentally. Direct your attention to the person with whom you wish to speak and mentally think the word just as you would say it to a person you are meeting. Frequently that person will look at you with a puzzled expression because he heard you mentally but did not hear audibly. Smile and let him wonder.

This same technique can be used when working with animals. Look at the animal you wish to read and listen to its voice. Say "hello" just as you would with another human. Request information in a mental voice so that he understands you. Once the animal realizes that you are indeed listening, he will talk with you.

In the same manner that you said "hello" silently to another human, you can read minds. This is not something that one generally does with conscious knowledge. Ordinarily a medium senses the person he is reading. Saying that person's thoughts without hesitation can cause trouble.

Once a person desires to become a medium, starts to focus and concentrate, then verbalizes what he receives, confirmation comes in the form of surprise — "How can you do that?!?"

Reading people who are physically alive is another form of channeling. Giving yourself permission to be a medium is the first and foremost step toward becoming a gifted medium. Getting permission from those you read is another initial action, whether that entity is physically alive or dead. Most always, permission is implied if a person or spirit entity visits you for a reading, but if you have a doubt, then ask mentally if you have consent. It is highly unlikely that approval won't be given.

At this point, you are ready to begin reading another person. You may either look at the person being read, close your eyes, look around, focus on a wall, or whatever makes you comfortable. If this is the first time for you, then taking the person's hand might make it easier to start the channeling process. Immediately, touch makes one's vibrations stronger and allows more access to the channeling process.

Remember to say anything you hear, feel, think, see, smell, or sense. The only exceptions that need to be made is if you see the person or someone he or she loves dying soon. Whether you are right or wrong, telling the person you are reading this information might not be helpful. Using less hurtful methods of imparting the information might be just what the person needs to hear in order to be convinced that you are truly channeling. There are ways of giving unwanted information without hurting the person being read too much. Use discretion in doing so.

Fear of being ridiculed is your worst enemy. Give yourself the freedom to acknowledge that you may say what you think is the wrong thing but may be right on for the listener.

If you find that you are having a little trouble beginning the session, always keep in mind that you need to ask questions of your inner self or other spirits, who are visiting, that you would like to have answered.

Another possibility for problems in a channeling session is that you might worry because you know the person you are reading. This happened with a next-door neighbor. She told me to tell her something about her life if I was truly a medium. I told her that since she was so skeptical, anything I revealed she would think I already knew. But she insisted that she would not

My guides helped immensely, but the neighbor was so shaken she rarely spoke to me afterwards. Knowing nothing of her family, I instantly gave her the name of her brother and asked why he felt as if he wasn't part of the family. Imagine the shock on both our faces. She replied she didn't know why he felt that way but had expressed that opinion continuously since they were children.

A similar case concerned a favorite cousin of mine whom I knew well, although we had been out of touch for a number of years. As I said in the first part of this book, most family members do not want to believe that you can really predict anything. Since they have known you always, they have a little problem with your abilities, just as Jesus' family did. My cousin, her friend, and I were sitting around talking when my cousin mentioned that I was psychic. She then challenged me, and I told her that she wouldn't give me credit for anything I said because we grew up together. I knew what her next statement would be, and I was right. It was, "But you don't know my husband. You have never met him."

She was right. And the particular question she asked is the kind that often comes up when three ladies are talking and laughing together. But after telling her that I didn't want to discuss her husband's

Channeling or Mediumship

anatomy, she continued to goad me, as cousins will. Finally, in front of her friend, I told her all about her husband's attributes and even went on to tell her what she and her friend had discussed — verbatim — on their way to my home. My cousin and her friend became believers at that moment.

Because this does not create the best of atmospheres, I would not recommend that other mediums go to such extremes. But it does make the case for asking for information that there is no way you could know.

When speaking with spirits, obviously you don't need to have anyone else other than said spirit with you unless you want a witness. There is no proper procedure for speaking with the "other side," and you may talk with them at any time. It could happen when you are dropping your children off at school or having lunch with a friend.

More than once my husband has asked that I look at him while talking with spirit in a restaurant. His concern is that others might think I am totally crazy, and he is too because he is my mate. Spirits are just as physical to me as any corporeal person. I forget at times that others can't see them and that they don't understand that I am speaking with ghosts.

A long-distance friend of mine will tell me while we are speaking on the phone to stop for a moment and talk with my dead friends because she doesn't want to share my attention. After learning the signs that I am speaking with both her and a ghostly entity, she says she has learned that if she will give me that second, I will then speak more freely with her.

Communicating with the "other side" is very easy. Sharing can occur anytime and any place. Being a good medium does not involve ritual — it involves being a good listener, just as any conversation requires.

Deciding that you want to become a medium is the sole requirement. Focus and concentration create a better medium. Being able to decipher what is heard is another requirement. We might all see a white house when looking at a picture of a white house but some who might be better at perception can tell you that the white house has seven rooms and thirteen windows. Being able to look beyond the flat picture to see the third dimension of rooms and windows — seeing the entire picture, in other words — is what makes a good medium.

Using logic is great when in a psychic mediumship mode,

but acknowledge the logic and accept that some material can be entirely illogical.

If one actually needs ritual, a good pre-channeling prayer might be, "God grant me the ability to be the best medium that I am capable of being. Keep your guiding hand over all that come to me and all that don't. Guide my tongue so that I hurt no one."

This prayer might even help in creating the atmosphere you need to start the channeling session. Use auras to help. Notice the person you are reading and his aura. Within a few moments, you might see other spirits joining you. Once they start to materialize, give your impressions of how they are appearing to you. As you continue to give your thoughts on the subjects, you might hear them speaking with you. Interpret what you are hearing and describe it to the person with whom you are reading.

Do not let the person being read interfere with your reading. He is there, just as all the spirits in the room, but some of the entities need to be tuned out while you work with the others. This does not mean that you should completely ignore the person you are reading, but he can cause you to have to start over again. When spirits are speaking, they sometimes talk very quickly. You have to listen closely to hear the message. There are times they are good enough to repeat the message, but at other times they seem to have too much to say and thus don't want to start over again. Be respectful of their feelings as well as the physical person with whom you are reading.

All the tools you need for channeling have been provided in previous chapters. Using those tools can assist you in getting started with your mediumship goals. Asking the proper questions can give added impetus for channeling. The most important feature is that you not be frightened.

Channeling can also be done to interpret past lives, future lives and present lives. Just as you did while assessing auras, stare at the person you are reading. Look for the aura and watch as the person begins to change before your eyes. He may appear as someone in past times, future times, or in the present, but you will be aware of information being given to you at the same time you are watching the transformation. This information is coming from the spirit world, allowing you access to knowledge that can help you and the person for whom you are reading.

It is not unusual to see clothing from another time being worn by the person being read. His hair might be quite different from the way he usually wears it. Just as ghostly entities appear in a fashion they feel is best for the period of time they want you to express, the person being read subconsciously uses the same abilities. In this way he can bring to the conscious all the items on which he needs to work.

Past lives generally reflect what is needed in this life when being channeled. Memories of the past life may evoke strong likes, dislikes, food, or otherwise in the present lifetime. They run parallel to the present life in some manner and create strong impressions in the lives of those living. Personalities of spirit entities change as quickly as the entities learn — just as babies' personalities change. Therefore, past lives do affect present lives and can help achieve spiritual growth.

Mediumship is a tool, just like any other psychic ability, and is there to assist you in spiritual evolution. All that it proves is the intangible that everyone is looking for: there is life after death. Any true medium should have proof positive that we never die.

Afterword

Hopefully what you have learned from this book is to take responsibility for your actions and to keep an open mind for your continuing learning experience. As a part of God, you are charged with remembering that each action has a consequence resulting in Karma. Your psychic ability is an inherited gift and, though taken for granted, should be used in thoughtful ways.